The
COAST of MAINE
Book

A Complete Guide

THE
COAST OF MAINE
BOOK
A Complete Guide

RICK ACKERMANN &
KATHRYN BUXTON

Berkshire House, Publishers
Stockbridge, Massachusetts

ON THE COVER AND FRONTISPIECE

Front Cover—Background—*Penobscot Bay Seacoast;* Inset—*Lighthouse with Sailboat, Lobster Buoys, Chair Caner,* all by Kip Brundage; *Lobster*—by Camilla Smith, courtesy Rainbow.
Frontispiece—*Burnt Harbor Light,* by Tom Hindman.
Back Cover—*Canoes, Kayaks, Backpacker at L. L. Bean; Woman and Child in Rowboat; Dansk Factory Outlet, Freeport,* all by Kip Brundage.

Excerpt on p. 16 from
E.B. White, *Writings from* The New Yorker, *1925-1976*
HarperCollins, New York © The New Yorker

Excerpt on p. 131 from
Calvin Trillin, *Alice, Let's Eat*
Ticknor & Fields, New York
© 1989 Calvin Trillin

Excerpt on p. 153 from
Sarah Orne Jewett, *The Country of the Pointed Firs*
Houghton Mifflin, Boston

Excerpt on p. 83 from
Marguerite Yourcenar, "Reflections on the Composition of Memoirs of Hadrian," from
  Memoirs of Hadrian
Farrar, Straus & Giroux, Inc.
© 1954 Marguerite Yourcenar

THE COAST OF MAINE BOOK: A COMPLETE GUIDE
© 1992 by Berkshire House, Publishers

Photographs © 1992 by credited photographers.

Library of Congress Cataloging-in-Publication Data
Ackermann, Rick, 1948-
    The coast of Maine book : a complete guide / Rick Ackermann & Kathryn Buxton.
        p.   cm.
    Includes bibliographical references and index.
    ISBN 0-936399-24-4 : $14.95
    1. Maine — Guidebooks.   2. Atlantic Coast (Me.) — Guidebooks.
I. Buxton, Kathryn, 1958-   . II. Title.
F17.3.A25   1992
917.4101'43 — dc20   92-15589
                                                                                         CIP

        ISBN: 0-936399-24-4
        ISSN: 1056-7968 (Series)

        Editors: Cia Elkin, David Emblidge, Sarah Novak
        Design of original text for Great Destinations series: Janice Lindstrom
        Cover design: Jane McWhorter

                        Berkshire House, Publishers
                        Box 297, Stockbridge, MA 01262
                Manufactured in the United States of America

                        First Printing 1992
                        10 9 8 7 6 5 4 3 2

The <u>GREAT DESTINATIONS</u> Series

- The Berkshire Book: A Complete Guide
- The Santa Fe & Taos Book: A Complete Guide
- The Napa & Sonoma Book: A Complete Guide
- The Chesapeake Bay Book: A Complete Guide
- The Adirondack Book: A Complete Guide (Fall 92)
- The Aspen Book: A Complete Guide (Fall 92)

Contents

CHAPTER ONE
From the Ice Age to Lobster Rolls
HISTORY
1

CHAPTER TWO
From The-ah to He-ah
TRANSPORTATION
29

CHAPTER THREE
Where Sea Captains Slept
LODGING
46

CHAPTER FOUR
What to See, What to Do
CULTURE
83

CHAPTER FIVE
Shore Food
RESTAURANTS & FOOD PURVEYORS
126

CHAPTER SIX
By the Sea, By the Sea
RECREATION
177

CHAPTER SEVEN
Something Old, Something New
SHOPPING
228

CHAPTER EIGHT
Practical Matters
INFORMATION
251

Acknowledgments

Wxe'd like to thank Wendy Keeler and Cynthia Hacinli for helping us get Old Orchard Beach and Kennebunkport under control; Jeff Isaac, Jonathan Nolan and Paul and Robin Fagan, former Outward Bound instructors and our upstairs and downstairs neighbors, for telling us how to dress for the Maine weather, for locating a half-dozen great places to eat, and for making us feel perpetually guilty for spending any time indoors.

Thanks also to Gary Lehy for one superb piece of pie and an invaluable shortcut; Barbara Ackermann for writing the birding section; Edie Armstrong for jewelry information; Jackie Carlton and Lisa Blinn for their thoughts about the Yorks, the Berwicks, Ogunquit and Wells; Bill Sweet for his input on history; Bill Connor, Arthur Kirklian, Elissa Conger, Joan Ackermann, Greg Clement, Nancy McCallum, Judy Paolini, Jim Thibault, Sara Young, Anne Webster and Chris Mathan for their help finding some of the best places to eat and stay on the coast. Vicki Walsh for her good information about Bar Harbor. Julie Michaels for her kind recommendations and encouraging words. Thanks to Alison Kolesar for the maps; without them some of us might never have left home. David Emblidge, Sarah Novak, Mary Osak and the staff at Berkshire House for their patience — with special thanks to editor Cia Elkin for playing us like violins. Also thanks to Monica Delehanty, our trusty researcher and fact checker who was undaunted and wonderfully resourceful; Tracy Lord and her phalanx of photographers for accomplishing the impossible; and Kip Brundage and Camilla Smith for their wonderful cover images. We also are indebted to our dog Argos for taking us on a few side trips we might otherwise have overlooked.

Introduction

Half of all Mainers vacation in the state. When they're not vacationing, they're getting away, *in Maine*, for the weekend. That's why so many cars in our Portland neighborhood have bike or ski racks on the back, an Old Town canoe or a sea kayak on top, and fishing gear, sail bags, extra battens, camping or beach equipment (including lobster bib) in the trunk. We suspect many have several of the above ready and waiting to go at a moment's notice. Carwise, it's hard to tell a Mainer from an out-of-stater.

Of course, vacationing is not a way of life suited to everybody. Some cars that pass through the state look as if the only thing that's ever been in them are people. Every year more than four times as many people as live in Maine visit Acadia National Park. Most of them, after a brief detour to L. L. Bean, go home again. And every year a small group of visitors decides to give up whatever it was they were doing and move here. Many open new restaurants, which is fine, since in addition to vacationing, Mainers love to eat. In Portland there are more restaurants per capita than any other city in the country except San Francisco, and more than just a few of them are busy cooking up things as exciting as the best of what's served in much larger cities. Others among the newly relocated open bed & breakfasts or inns. Traveling the coast we have met an investment banker, a pilot, a state department official, a social worker, and a psychologist, all enjoying their new occupations. One woman, from Houston, had looked out her snow-covered window at sunset a few days earlier and cried. She said she cried not out of frustration with Maine's winter, which can be long, but because she was "so happy to be here."

She came for the same reason people as far back as the Abenaki Indians and European settlers came — for a better life. They came for the rocky coast, ocean storms, fog thick enough to stuff a pillow, wildflowers in spring, vast sandy beaches at low tide. Visitors and new residents on Maine's coast come so that every day they can look out on the pen-and-ink lines of fish weirs in Johnson Bay off Lubec. They like watching the colors change during fall in the Camden Hills. They want to be able to cross-country ski the carriage paths in Acadia — one of the great off-season joys of the coast.

People are not only taken with the coastal Maine landscape and all it has to offer, but with the way of life. The state tourism office bottled this phenomenon with the slogan "Maine. The Way Life Should Be," a phrase ridiculed among residents and recent transplants for its obviousness. Maine is a place people come to change — to slow down and try something new — and Mainers encourage this kind of behavior. People here are highly independent and extremely resourceful, and it is not rare to know someone who has done what may seem impossible — take up mountain climbing at 80, start an opera company in a tiny seaside village, write a novel, or capture the coastal light on canvas.

Life here — and vacations — represent an ethic different from most other parts of the country. Small, family-run operations are the rule. Big shopping malls and chain restaurants are the exception (in fact, they are virtually non-existent east of Portland, the state's largest city). Shops, inns and restaurants are run by individuals who are unremitting in their quest to offer good value. That comes from a particularly Yankee characteristic, which is to get the most out of something.

That's why almost everybody in Maine, rich or poor, knows two things: how to conduct a yard sale and how to shop at a yard sale. Someone's discarded sofa easily becomes someone else's treasured antique. Likewise, old wooden lobster boats or vintage friendship sloops, once popular coastal working boats, now are prized by weekend sailors, and sea captains' homes are made over into inns. Recycling and rejuvenation take on new meanings here.

Rick Ackermann and Kathryn Buxton
Portland, Maine

THE WAY THIS BOOK WORKS

ORGANIZATION

This book is divided into eight chapters, each with its own introduction. If you are interested in one chapter or another, you can turn to it directly and begin reading without losing a sense of continuity. You also can take the book with you on your travels and skip around, reading about the places you visit as you go. Or you can read the entire book through from start to finish.

If you're interested in finding a place to eat or sleep, we suggest you first look over the restaurant and lodging charts in the *Index* (organized by area and price); then turn to the pages listed in the general index and read the specific entries for the places that most interest you.

Entries within most of the chapters are arranged alphabetically by towns under **five regional headings**: "South Coast," "Casco Bay," "Midcoast," "Down East/Acadia" and "East of Schoodic." A map showing the entire coast divided into these five regions appears at the end of the *Introduction* and at the end of the book.

LIST OF MAPS

	Chapter
Coast of Maine — Five Regions	*Introduction*
Maine — Topography	1
Maine Access Maps	2
Five Regional Maps	2
Acadia National Park	6
Portland	Follows *Index*
Coast of Maine — Five Regions	Follows *Index*

Some entries, most notably those in the lodging and restaurant chapters, include specific information (telephone, address, hours, etc.) organized for easy reference in blocks in the left-hand column. The information here, as well as the phone numbers and addresses in the descriptions, were checked as close to publication as possible. Even so, details change with frustrating frequency. It's best to call ahead.

PRICES

For the same reason, we have avoided listing specific prices, preferring instead to indicate a range of prices. Lodging price codes are based on a per-room rate, double occupancy, in the high season. Low season rates are likely to be 20-40 percent less. Again, it's best to call.

Restaurant prices indicate the cost of an individual meal including appetizer, entree and dessert, but not including cocktails, wine, tax or tip. Restaurants with a *prix-fixe* menu are noted accordingly.

Lodging rates generally increase close to Memorial Day when the summer season begins, and they are highest through the fall foliage season in mid- to late October. Special packages are often available for two or more nights' stay, and frequently there are even better values during the off-season. If breakfast and/or dinner is included with the price of a room, we do not alter the rate category, we just note that the room rate includes one or more meals.

These lodging rates exclude required room taxes or service charges.

PRICE CODES

	Lodging	*Dining*
Inexpensive	Up to $50	Up to $10
Moderate	$50 to $110	$10-20
Expensive	$110 to $180	$20-30
Very Expensive	Over $180	Over $30

Credit cards are abbreviated as follows:

AE — American Express	DC — Diner's Card
CB — Carte Blanche	MC — MasterCard
D — Discover Card	V — Visa

AREA CODE

There is one telephone area code for Maine: 207. For all numbers in the 207 area, we cite local exchanges only.

TOURIST INFORMATION

The best sources for year-round tourist information are: the *Maine Publicity Bureau* (P.O. Box 2300, Hallowell, ME 04347; 582-9300 in state and 800-533-9595 out-of-state) and the various chambers of commerce listed in Chapter Eight, *Information*.

WELCOME CANADIANS / BIENVENUE AUX CANADIENS

We hope this book will give Canadians an idea of all the good things there are to do on the Maine coast. We have kept our northern neighbors in mind and have tried to provide pertinent information.

Nous voulons que ce livre donne aux Canadiens une idée de tous les endroits où on peu s'amuser sur la côte du Maine. Nous apprécions la visite de nos voisins du nord, et nous essayons de leur fournir des renseignements pertinents sur cette partie du Maine. Il y a beaucoup d'aubergistes et de restaurateurs sur la côte qui parlent français. Si vous êtes en train de planifier un séjour sur la côte du Maine et vous aimeriez consulter quelqu'un qui peut vous renseigner en français, communiquez avec le Maine Publicity au 207-582-9300 (P.O. Box 2300, Hallowell, ME 04347). Ce service publie plusieurs brochures en français.

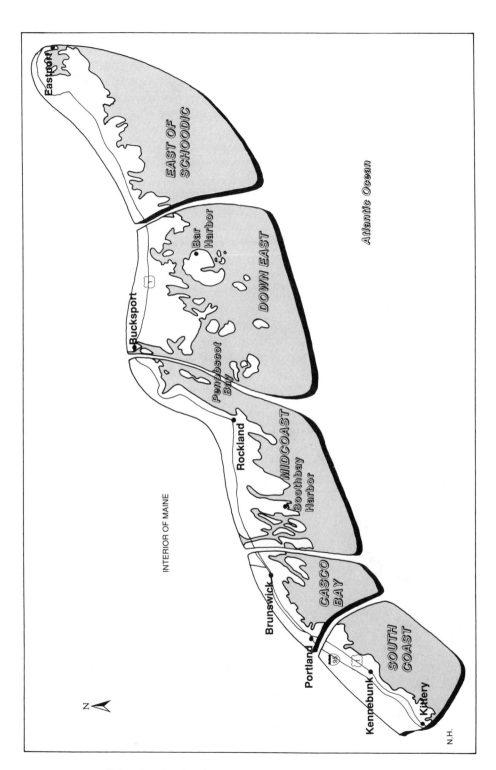

COAST OF MAINE — FIVE REGIONS

The
COAST of MAINE
Book

A Complete Guide

CHAPTER ONE

From the Ice Age to Lobster Rolls
HISTORY

Long before Europeans discovered the New World, tribes of the Algonquin nation came every summer to the coast of Maine where the sun was tempered by cool ocean breezes. Down East, as 19th-century sailors termed the land governed by the prevailing west winds, is a place to come back to.

Mainers built and sailed the wooden ships that traded with the

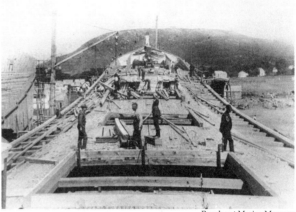

Penobscot Marine Museum

Shipbuilding at Camden Harbor during the mid-19th century. Mount Battie is in the background.

world and rode those westerly winds "Down East" to their homes on the Maine coast.

People still come to cool off and trade. Today, the major trading route connecting the Maine coast to the rest of the world has shifted inland to coastal Rte. 1. Tourism is second only to the paper industry in total revenues for the state. Visitors shop Maine's outlets and relax by its inlets. Many of the old working harbors have been transformed into pleasure harbors. Visitors from all over the world come to sail windjammers on Penobscot Bay, peep at the autumn leaves on Rte. 182 north of Ellsworth, cross-country ski on the carriage trails in Acadia National Park and bed and breakfast in old sea captains' homes. For many Canadians, the south coast of Maine is the closest beach.

What visitors find is a coast and a people that have much in common with the Maine coast and people who lived here in the 19th century. Artists are still intent on capturing the region's fugitive colors. Mainers today have to work just as hard to make a living.

All Yankees, and especially the people who live along Maine's coast, have a reputation for keeping to themselves. Mainers are a people of few well-chosen words — all delivered with an accent flat as a clam bed at low tide. Underneath this crusty exterior, they are adventurous, inquisitive and have a great sense of humor, as Benedict Thielen discovered 30 years ago writing for *Holiday* magazine: "They never seem to look at you," he mentioned to an acquaintance. "Oh, they do, sideways, or when your back is turned," the man replied.

"That fellow, he's probably off around the corner right now, looking at the license plate of your car."

The writer E. B. White once wrote to his wife, Katharine, about the apparent indifference he found frustrating but infinitely attractive. "Dear K, Santayana, whom I read on the train last night, holds out little hope for our achieving any satisfactory relationship with the Maine people." The Whites ended up spending the second half of their lives on the Blue Hill peninsula among these laconic people. Like the Whites, people "from away" find the coast a place they want to come back to year after year. It's not a fashionable place. It's one where you find delicious traditions, like the four-decades-old lobster festival in Rockland. It's also a place to enjoy some of nature's most enduring pleasures, such as Ogunquit's broad sandy beach, Acadia National Park's rocky headlands, and the dramatic 18-foot tides at Cobscook Bay.

NATURAL HISTORY

Visitors are astounded by the topography of the Maine coast. Enormous tides expose rocky headlands that rise abruptly from the ocean. Two thousand to three thousand islands dot its length; inlets and fingers of land provide infinite variety. To understand what forces created the "rocky coast of Maine," you have to look at its geologic past.

ROCKS OF THE ROCKY COAST

According to the plate tectonics theory of continental drift, the European and North American tectonic plates began to collide about 450 million years ago. The impact caused the edges of both plates to buckle and crack as the ocean floor separating the two plates began to slide under the North American plate. Tons of rock were forced upward into huge mountains. Rivers of magma forced their way through cracks and formed volcanoes. In some places, magma pushed its way through cracks in the hardened granite crust to form what geologists call "black dikes." Today you can see black dikes cutting through the pink granite at Schoodic Point at the far eastern reach of Acadia National Park.

Tom Hindman

The Atlantic surf smoothes the rough edges of the hardest stones, like these on a beach in Acadia National Park on the Isle au Haut.

Roy Zalesky

Cadillac Mountain in Acadia National Park. At 1,530 feet, it is the tallest coastal mountain in the eastern United States and affords splendid views of the bay.

The geologic past is also evident in the makeup of Maine's islands. Look at the mostly long, skinny southern coastal islands, and you'll see the remnants of the mountains that were formed when the two tectonic plates pushed together and forced the coastline to crumple. Further up the coast, islands such as Monhegan and Mount Desert are distinctly rounded mounds. These were created when molten magma forced its way up through the plate and formed volcanoes.

The two plates continued to slide together, and about 390 million years ago, the coastal lands' layers of sedimentary materials were transformed into metamorphic rock by the immense pressure and heat of the collision. The collision created a diverse collection of rock formations and minerals along the Maine coast — sandstone, shale and limestone in the south; shale, slate and impure limestone in the north. The European and North American plates eventually began to drift apart, and 70 million years ago the Atlantic Ocean was already formed. Today the continental plates continue to shift and the ocean to expand at the hardly perceptible rate of one inch every year.

THE DROWNED COAST

The most prominent feature of Maine's coast is a consequence of the Ice Age. Twenty thousand years ago great glaciers covered much of the northern hemisphere, including Maine. Weighed down by thousands of tons of ice, the coastal plains and many of the bordering mountains were forced downward. Water from the melting glaciers rushed into the ocean and the rising waters poured into the depressed valleys and lowlands of Maine, forming what is now called the drowned coast.

The glaciers have disappeared, and coastal lands have bounced back, at least partially, to their pre-glacial elevation. Still much of Maine's coastal lowlands, marshes and wide sandy beaches, part of a giant alluvial plain that once stretched the entire length of New England, now lie hidden by Gulf of Maine waters. The result of the lingering glacial depression is a meandering line where land meets water. The state's coastline stretches for 2500 miles from Kittery to Eastport — a distance that is only 225 direct miles or 290 miles by car. Several major rivers empty into the ocean in Maine: the Piscataqua at the Maine-New Hampshire border; the Saco River between Biddeford and Saco in the south; the Androscoggin between Brunswick and Topsham; the Kennebec at Bath; the Penobscot near Bucksport, and the St. Croix at the border between the U.S. and Canada.

The coast has hundreds of deepwater approaches and safe ports protected by thousands of islands. Some are small piles of rocks that appear at low tide. Others are larger, like Mount Desert Island, which is the second-largest island in New England. It has 17 mountains, several towns and villages and the eastern United States' only fjord.

The Major Bays of Maine

Casco	Dyer
Merrymeeting	Narraguagus
Sheepscot	Pleasant
Muscongus	Western
Penobscot (by far the largest)	Chandler
Isle au Haut	Englishman
Blue Hill	Machias
Union River	Cobscook
Frenchman	Passamaquoddy

THE ICY LABRADOR CURRENT

The Atlantic Ocean gives the coast much of its character. The waters off Maine's shore are kept cold by the icy Labrador Current that runs from the northeast over the Grand Banks off Newfoundland southwest past Nova Scotia and through the Gulf of Maine before veering east off Cape Cod.

The ocean is also responsible for two other Maine coast phenomena: fog and tide. Fog, which frequently enshrouds Maine's coast and islands between May and September, occurs when warm moist air traveling overland from the southwest encounters cooler ocean temperatures. The air is cooled and moisture in the air condenses to form low-lying clouds — or fog. Maine's tidal range increases dramatically as you head east: the tide at Kittery is about nine feet; it reaches nearly twenty feet at Eastport, as the sea rushes in and out of the Bay of Fundy's narrow confines.

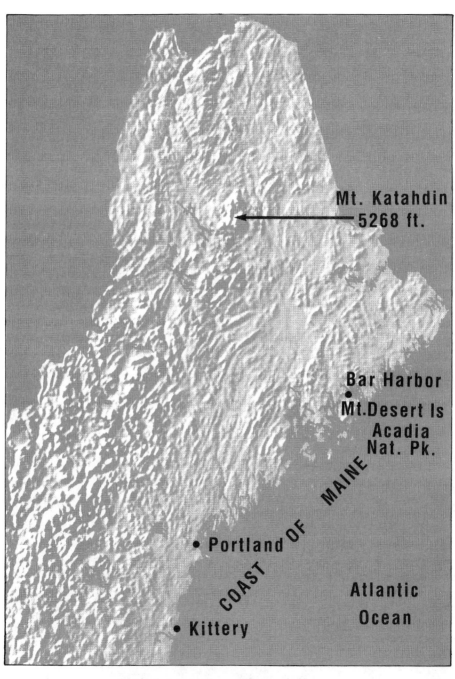

TOPOGRAPHY OF MAINE

The coast of Maine is a haven for birds migrating north and south, including the Arctic Tern.

Tom Hindman

THE PINE TREE STATE

The coast of Maine and its islands are home to more than 300 types of birds, which make the state a birder's paradise. It's not unusual to see an eagle on Mount Desert Island and places further Down East. Herring gulls are common, as are terns, great cormorants, snowy egrets, blue herons, sandpipers, osprey and Canada geese. Mergansers dive in the ocean for fish. Teals swim on the rivers. Puffins, nicknamed "sea parrots," and once near extinction, nest on Matinicus. Visitors also frequently meet with other Maine wildlife, including black bears, deer and moose.

Hundreds of wildflowers are found along the coast and its islands, including the spiky purple wild lupine, white Queen Anne's lace, yellow goldenrod, orange Turk's-cap lily, pink rhododendron and laurel, and pale green jack-in-the-pulpit. Wild blueberries stain the hillsides and coastal mountaintops from Ellsworth to Eastport (in the fall, the blueberry barrens Down East turn bright red).

There are the 76 species of trees in Maine. Softwoods like the white pine, balsam fir, white spruce and hemlock account for only 14 of the different species of trees but more than 80 percent of the forested land. Even today 80 percent of the state is forested.

The most famous of the state's trees is the white pine. Maine takes its nickname, "The Pine Tree State," from the tall and stately coniferous tree that grew in such abundance near the shore when the first Europeans arrived in the 1600s. The British crown government had all pines more than 74 feet tall with a diameter 24 inches and greater marked with the King's Arrow and reserved for use in the making of masts for his navy. The colonists exploited the white pine for their own uses — as beams and clapboards in their new homes. Later, paper manufacturers cut the pine for use in pulp mills. As a result, few of these great trees, many of which measured 6 feet around and stood 200 feet tall, remain today. The pine that do exist are not the abundant virgin forests the early explorers saw lining the coast, but second and third growths on land once cleared by coastal farmers.

Fishing the rich waters Down East. The barrel contains sea urchins, one of the many edible forms of sea life found off the coast of Maine.

State Development Office

The balsam fir is an easily recognized denizen of the coastal forests. It is the tree seen most often growing in the thin topsoil on the islands and near the coast. On a cool, moist day in late summer or early fall you can smell its rich firry aroma as you drive or walk through a grove of balsams.

The white birch grows in the state's northern reaches and along the eastern-most shore. Coastal Native Americans used to make their canoes from birch bark. Coast white cedar and butternut is found in York County, but as a rule not further north. Maples and fast-growing aspens are abundant. The American elm was once so plentiful around the city of Portland that it was called "Forest City." The trees, which had survived two devastating fires that raged through the city, fell prey to Dutch elm disease during the middle of this century.

Maine's waters are home to hundreds of species, including cod, haddock, flounder, whiting, yellowtail, pollock, lobster, mussels, oysters and clams. Wild

Atlantic salmon occasionally are found in the waters of Merrymeeting Bay near Bath. More often the salmon one finds has been farm-raised in aquaculture pens near Vinalhaven and Eastport. Whales frequent the coast. Pilot whales sometimes become stranded near the South Coast's beaches, because they follow squid too far into shore. Humpbacks and finbacks visit late in summer after warmer water temperatures lure the fish they feed on close to shore. Seals are as numerous as boats in many Maine inlets.

Tidal Pools

The importance of tidal pools cannot be underestimated. They are a miniature saltwater empire that can tell us a great deal about life in the ocean at large. The food chain in a tidal pool is much the same as it is in the ocean. Hermit crabs take over empty snail shells and dine on smaller animals. Clams bury themselves in the sand and at low tide you can see airways leading down to their hiding places. Mussels and barnacles cling to rocks and ocean debris with periwinkles, starfish, kelp, rockweed, Irish moss and hundreds of other plants and animals.

The Maine coast has an abundance of tide pools, from the small puddles left at low tide to Biddeford Pool, which is a mile in diameter. Another great place to observe the ocean cooperative at work is at Two Lights Park in Cape Elizabeth, where the receding waters expose hundreds of small saltwater pools and the marine organisms that make them hop.

SOCIAL HISTORY

RED PAINT AND OYSTER SHELL PEOPLE

Remains from the first known inhabitants of Maine date from approximately 4000 B.C. to 3000 B.C., well after the glacier's ice began to recede from the coast. These early Native Americans were well developed in their ability to make and use implements. Spears, knives and fire-starting tools fashioned from stone indicate that the first known human residents of Maine were hunters who eventually evolved into farmers and fishermen. Found among their remains were heavy woodworking tools, including adzes, gouges and axes. They had elaborate rituals, including the practice of burying their dead in graves lined with a mix of clay and iron oxide. For that they have been named the "Red Paint People." To collect the iron oxide, they had to travel inland to Katahdin, Maine's highest peak. Their grave sites have been found near Blue Hill and Ellsworth, as well as several locations inland.

The Red Paint People have provided the basis for a great deal of speculation and romanticizing among historians and archaeologists. For a long time it was believed they were a lost race washed away by a huge tidal wave or erased by some other natural catastrophe. While scholars speculated, no archaeological record was uncovered to support the theory. Today most historians believe the Red Paint People are ancestors of the Native American tribes Europeans found when they first came to Maine. It is believed that their burial rituals — like their reliance on wildlife and game for food — changed with time.

The next archaeological record of Maine's native population occurs around A.D. 80 to 350. Giant piles of oyster and clam shells were left in waste heaps near rich oyster-breeding grounds. The largest of these middens, or collections of everyday "kitchen" waste, was called the "Whaleback Heap," and was removed in the 1900s. Today several smaller middens remain, measuring up to 400 feet in length and almost 25 feet high. They can be seen near Damariscotta on Rte. 1 in the Midcoast region.

Few Native American artifacts have been found among the oyster, clam and mussel shell mounds. The implements that were discovered — spoons of copper and well-formed pottery — indicate that the Oyster Shell People, like their predecessors the Red Paint People, were sophisticated in their use of tools and natural resources.

Courtesy of Penobscot Marine Museum

Members of the Micmac tribe in Bar Harbor at the turn of the century.

THE FIRST SUMMER VISITORS

By the time of the Oyster Shell People, life had developed a rather peaceful rhythm for Maine's natives. They summered in relatively large colonies on the coast and sometimes on its islands. When the cold weather arrived, they dispersed to smaller communities inland. That seasonal way of life was carried on by the Oyster Shell People's successors, the Abenakis, or "people of the dawn."

The Abenakis, a branch of the Algonquin nation, were divided into four distinct tribes: the Androscoggins, the Kennebecs, the Penobscots and the Passamaquoddies. In summer they tended gardens of beans, squash and corn. They also picked wild berries and harvested and dried fish and shellfish. During the winter they hunted game, fished the rivers and inland lakes and made maple syrup.

When the Europeans "discovered" the New World in the 15th century, historians estimate there were approximately one million Native Americans living in North America. Some 3,000 of the more fortunate of those — the Abenakis —lived along Maine's coastal region.

FROM AWAY

About A.D. 1000 Vikings may or may not have sailed down Maine's coast. They even may have landed, but contrary to popular opinion, there is no proof they did.

The first European documented to have landed on the Maine coast was an Italian in the service of an English king during the late 1400s. King Henry VII hired Italian navigator and explorer John Cabot (his unAnglicized surname was "Caboto") to sail up and down the northeastern seaboard and explore endless rivers to find a passage to the Indies. All Cabot found was dense forest, much of it in Maine, but he drew a map later used by England as the basis for its claim to North America.

After Cabot, the exploration of the land was left mostly to the French. They were not only interested in treasure, but also wanted to establish a New France. King Francis I of France hired another Italian explorer, Giovanni da Verrazano, to explore and chronicle the prospects of the new world. Although Verrazano reached Maine's coast in 1524, he had no great interest in what he found. On a subsequent trip Verrazano was eaten by natives at the age of 42 on a beach in Guadeloupe.

Maine also held little attraction for the Spanish explorer Gomez, who arrived one year later. Nor did it promise enough riches to hold the interests of several other explorers who set ashore here during the 1500s. The Frenchman Jean Allefonsce did stay long enough to explore a cape and river he called "Oranbega," which in native Abenaki means "stretch of quiet water between two rapids." He probably described the land near the mouth of the Penobscot River.

Sometime during the 1500s, "Norumbega" achieved notoriety in Europe as a city filled with precious minerals and gems and inhabited by wealthy, regal Indians. One of the first to write extensively about Norumbega was David Ingram, an Englishman who in 1568 sailed to the New World on a pirate ship. He was left ashore in the Gulf of Mexico, and claimed to have walked to Maine, where he said he saw the fabled city. He found a ride home on a French trading ship and wrote a book documenting his adventure and perpetuating the myth.

Several other Frenchmen came and went, but the team of Samuel de Champlain, Pierre du Gast and the Baron de Poutrincourt left the era's most notable mark. In 1604, after Champlain and du Gast already had spent considerable time exploring the Atlantic coast, they established a settlement with de Poutrincourt on an island at the mouth of the St. Croix River (which now forms the border between Maine and Canada).

While his partners built their new town, Champlain toured the nearby coast. He sailed into what is now known as Frenchman Bay, saw an island with ancient treeless mountains and named it *L'Isle des Monts Deserts*, or Mount Desert Island. Today it is the most visited spot in all of Maine.

A WEALTH OF FISH

Ironically, European fishermen looking to fill their nets had been rummaging about the Gulf of Maine for years. They camped ashore for months at places such as Pemaquid Point, drying their catch and co-existing peacefully with the Abenakis. These fishermen didn't keep records. Finding a good fishing hole is not something a smart fisherman boasts about, and the Gulf of Maine may have been the best fishing spot in the known world. In 1604, Champlain claims to have met one industrious boat captain along the coast who had made more than 40 fishing trips across the Atlantic. By the 1600s more than 300 fishing boats were harvesting Maine fish to feed Spain, Italy, France, England, Portugal and Scandinavia.

In 1605, Captain George Waymouth explored the New England coast. Returning home, he convinced King James I of England of what the French already knew. This was a region worth more than gold; it was worth developing. To make the king feel a part of the exploration, Waymouth kidnapped five Native Americans and brought them with him to England. This did not endear the English to the Native Americans. More of that later. The king backed Waymouth's bid for future colonization.

FRENCH AND ENGLISH SETTLERS

The French and English were eager to colonize the coast, although the French at first were less aggressive than the British. The French tended to learn the languages and fit in with the local tribes in order to foster a profitable fur trade. A few Frenchmen came to spread their religion. In 1613, nine years after Champlain gave Mount Desert its name, a group of Jesuits established a religious community there.

One month later, the British razed the Mount Desert settlement and set the Jesuits out to sea. This marked the beginning of a long and bloody feud between the two nations. The region that is now Maine was, in fact, part of two overlapping territorial claims established by both nations. The territory played heavily in the struggle for supremacy that continued until the Peace of Paris in 1763, when France gave up its claim to the vast timberlands, excellent deepwater harbors and potential fur trade.

DREAMS FOR "THE MAIN"

In 1606, James I granted a charter for southern Maine to the Plymouth Company. In 1607, the same year the British established a permanent settlement at Jamestown, Virginia, a group of British settlers established the Popham Colony (they called it St. George) at the mouth of the Kennebec, in what is today Phippsburg. This was the start of British colonization in New England (the Popham Colony preceded the settlement at Plymouth, Massachusetts, by 13 years). Although the colonists endured only one long and unusually harsh winter, this is where Maine's famed shipbuilding history began. In 1608 the colonists built the fifty-foot pinnace *Virginia* to take them back to England. The *Virginia* was much hardier than the colonists who had built it; it sailed the Atlantic for many years.

The first permanent European settlements in Maine were at Monhegan in 1622, Saco in 1623 and Agamenticus (later York) in 1624. In 1629 the Pilgrims of the Plymouth Colony in Massachusetts established a trading post at

Archaeological dig done in the late 19th century under the direction of antiquarian John Henry Cartland uncovered British officers' quarters at Fort William Henry, Pemaquid Point, first built in 1692.

R. L. Bradley. Courtesy, Maine Historic
Preservation Committee

Bagaduce, on the Penobscot peninsula. From there they sent their English sponsors furs and other goods to pay off the debt for their New World voyage. The French didn't like the English being in what they considered their territory. Forty years later Baron de St. Castin took it by force.

In 1635 King Charles I of England, assuming it was his to give, gave Maine to Sir Ferdinando Gorge and named him "Lord of New England." Sir Gorge chose Agamenticus, which had grown into a small village, as the center of his empire. Five years later, he named it after himself, Gorgeana. Sir Gorge's hopes to develop "the main" — or the mainland and later "Maine" — were never realized. His heirs sold out his dream in 1677, and Gorgeana was reorganized as the town of York.

PRELUDE TO THE FRENCH AND INDIAN WARS

The uneasy relations between the French and English existed for years before formal war was declared. The coastal lands of Maine, particularly those east of the Penobscot River, were in a fairly constant state of dispute.

Although the French controlled most of the area east of the Penobscot, the English had managed to establish two trading centers there — one at Machias and one at Penobscot village. The French raided the posts in 1634 and 1635, and the English retook them in 1654. In 1664, the Duke of York was granted the lands between Pemaquid Point and the St. Croix River. In 1667, the English King Charles II surrendered his claim on lands including Nova Scotia, Acadia and Penobscot to the French under the Treaty of Breda. At the time, Baron de St. Castin established himself in Penobscot and proceeded to protect France's interest while trading with both the English and the Native Americans. He remained there until Sir Edmund Andros, the governor of New York and Massachusetts, forcibly took the town for the English.

Official hostilities between the two countries lasted from 1675 to 1763. In the British colonies it was known as the Indian War. Saco, Scarborough and Casco were the first towns to be attacked in September 1675. The Native Americans perhaps were still angry with Waymouth's kidnapping of their five kinsmen 70 years earlier. Certainly they were threatened by the English colonials' encroachment on their land. They sided with the French, who largely had left them and their ancestral claim to the land alone. The acrimonious 88-year struggle preoccupied the small native and colonial populations of Maine and was the reason why colonization nearly halted during that time. Following the defeat of the French at Quebec in 1759, English colonists began to settle on the coast in larger numbers.

By 1790 the few Native Americans who had survived the French and Indian Wars were made wards of the Commonwealth and confined to two reservations — one at Old Town, near Bangor, and the second at Perry, near Eastport. They had no documents on which to base their claims to the land, no guns, and were highly susceptible to diseases that had crossed the ocean with the Europeans. "In the end," writes historian James MacGregor Burns, "the less numerous and less sophisticated [Native American] society crumbled before the aggressive expansion of history's largest migration."

In 1953, Native Americans were given voting rights. In 1977 the Penobscot, Passamaquoddy and Maleseet Indians sued the state claiming that all treaties granting land to Maine were null and void, because they were never ratified by Congress. They asked for $25 billion and 12.5 million acres of land. In 1980 they received a settlement of $81.5 million, but no land.

THE REVOLUTIONARY WAR

In the mid-18th century, Maine was still very much a part of Massachusetts. Whereas Bostonians threw tea into the harbor, a Falmouth (now known as Portland) mob seized the Imperial tax stamps in 1765. Still many residents along the coast of northern Massachusetts were actively doing business with the British. Although Boston was the capital of Maine, Mainers valued above all their independence from London *and* Boston.

Once the Revolutionary War started, Mainers refused to ship their highly prized masts to the British fleet. The Royal Navy bombarded the city then called Falmouth and burned much of it to the ground. Even before that, zealous Maine patriots claimed the first naval victory of the war when in 1775 colonists captured the British cutter *Margaretta* in Machias Bay, a battle James Fenimore Cooper called the "Lexington of the seas."

The first colonial warship, *Ranger*, was built at Kittery in 1777. Two years later the colonies suffered a disastrous setback when 19 armed ships and 24 transports with more than 1,300 soldiers and marines were lost to the British at Castine. At the war's end in 1783 the Treaty of Versailles established Maine's most easterly border at the St. Croix River.

POSTWAR PROSPERITY AND THE WAR OF 1812

After the Revolutionary War, Maine prospered and grew. The era of logging began. Maine became a center for production of lumber for houses, barrels for trade, masts for ships, and wood for fuel. Ships from safe harbors all along the coast established trade routes around the world. Maine began to think about breaking away from Massachusetts.

Then France declared war on England in 1793. Short of men, England's navy began boarding American ships and impressing sailors with naval duty under pretense they were still subjects. For this reason President Jefferson finally ordered an embargo in 1807 disallowing trade with any foreign country. The embargo was particularly tough on the people and ports of Maine.

Many of the region's maritime businesses turned to smuggling. Eastport, just south of Canada, became the busiest port in the country. When the United States went to war against England in 1812, Mainers at first offered little resistance to the British, who were their best customers. People along the coast also continued trading with their own government. Worse, for the British, they continued building ships used by the American navy. The British set up a blockade and captured Castine and the surrounding towns.

With the Treaty of Ghent in 1814, the war ended as did England's blockade. The people of Maine started thinking again about breaking off from Massachusetts. In 1820, Maine was granted statehood as part of the Missouri Compromise. The separation papers were signed at the Jamestown Tavern in Freeport (the tavern still operates today down the street from L. L. Bean). The 23rd state to join the union established its current-day capital inland at Augusta 12 years later.

Fish drying on a pier in Friendship during the mid-19th century.

WOODEN SHIPS

"There are still any number of working lobster boats, plenty of yacht yards, and even a few deep-sea fishermen. . . . These are inadequate compensations, though, for anyone brought up in the knowledge of Maine's deepwater supremacy, those great times when Maine skippers were admired from the Elbe to the Amazon, and Maine-built ships were the world's criteria of seaworthiness. In those days, local prodigies like the stupendous six-masted schooner *Wyoming* were legends of the sea," wrote Jan Morris in *New England Monthly*.

By 1850, Maine was considered the preeminent shipbuilding capital of America. By 1860, one fifth of the state's population were mariners, 759 of them masters of ships. Ten percent of the nation's deepwater shipmasters lived in Searsport at the top of Penobscot Bay. Bath, midway up the coast, was the United States' fifth busiest port. A little farther up the coast, Wiscasset was the busiest international port north of Boston.

Maine's romantic era of wooden shipbuilding ended with a complex set of economic events that came just before the Civil War. The invention of ironclad ships didn't help. Foreign trade moved to other ports. Maine businessmen began looking for other industries to bank on; they didn't have to look far. Forests that once supplied timbers for masts and lithe hulls now are devoted almost entirely to the production of paper.

Fisheries were among the industries that flourished, with fishermen reaping a bounty from the cold waters off northern New England, including the fish-rich St. George's Bank. At its peak in 1902, the state landed and processed 242 million pounds of cod, cusk, hake, haddock, ocean perch, mackerel, halibut, pollock, crabs, clam, shrimp, mussels, lobster, herring and sardines. Canneries built during the height of this fishing boom, and now abandoned, are still in evidence from Yarmouth to Eastport. The canning industry fell on hard times. The nation's hunger for canned herring and sardines slaked with the advent of refrigeration and the easy transport of fresh fish at the turn of the century. Other popular whitefish species, such as cod, halibut, haddock and pollock, have become scarcer as fishermen have overfished the waters off Maine's coast.

ARTISTS "DISCOVER" MAINE'S COAST

In 1844, Thomas Cole, founder of the Hudson River School of painting, visited Bar Harbor, loved what he saw and spread the word around the art community. He also told his wealthy patrons. More than 200 lavish summer "cottages" were built. Grand hotels appeared. Developers were quick to claim Mount Desert Island's thick fogs were "as healthy for the body as basking in the sun." Bar Harbor became as well known as Newport, Rhode Island.

The Maine Almanac, compiled by the *Maine Times,* reported in 1870 that "Tourists begin arriving in Maine." Not only did they come to see Maine's rocky coast, they came to see and be near the rich people who lived on the coast. Then in 1912 Leon Leonwood Bean invented the Maine Hunting Shoe, an ugly duckling of a shoe, half-leather, half-rubber that nevertheless has made many a hunter happy. "L. L.," as Freeport residents and shop clerks still call him, might as well have invented shopping. The shoe, and the store that grew up around it, eventually turned the little village of Freeport into the second most popular place in Maine.

THE BIRTH OF ACADIA

The most visited place in Maine was also being established about the same time. A group of wealthy Mount Desert "rusticators" decided to donate large parcels of land to be used for a national park. Today Acadia is a public toe-hold on a coast that is 98 percent privately owned. In 1947 much of Bar Harbor was destroyed in a forest fire. The French paper *Le Figaro* mistakenly reported the peasants of Maine had struck a blow against feudalism. The town's year-round residents did not like being called peasants.

The fact is there are no aristocrats in Maine. It is a place where millionaires, lobstermen — Yankees who above all value self-reliance — talk about politics, the weather and their boats over pie and coffee in homespun diners. The beauty of the coast and the ocean is considered more important to the people who live and visit here than what is being worn on the streets of Boston or New York. "We are hardly fashionable," wrote Frances Fitzgerald, whose family members have been longtime summer residents of Northeast Harbor, in the August 1989 *Vogue*. "You might say we are consistent to the point of atavism."

"Come one, come all.

"There are many facets of the promotional spirit which beguile us, but our favorite is the promotion of states of the Union by their development commissions. It is common practice for a state to recommend itself as a sanctuary to people of other states, extending a blanket invitation to all to come and romp in the peculiar sunlight within its borders. Maine, conscious of its paradisiacal quality, doggedly advertises its 'unspoiled wilderness,' presumably in the hope that millions will shortly arrive to cry in it. This is an odd quirk. Obviously, if a state valued its wildness, it would keep silent and not let the secret out among the tame. The very idea of 'development' is inconsistent with natural beauty, and there is, of course, little likelihood that the Maine woods will be thoroughly appreciated by Maine until after they no longer exist, except in the joists and rafters of the wayside soft-drink parlors. . . ."

— E. B. White, *Writings from* The New Yorker, *1925-1976*

A JOURNEY UP THE COAST

Today there are many destinations on the coast that could be described as still having the "wild" feeling of a place barely settled. Throughout Washington County far Down East, there are long stretches of shoreline without summer cottages where the homes of year-round residents lie hidden within a dense, second-growth forest of spruce and pine. Even in the populated Midcoast section, there are meandering peninsulas punctuated with small fishing villages that seem to have only a tenuous hold on the landscape.

An occasional coastal visitor.

State Development Office

The coast also is home to several cities where a seat at the symphony can be hard to come by, and where the pastrami on rye is almost as satisfying as that you find on Second Avenue in New York. There are the bustling old summer resorts, many of which have expanded their seasons during the past decade and now host visitors year round. Visiting the Maine coast can be a matter of choosing between more than 200 towns and villages, each of which is a small, distinct world unto itself.

KITTERY AND THE YORKS

Depending on what direction you're coming from, Maine begins or ends in Kittery, Maine's first city, incorporated on Oct. 20, 1647. The Warren Lobster House, on the banks of the Piscataqua River, displays the first or last of many giant red lobster signs used to woo visitors along a several hundred mile long strip.

Ships for the Civil War were built here, so was the nation's first submarine. The shipyard, which is open to the public and sits on Seavey Island in the middle of the Piscataqua River, is actively functioning today.

Recently Kittery has shifted to a retail economy that is based around factory outlet and discount designer stores. This is the beginning — or end — of a long stretch of what could be called the "shopper's coastline." The oldest residential part of town is in the pretty area called Kittery Point, which can be reached by Rte. 103, a winding, wooded state road that intersects with U.S. Rte. 1 and leads on toward Rte. 1A and York.

The Yorks are a group of small villages — York Village, York Harbor, York Beach and Cape Neddick — that were among the first areas of the coast to be settled during the 1600s.

York has a well-preserved historical district. The Old Gaol Museum at the heart of York's "living history district" is the earliest example of stone architecture in the U.S. For most people, though, the Yorks have other charms. Some of the coast's best beaches are right here. Cape Neddick was one of the state's first summer resorts. Today York's coastal routes and shoreline is marked by an eclectic mix of stately homes, antique shops, working lobster boats and striking stretches of fine white sand.

The broad stretches of sand at York Beach make it a favorite on the South Coast for families.

State Development Office

OGUNQUIT AND WELLS

During the high season in July and August, these two towns have almost a carnival-like atmosphere and are packed with visitors from New York, Boston, Montreal and Quebec who come for the cool ocean breezes, good restaurants, a healthy cultural calendar — and great beaches. Wells and Ogunquit together have about seven miles of beachfront, roughly the same amount as Old Orchard.

Once a fishing village, Ogunquit, which in Algonquin means "beautiful place by the sea" was discoverd by artists during the mid- and late 1800s. These days, you still can see painters with easels perched at the side of the road trying to capture the elusive southcoast light as it plays on Bald Head Cliff, which rises a sheer 100 feet from the ocean. This area is a favorite vacation spot for artists of all kinds and tourists who come to shop quaint Perkins Cove and walk Marginal Way, the mile-long coastal footpath.

While Ogunquit caters to an art-minded crowd, Wells, with a beach rimmed with shops and family-style restaurants, is a favorite stop for travelers with children. Birders and naturalists also flock here to visit the Rachel Carson Wildlife Refuge, 1600 acres of fragile coastal wetlands, a haven for an amazing number of migrating birds during spring and summer.

THE KENNEBUNKS

Until George Bush was elected president, the Kennebunks flourished in relative obscurity. Now Bush's stone manse-by-the-sea is a familiar backdrop. Judging from the queue of cars and amateur cameramen setting up tripods across the Bush estate, the tourist trade is alive and well in Kennebunkport. Once the most popular roadside stop, Blowing Cave, with its dramatic 30-foot spray of water that announced the coming high tide, now ranks a pale second to the Bush family compound.

This affluent community has all the makings of a resort town. Winding country roads, acres of coastline, stately pines, gracious inns, interesting restaurants, shops, boutiques and galleries, sandy beaches and the sea.

First settled in the 1620s, the area's early history was peppered with Native American raids. The Kennebunks evolved into fishing and shipbuilding towns, and many of the historic captains' mansions are now handsome inns. The Kennebunks became known as a summer "watering place" in Victorian times, when city folk arrived by train to take in sea air and rusticate.

Kennebunkport is the most often visited. Dock Square, a lively hub of shops and restaurants, is a major draw, as is Ocean Avenue, which snakes past Cape Arundel and the Bush estate at Walker's Point. To the south, Kennebunk Beach offers fine sand and a sheltered cove. A short drive north on Rte. 9 to Cape Porpoise gives one a glimpse into the past. The cape is still very much a fishing village, and its harbor is a working one. The waters are so thick with lobster traps, it is almost impossible for pleasure boats to anchor anywhere near shore.

To the west, Kennebunk itself is a period piece. Eighteenth and nineteenth century homes offer a primer of architectural styles from Colonial and Greek

Surfers and families enjoy the water at Kennebunk Beach along with a view of the historic houses in the town.

State Development Office

Revival to Federal and Victorian. Best known is the Wedding Cake House, so named because of its icing-like embellishments, and a sterling example of Victorian excess. The bell swinging in the steeple of the First Parish Church was cast by Paul Revere and the steeple itself designed by Christopher Wren.

A good drive is Rte. 9, which was the main road to Bangor before Interstate 95. It starts in the Kennebunks and travels through Cape Porpoise, Pine Point and past the wealthy seaside community of Biddeford Pool.

OLD ORCHARD BEACH

Americans call it the "Maine Riviera" for its summer population, 60 percent of which is French-speaking Canadian. Or the "Coney Island of Maine" for its predominance of asphalt and its honky-tonk, boardwalk atmosphere.

French-speaking Canadians don't care what Old Orchard Beach is called — many consider it the capital of Maine. Since the 1850s, when the Grand Trunk Railroad opened between Montreal and Portland, French Canadians have been flocking to Old Orchard Beach and its centerpiece — a 7.5 mile sandy beach — the closest to Montreal and Quebec City.

In the old days, only wealthy French Canadians came to Old Orchard, and they came for weeks at a time. After World War II, working-class Canadians had money to spend and vacation time. Old Orchard was where they headed.

Today wealthier French Canadians favor tonier Ogunquit and Kennebunkport to the south, where there are no amusement parks, where hotels, not motels, are the rule and where shops are boutiques — and don't sell T-shirts with messages like "It's Not How Deep You Fish, It's How You Wiggle The Worm."

There's still a devoted French-speaking following for Old Orchard Beach with its 4,000 campsites, 90 motels, 350 cabins, 120 restaurants and 15 arcades. They come for the beach, one of the most spectacular and well-groomed stretches of sand in New England.

Old Orchard Beach does all it can to make French Canadians feel at home — perhaps because so many year-round residents of Old Orchard and nearby Biddeford and Saco are of French ancestry. Everywhere is the sign, "Ici on parle Francais." Restaurants feature bilingual menus. You can buy a cup of coffee at Dunkin' Donuts on Elm Street in nearby Biddeford and hear fellow patrons trade thoughts on politics and the weather — in French. St. Margaret's Catholic Church on Old Orchard St. holds a mass in French every Sunday. Many of the corner stores sell French-language newspapers from back home in Quebec and Montreal.

These days, both French- and English-speaking Canadians have another reason to visit Old Orchard Beach — shopping. The exchange rate has been very favorable in recent years. There's also the "TPS," or "GST" — 7 percent tax levied on all goods and services purchased in Canada since 1991. Visitors from the province of Quebec also pay an 8 percent sales tax on top of the TPS, making Maine's 6 percent state sales tax (as of the printing of this book) seem quite reasonable, indeed.

Old Orchard Beach has plenty of what many Canadians can't get enough of: electronics. Old Orchard St., the town's center strip, has at least nine electronic/T-shirt stores —a popular combo here — in its several downtown blocks.

PORTLAND

If there is one city on the coast that is an anomaly, it is Portland. Outsiders may not be able to understand this at first. To the rest of Maine, Portland is considered more a suburb of Boston than the state's largest city and home to one fifth of Maine's approximately one million inhabitants.

Maybe that's because of its big city ways. Boutiques. Ethnic food and more restaurants per capita than all but one other U.S. city (San Francisco). A full-time, professional symphony orchestra. The I. M. Pei-designed Portland Museum of Art. An international ferry (to Nova Scotia) and an international airport. And, of course, the Old Port, the old waterfront commercial district that has been made over into a mecca for shoppers and business people who eat lunch here. A writer for *The New York Times* once described it as the "San Francisco of the east."

The city sits on a moderately hilly peninsula framed by the Fore River to the west, the Presumpscot River to the East and Casco Bay to the north. With its working waterfront and underneath its big city ways (only a Mainer would call this cosmopolitan), it is the latest incarnation of a 19th-century seaport.

There are hundreds of islands large and small in Casco Bay, several of which have become bedroom communities for working Portlanders, that are interesting to explore, as well as good swimming, biking and walking ground.

FREEPORT

A newcomer to Freeport will certainly note that this town was built for shopping. Rte. 295 off the Maine Turnpike deposits the traveler on a two-lane road leading right through town. For the most part, the view from the car window is good enough to eye the buttons on a Ralph Lauren shirt or catch the winsome line of a canoe bow at L.L. Bean.

Way back before there were factory outlets, and before there was even an L. L. Bean, this was a favored stopping place for the British navy. His Majesty's ships would berth and pick up the famous Maine white pine the navy used to make their masts. Even today, two major landmarks commemorate this early trading route — Upper Mast Landing and Lower Mast Landing where the mast pines were collected before being shipped.

Until 1981, there was L. L. Bean and the kind of stores you'd find on Main St. in any small town. Now it is wall-to-wall factory outlets. But the true beauty of Freeport isn't in the great bargains to be found there. It's that the town has retained much of its feel as a New England village. That and knowing that only two minutes' drive east on Bow St. and you're out in the country. Then you get a sense of the way it used to be: hilly, green pastures, tidy 18th-century farmhouses, country lanes, pines and firs.

BRUNSWICK TO WISCASSET

Bowdoin College is the overwhelming presence in Brunswick, but there's much more here than just the school, including the Peary-MacMillan Arctic Museum and the Maine State Music Theatre. This is also where Harriett Beecher Stowe wrote *Uncle Tom's Cabin*. For most visitors, this town is a place to get serious about their visit. This is the point in the coast where little-known detours can often be more rewarding than the better-known vacation destinations like Bar Harbor, Portland and the South Coast beaches. Brunswick is certainly the place where one has to start picking and choosing.

Case in point, just a little to the southwest of here are the Harpswells, skinny fingers of land that stretch into Casco Bay and are connected by bridge to the rounded and rocky terrain of Sebascodegan, Orrs and Bailey islands. Making your way to the edge of Mackerel Cove on Bailey Island is only a matter of about 15 miles, but it can seem like time-traveling through decades. There's also Cundy's Harbor off on its own, a fishing village so heavily populated with photographic subjects that local stores do a brisk business selling film.

Bath is a city of ships and shipbuilding that hugs the shores of the Kennebec, a deep and navigable waterway that has an ocean-like feel to it — as if it were capable of handling any oceangoing vessel large or small. During World War II, Bath built more destroyers than all the shipyards in the entire Japanese empire. Not far from here is the Phippsburg peninsula, the cradle of Maine civilization and its shipbuilding industry.

Across the Kennebec is Georgetown Island, a sprawling network of summer communities and fishing villages with names like Robinhood, Five Islands, Marrtown and Arrowsic. Robinhood Cove, which cuts into the island's northeastern side, is often filled with the yachts of summering residents, and Reid State Park at the outermost reaches of the Sheepscot River is a wonderful family park with one of the better beaches in the Midcoast.

Wiscasset has billed itself as the "prettiest village in Maine." That title could be disputed, but it is one of the prettiest many visitors will see, because of its highly visible location where Rte. 1 crosses the Sheepscot River. Making the town even more romantic are two old schooners lodged haphazardly on the west bank of the river. The *Hesperus* and the *Luther Little* once carried cargo between Boston, Haiti and Portugal. They were two of thousands of ships that plied the seas until well into the 1920s. Today they are one of the most photographed sites in Maine.

BOOTHBAY HARBOR

Formerly a trading center, and later a shipbuilding center, Boothbay Harbor today is mostly about boats, activities attached to boats and people who find the boating way of life appealing. The shady streets of the town, at the tip of a rocky peninsula, are lined with summer-people-minded shops and a wealth of art galleries. The pretty harbor is jam-packed with boats to rent, boats to hire, boats to envy and boats to drool over and make one consider Captain Kidd's occupation. (The notorious pirate also liked to summer here and reportedly left a buried treasure on nearby Damariscove Island.) This is also the port of call for Windjammer Days and the Friendship Sloop Races, two famous Maine boaters' events.

Within half an hour's drive you can see the great boats being built in East Boothbay. Nearby are the summer retreats of Newagen on Southport Island to the west and Ocean Point to the east.

NEWCASTLE / DAMARISCOTTA TO PEMAQUID POINT

For centuries Native Americans summer camped here and left behind giant piles of oyster shells, a feat which today is celebrated at the annual Damariscotta River Oyster Festival. Not far off Rte. 1, you can still see one of the great shell heaps where the Damariscotta River and the inland Great Salt Bay meet.

Here is another one of those famous coastal junctures, where travelers can push on toward Rockland and Camden or veer off the main road onto picturesque Rte. 129. This road runs down the Pemaquid peninsula along the river to South Bristol, a fishing village, and Christmas Cove, a yachting basin so named by Captain John Smith, who anchored here on Christmas Day in 1614. Rte. 130 picks up in the fishing village of New Harbor and meanders on through the historic peninsula to Pemaquid Point, where there is one of Maine's most stunning lighthouses — Pemaquid Light. This spot shows off the Maine coast at its stormy best with the power of the ocean pounding against the rockbound coast. Rte. 32 takes you back up along Muscongus Sound through pretty Round Pond, to Waldoboro.

WALDOBORO TO ROCKLAND

Waldoboro was settled by Germans in the mid-18th century, and today is famed for two of the state's culinary landmarks — Moody's Diner and Morse's Sauerkraut. The first five-masted schooner was built here in 1888.

From here, Friendship is just a short trip down Rte. 220, which skirts the western shore of the Medomak River. It's hard to believe Friendship exists. Where are the shops, the hotels, the gas stations, restaurants? Here on beautiful, isolated Hatchet Cove are a few summer homes, a handful of lobster boats and a Friendship sloop or two, that famous gaff-rigged working boat now prized by wealthy modern-day sailors. Rte. 97 leads past Cushing, another quiet fishing village, made famous by painter Andrew Wyeth.

From Thomaston, home of the state prison, you can veer off onto Rte. 131, which leads down yet another peninsula filled with history. Tenant's Harbor looks simple, but look again. Those are mighty big yachts anchored so casually in the harbor. Southwest from here is Port Clyde, once called Herring Gut. Port Clyde is the point of departure for the hour-long boat ride to Monhegan, eleven miles off the coast. Measuring only one mile by 1/2 mile, Monhegan literally is besieged with painters, and the salt breezes alternately smell of turpentine. The dark forests and dramatic cliffs make the island a hiker's paradise as well.

Once known for its quarried limerock, shipped to the four corners of the earth, today Rockland bills itself as the lobster capital of the world. It is the Penobscot Bay region's central working town, and its harbor is filled with lobster boats and commercial fishing boats that regularly fish the waters of the Grand Banks. Rockland is a bustling town that in recent years has become gentrified with artists' studios, galleries and moderately expensive restaurants that clearly aim to serve tourists. It also is a hub of the windjammer trade, and from here ferries regularly travel to Vinalhaven, Matinicus and North Haven.

Emblidge

Salty spray and brilliant sunlight inspire artists on the rocky edge of Monhegan Island.

Sitting fifteen miles out in Penobscot Bay, Vinalhaven flourished when granite was quarried here. Today the island has a tenacious year-round population of lobstermen and fishermen and a dedicated coterie of summer residents who seem to like keeping the secret of this island to themselves. To the north is the small and exclusive summer community of North Haven on North Haven island. Windjammers and large pleasure boats often anchor in Pulpit Harbor where passengers can catch a glimpse of the large seaside estates owned by the island's reclusive summer residents.

In striking contrast there is the quiet, tiny island of Matinicus. Approximately 100 people make their living here, most of them lobstering and fishing the outer waters of Penobscot Bay. It takes about two hours by ferry to ply the 23 miles of water to the island. Dedicated birders often opt to charter a local boat and keep going another five miles to Matinicus Rock, where nesting puffins often can be seen.

CAMDEN

Just off Rte. 1 before Camden is Rockport, a pastoral village where Galloways munch in green meadows and actors, photographers and boatbuilders live in mansions by the sea. Rockport was also the home of Andre the Seal; today a statue on the harbor commemorates him.

The storybook beauty of Camden was captured in the film *Peyton Place*. Today it's considered the shoppers' resting place between Freeport and Bar Harbor. It's a destination in its own right and a hard town in which to find a parking space. Space in the harbor is also scarce. Luxury yachts moor next to giant windjammers that ferry passengers on weeklong cruises. Lincolnville Beach just to the north offers an expansive view of Penobscot Bay. This is also where you catch the ferry to Islesboro, the exclusive summer community three miles off shore.

BELFAST TO BUCKSPORT

The towns along this part of the coast keep promising to be the next Camden. The fact each is still waiting to be discovered makes this a wonderful place to

A mooring in beautiful Camden Harbor is one of the most valuable pieces of real estate on the coast.

Tom Hindman

visit. Antiques and sea captains' homes abound. Beautiful old houses with ocean views are still more than reasonable. There are art galleries, theater groups and big city restaurants in Belfast.

The deepwater port of Searsport at the head of Penobscot Bay was once known in ports around the world. The town still has the grand waterfront houses to prove it, many of them now converted to inns and bed and breakfasts. Today it bills itself as the antique capital of Maine.

BLUE HILL PENINSULA

Rte. 175 off Rte. 1 just past Bucksport takes you down to Castine. This former trading post is one of the most attractive towns on the coast, with its tree-lined streets, grand homes and spectacular views of Holbrook Island Sanctuary, Isleboro and Cape Rosier, where authors Helen and Scott Nearing built their own Walden. The Maine Maritime Academy is in Castine and so is its training ship, the *State of Maine*, which is open for tours when in port. Rte. 15 to Stonington on Deer Island at the end of the peninsula is a good hour and a half off Rte. 1 and prefers it that way. The fishing industry is very much alive here. The mail boat leaves here for Isle au Haut, Acadia National Park's least-visited outpost shared with a small community of fishermen and farmers.

Blue Hill, named after the nearby blueberry-crested mountain, has abundant views of Mount Desert Island. This is obviously ample inspiration, because it is a thriving center for artists and writers who live here and in nearby villages including Brooklin and Sedgwick. It is also the sight of the annual Blue Hill Fair, made famous by local writer E. B. White in *Charlotte's Web*. Surry, on pretty Rte. 172, which leads up to Ellsworth, may be the only village of its size with its own opera company.

Stonington, on Deer Isle, is a quintessential coast of Maine fishing and lobstering town.

Roy Zalesky

MOUNT DESERT ISLAND AND THE SCHOODIC PENINSULA

If only the French explorer Champlain had known what he had discovered when he first set eyes on this island of rounded mountains almost 400 years ago. Today Mount Desert, which includes Bar Harbor and most of Acadia National Park, is the most visited place in Maine. Visitors come here to walk the famed carriage trails that were built in the early part of this century as a kind of social lifeline connecting the homes of summer residents like the Rockefellers and the Pulitzers. They also drive the twenty-mile Park Loop Road along Frenchman's Bay and the road to the top of Cadillac Mountain to watch the sun go down at Sunset Point, which has been renamed Blue Hill Overlook by park officials to help reduce overcrowding at dusk. The hike up Cadillac is usually a lovely, lonely climb.

Mount Desert Island is also home to Bar Harbor, a lively, unabashedly tourist town that somehow manages to keep its dignity. Maybe the stately Victorian townhouses lining the streets, many converted to small inns and bed and breakfasts, keep check on the proliferating T-shirt and souvenir stores. Maybe also because the people who get the most out of their visit here only stop mountain climbing, biking, canoeing and kayaking long enough to grab a bite and a good night's rest. If you like it quieter, there are the civilized charms of tea at the Jordan Pond House in Acadia and the famous Mount Desert gardens bursting in bloom at the height of summer. There also are more secluded island spots like Northeast Harbor, Hulls Cove, Southwest Harbor and Bass Harbor and the islands — including Little Cranberry Island, the lovely home of the tiny village of Isleford. Or do what many Mainers do, and visit in the spring, fall and winter — when the island is less crowded.

Just east of Mount Desert is the Schoodic Peninsula, the tip of which is part of Acadia National Park, a smaller, wilder version of the main portion of the park. The rest of the peninsula is characterized by an anything goes feeling. Lobstermen rub elbows with the sons of captains of industry and movie stars. Army personnel venture about, caring for a secretive military installation on the point. Year-round residents like to tell the story of one neighbor who bought a whole fleet of little wooden sailboats and every year rounded up family and acquaintances to compete in friendly regattas.

EAST OF SCHOODIC

For the majority of coastal Maine visitors, the world ends at Bar Harbor. The former Washington County, thoughtfully renamed Sunrise County by the state's publicity department, is thought to be dirt poor, flat and endless. It's not. In fact, it has a beauty all its own, stark as a blueberry barren, religious, pure — probably thanks to the fact that developers have largely ignored it during the last 50 years.

Everything up here is out in the open, exposed to the elements, and here they seem more, well, elemental. Like Jonesport. It's terrifyingly close to the sea. In the hilly fishing village, weatherbeaten clapboard and shingled houses huddle together as if to draw comfort from one another. There's also Dennysville, tucked into the countryside on the Dennys River where stately Georgian homes rise up from the rolling landscape and make this look more like the manor-strewn countryside of England than Down East.

MACHIAS TO LUBEC AND EASTPORT

Machias, which is Indian for "bad little falls," is the most businesslike of towns. It's a get-em-in-get-em-out place where waitresses wait on busloads of people headed out of town almost as quickly as they drove in. No questions asked. Settled by the English in 1633, this was a favorite repair and refueling spot for pirates in the late 17th century. For those American history students who thought the Revolution was a unanimous undertaking by all colonists, think again. Prosperous lumbermen, who understood quite well that England was their best customer, argued for a long while about whether or not to support the revolt. They did, and a few months later nearby Machiasport was the site of the first naval battle of the Revolutionary War. Stalwart Mainers, you'll be glad to know, won the skirmish, captured the British armed schooner the *Margaretta* and inspired leaders in Philadelphia to establish a navy.

Lubec sits on a narrow strip of land that juts into Cobscook Bay and is a quiet town with tree-lined streets and wonderful views of the bay. Just down the road is West Quoddy Head, the easternmost point of land in the United States and site of a beautiful state park and a lighthouse that is enshrouded by fog 59 days of the year. Lubec is also the only auto route (via bridge) to Campobello Island, the summer home of President Franklin D. Roosevelt. To get there, you have to go through customs — Campobello is within Canadian territory — although the presidental landmark is operated jointly by the U.S. and Canadian governments. The island is also a birdwatcher's haven, part of the famous Quoddy Loop that extends through northeastern Maine and southeastern Nova Scotia.

Eastport has been described as a city of dreamers, and there are ample examples of the city's saga of boom-and-bust. During the early 1800s, when trade between the United States and England was embargoed, Eastport gloried as a smuggler's port. It was certainly far enough down east to escape diligent enforcers.

Fishing was and remains today the city's main industry. Cod, pollock, haddock, halibut and herring once flourished in the cold offshore waters, but during the past 25 years have dwindled. During the late 1800s to mid-1900s, sardines were big business, and canneries lined the waterfront (sardines are actually small herrings). During the 80s, the bay's sweeping tides and deep coastal waters were discovered as ideal for farming salmon in offshore pens. Now, every year the town celebrates the domesticated Atlantic salmon with a festival in early September. Most recently, the paper manufacturer Georgia Pacific stirred up local dreams of grandeur when they announced the company would make this the major place for exporting their paper goods. To the outsider this hillside town, with a startlingly minimal number of gift shops and art galleries, has almost a Wild West feel and is a great place to make home base when exploring the beautiful country that surrounds it.

However much Mainers and summer visitors curse its traffic and tack, Rte. 1 from Kittery to Eastport links everything together and is a journey unto itself. Rte. 1 takes you through the heart of many coastal towns, letting you see real Mainers going about their everyday business. Over the years landmarks of good taste and bad and a mix of both have made it a destination in its own right. Take Rte. 1 to Flo's Hot Dogs, the Sleepytown Motel, the Ogunquit Playhouse, L. L. Bean, Moody's Diner and Helen's. That's a classic vacation right there.

CHAPTER TWO

From The-ah to He-ah

TRANSPORTATION

Sections of coastal U.S. Rte. 1 in Maine, which today runs from Kittery to Fort Kent by way of Rockland, Ellsworth and Machias, follow ancient Native American trails. Settlers marked the trails during the 1600s and named the resulting road the King's Highway. The route first was used by mail couriers traveling from Boston to Machias; later, as settlements grew up along the coast, the public highway was traversed by horse-drawn vehicles.

Prince of Fundy

Passengers save several hundred miles of road travel on the Scotia Prince, *shown here off Portland Headlight, bound for Yarmouth, Nova Scotia.*

The first stagecoach began operating between Portland and Portsmouth in 1787. The 90-mile journey took three days. Keep that slow crawl in mind as you're creeping across the Carlton Bridge east of Bath. (Later we will tell you about some of the most famous bottlenecks along the coast, including the Carlton Bridge; we'll also suggest ways to avoid them.)

Despite the early full-fledged "highway," most of the coast was serviced by roads that were muddy and impassable during much of the year. Because this is a coast, the preferred method of travel then was by sea; ships and shipping were the industries that made Maine.

By the 1850s, 246 sailing vessels and 12 steamships called regularly on the port of Portland while 31 different railway lines carrying lumber and passengers crisscrossed the state. At the turn of the century electric trolleys carried tourists from Boston up the coast to Kennebunkport and Bar Harbor.

With the creation of the Interstate Highway System during the 1950s, suddenly half the populations of the United States and Canada were within a day's drive of the Maine coast. Today, most visitors come by highway.

PRESENT POSSIBILITIES

Airports at Boston, Portland and Bangor service domestic and international airlines with direct flights from Canada and Europe. Smaller airports, including

Rockland and Bar Harbor, serve as connecting points for air travelers. Passenger train service to Maine ended during the 1950s. Today there are several groups advocating an extension of Amtrak that would connect Portland with Boston and New York. Car ferries run regularly between the maritime provinces of Canada and Bar Harbor and Portland.

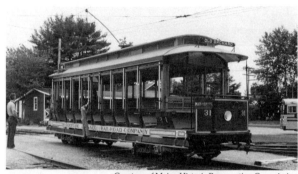

Trolleys like this were a popular form of transportation. This one and many others from around the world may be seen at the Seashore Trolley Museum in Kennebunkport.

Courtesy of Maine Historic Preservation Commission

GETTING TO THE COAST

BY CAR

From Connecticut, New York, New Jersey and South: I-95 goes right across the Piscataqua River separating New Hampshire and Maine, into Kittery, the first and oldest town on the coast.

From New York: I-95 runs along the coast of Connecticut, up through Providence, Boston and Portsmouth. For a more direct route take I-95 to New Haven, I-91 north to Hartford, I-84 northeast until you get on the Mass. Pike at the Sturbridge entrance. Take the Westborough exit and follow I-495 northeast to where it joins I-95, just south of the New Hampshire border.

From Boston: Although this route adds a few more miles, it is faster than fighting your way up Rte. 1. Take I-93 north to Rte. 128 east until it rejoins I-95. On the way home there's also the added benefit of saving the Tobin Bridge toll — and avoiding traffic.

From Montreal: AAA recommends you take Rte. 10 to Magog; 55 south to the international border just north of Derby Line, Vermont. Pick up I-91 at the border and follow to Rte. 2 in St. Johnsbury. Continue east on Rte. 2 through Gorham, New Hampshire, and on to Bethel, Maine.

If your destination is the Midcoast, Casco Bay or South Coast region, pick up Rte. 26 in Bethel and follow to Portland.

For the Down East/Acadia and East of Schoodic regions, continue on Rte. 2 from Bethel to I-95 near Newport, Maine, and follow to Bangor. From there you can take Alternate Rte. 1 to Stockton Springs and Belfast. Or you can take Rte. 1 south to Ellsworth and points east.

From Quebec City: Take Rte. 73 to Rte. 173 and the border, about 10 miles south of Armstrong. Pick up Rte. 201 at the border and follow all the way to Skowhegan, Maine. To access the South Coast, Casco Bay and Midcoast regions, continue on Rte. 201 to Waterville where you pick up I-95 south. If you're headed to the Midcoast or Down East, pick up Rte. 2 east of Skowhegan. It connects with I-95 near Newport, Maine, and goes to Bangor. From there you can take Alternate Rte. 1 to Stockton Springs and Belfast. Or you can take Rte. 1 south to Ellsworth and points east.

From Saint John or Fredericton: Take Rte. 1 from St. John to the international border at St. Stephen, then south to Calais, Maine. Continue on Rte. 1 toward Machias and points south. Rte. 190 in Perry veers off toward Eastport. An alternate route to the Midcoast, Casco Bay and South Coast regions is to follow Rte. 1 to Rte. 9 near Calais. Follow Rte. 9 to Bangor.

From Toronto: You have the choice of traveling north or south of Lake Ontario. Both routes take approximately the same amount of time. The southern route is super highways — and tolls — most of the way. The northern route is smaller roads and no tolls.

Traveling north around the lake, take Rte. 401 east to Cornwall, just north of the international border. Pick up Rte. 37 in Rooseveltown, New York, and follow that east to Malone. Take Rte. 11 East to Swanton, Vermont, where you get onto I-89 south. Take this highway to Montpelier. Pick up Rte. 2 east and follow all the way through St. Johnsbury on to Bethel, Maine.

If your destination is in the Midcoast, Casco Bay and South Coast regions, pick up Rte. 26 in Bethel and follow to Portland.

For the Down East/Acadia and East of Schoodic regions, continue on Rte. 2 from Bethel to I-95 near Newport, Maine, and follow to Bangor. From there you can take Alternate Rte. 1 to Stockton Springs and Belfast. Or you can take Rte. 1 south to Ellsworth and points east.

Traveling south around Lake Ontario, take the QEW to the international border. Take 190 through Niagara Falls, New York, to I-90. Follow I-90 to the connection with the Mass. Pike. Take the Mass. Pike to the Westborough exit and follow I-495 northeast to where it joins I-95, just south of the New Hampshire border.

BY BUS

Both *C & J Trailways* (800-258-7111) and *Greyhound* link Boston and Portsmouth with Portland (check your local phone book for Greyhound information). Greyhound continues up I-95 to Brunswick, Lewiston, Augusta, Waterville and Bangor. From Bangor there is service to Ellsworth and Bar Harbor. There is no direct bus link to points in Canada.

BY PLANE

If you are not traveling by car, you most likely will arrive in Maine via plane. There are major airports in Portland, Augusta and Bangor, all with connecting flights to smaller airports in Rockland and Bar Harbor. Many choose to fly into Boston's Logan Airport, only 1.5 hours to Kittery and 2.5 hours to Portland by car. All of the large airports are served by the major airlines. In addition, there are several small coastal and island airports with independent air services that have connecting regular and charter flights.

Augusta State Airport — 289-3185; Northwest Airlink.

Portland International Jetport — 874-8300; Delta, Continental, United, U. S. Air, Northwest Airlink and Northeast Express connecting with Boston, New York and Quebec. This airport also offers direct and connecting flights to other major cities in the U. S. and Canada, such as Chicago, Newark, Philadelphia, Washington, Toronto and Montreal.

Bangor International Airport — 947-0384; Delta, Continental Express, United, Northwest Airlink, Air Atlantic, Balair Ltd. (BGR-Zurich), Business Express, Air Belgium.

Knox County Regional Airport, Owls Head — 594-4131; Continental Express.

Hancock County/Bar Harbor Airport, Trenton — 667-7329; Continental Express.

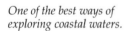
One of the best ways of exploring coastal waters.

Tom Hindman

MAINE ACCESS

The chart below gives miles and approximate driving times from the following cities to Portland:

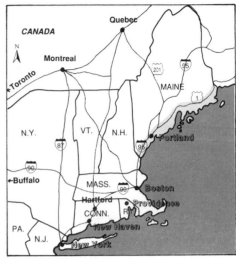

City	Time	Miles
Albany	5.5 hours	237
Boston	2.5 hours	109
Hartford	4 hours	200
Montreal	6 hours	255
New York	7 hours	317
Philadelphia	9.5 hours	424
Quebec	6.5 hours	278
St. John	7 hours	309
Toronto	14 hours	621
Washington, D.C.	12.5 hours	557

The chart below gives you miles and approximate driving times from the following cities to Bangor.

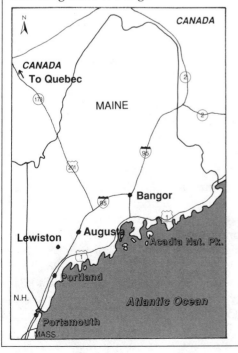

City	Time	Miles
Montreal	7.25 hours	306
Quebec	5.75 hours	236
St. John	3 .5 hours	163
Toronto	13.25 hours	609
Yarmouth	19 hours	850
Boston	5.5 hours	249
New York	9 hours	452

Maine Turnpike

To find out what the weather or traffic is like on the turnpike, call 800-675-PIKE. Following is a list of Maine Turnpike interchanges and their numbers.

Exit No.	Location
1	Kittery, York
2	Ogunquit/Wells
3	Kennebunk
4	Biddeford
5	Old Orchard, Saco
6	Scarborough Downs (summer)
6A	Portland
8	Portland
9	Falmouth Spur, Freeport, Yarmouth
12	Auburn
13	Lewiston
15	Augusta

GETTING AROUND THE COAST OF MAINE

BY CAR

There are three ways to drive up the coast: the fast way on I-95; the medium-fast way on U.S. Rte. 1; and the slow-and-easy way on smaller state highways and roads that often turn out to be the fastest of all. Which route you take depends on your destination — or how serendipitous you want to be.

The three most-visited spots in Maine and on the coast are: Acadia National Park, L. L. Bean in Freeport and Old Orchard Beach. Depending on your intentions and schedule, you may wish to see — or avoid — all three.

Acadia is one of the most beautiful parks in the national park system. To get to Acadia, take Rte. 1 or Rte. 1A to Ellsworth, which is in the center of the Down East/Acadia region. From Ellsworth take Rte. 3 to Bar Harbor. The park is less than a mile from Bar Harbor. Bar Harbor is 211 miles from Kittery, 122 miles from Eastport and 46 miles from Bangor. The portion of Acadia on the Isle au Haut can be reached by ferry from Stonington from late June through mid-October. Most of Acadia's 5 million yearly visitors speed up or down I-95 to Augusta or Bangor before heading coastward along Rte. 3 or Rte. 1A. Once they arrive, they drive the famed Park Loop Road, a 20-mile winding road through the 35,000 acre park, which culminates at the top of 1,530-foot Cadillac Mountain with views of Blue Hill, Penobscot and Frenchman Bay. In recent years, the number of vehicles on the loop has been so heavy that there have been traffic jams.

Roy Zalesky

Bar Harbor is a popular stop for the Queen Elizabeth II, *where passengers explore the seaside town and national park.*

To reach Freeport, most visitors opt for Exit 17 or Exit 19 off I-95 (the coastal extension that spans from South Portland to Topsham before rejoining the Maine Turnpike). The signs from the highway lead directly into Freeport, home of L. L. Bean and a growing community of factory outlets from Ralph Lauren to Maidenform lingerie (see *Shopping*, Chapter Seven).

To get to Old Orchard Beach, most travelers take Exit 5 off I-95, which leads to Rte. 5 and Old Orchard Beach. The town is home to a seven-mile long beach — one of the state's most significant sand beaches and the closest to Canada. During July more than 80 percent of the vacationers in Old Orchard Beach are French Canadian.

Then there is the rest of the coast. A small road sign leading off Rte. 1 on the right reads "Friendship." The whole Penobscot peninsula gets a similar simple sign or two. If you opt to heed one of these signs and turn off —and deciding which one or two to take can be the hard part, since any one could be considered a vacation destination — most likely you will find other tourists. You won't find nearly as many tourists as you will find in Acadia, Freeport and Old Orchard Beach. You could also find a place like Jonesport, where fishermen's houses are piled around the waterfront like lobster traps.

The best way to see the area is by car. Given the relatively long distances between towns on the coast be sure to plan carefully before you leave. Many secondary routes that access towns along the coast are narrow, two-lane roads, and they make travel slower than you might expect. For example, it takes a full hour to get from Rte. 1 at Orland to Stonington via rtes. 175 and 15.

If you want help getting around the coast, and you're a member, check in with AAA. They can map various routes to your particular destination. Their offices on the coast are:

Portland — AAA Maine   South Portland—AAA Maine
425 Marginal Way; 774-6377   Marshall's Plaza
Mailing address: 443 Western Ave.
P.O. Box 3544   So. Portland, ME 04106
Portland, ME 04104   775-6211

CAR RENTALS

If you are flying into Boston, Portland, Bangor or Bar Harbor, chances are you will rent an automobile to explore the coast. It is best to call well ahead of your visit to reserve a rental car, particularly during the busier season between Memorial and Labor days.

Agency: 800-321-1972 (Portland Jetport, 797-8331).

American International: 800-IAM-HERE (Portland Jetport, 761-5955).

Avis: 800-331-1212 (Portland Jetport, 874-7500; Bar Harbor Airport, 667-5421; Rockland Airport 594-5275; Augusta Airport 623-8550; Bangor Airport 947-8383).

Budget: 800-527-0700 (Portland Jetport, 772-6789; Bar Harbor Airport, 667-1200; Augusta Airport, 622-0210; Bangor Airport, 945-9429).

Dollar: 800-800-4000 (Portland Jetport, 773-0271; Bangor Airport 947-5474).

Hertz: 800-654-3131 (Portland Jetport, 774-4544; Bar Harbor Airport, 667-5017; Bangor Airport, 942-5519).

National: 800-CAR-RENT (Portland Jetport, 773-0036; Bangor Airport, 947-0158).

Rent-a-Ride: 800-323-3195 (Portland, 773-3367).

Thrifty: 800-367-2277 (Portland Jetport, 772-4628).

Statewide Airport Transportation
Jet Limo: 800-834-5500; outside Maine: 800-992-1401.

BY PLANE

A fast way to get around the coast is by air. Following is a list of air charter services that fly on the coast.

Maine Aviation Corporation, Portland Jetport	775-5635
Down East Flying Service, Portland Jetport	774-2028/800-752-6378
Echo Helicopters, Portland Jetport	775-5440
Penobscot Air Service, Rockland Airport	596-6211/800- 777-6211
Acadia Air Inc., Bar Harbor Airport	667-5534
Snug Harbor Airways, Bangor Airport	942-4557
Maine Beechcraft, Augusta Airport	662-1331
Ace Aviation, Belfast Airport	338-2970

COASTAL TOWN ACCESS

Here are approximate distances between selected cities and towns within the state. The time it takes to travel these distances varies widely, depending on time of year, traffic conditions and the route traveled. The highway speed limit in Maine is 55 mph in populated areas, 65 mph in rural regions.

From Kittery to:	Miles	From Eastport to:	Miles
Old Orchard Beach	37	Machias	44
Portland	50	Bar Harbor	122
Freeport	66	Belfast	141
Brunswick	76	Camden	160
Augusta	107	Rockland	167
Boothbay Harbor	109	Boothbay Harbor	207
Rockland	131	Brunswick	217
Camden	135	Freeport	227
Belfast	153	Portland	243
Bangor	183	Old Orchard Beach	262
Bar Harbor	211	Kittery	293
Machias	249		
Eastport	293		

Others:	Miles
Bangor to Bar Harbor	46
Augusta to Rockland	42
Augusta to Belfast	47

BY FERRY

One of the advantages of visiting the coast of Maine is that you have so many opportunities to ride a ferry. Island residents live with their inner clocks set to the ferry schedule, and so will you when you plan to visit one of the coastal outlands. For information on ferries statewide, write to or call the *Maine State Ferry Service*, P.O. Box 645, 517A Main St., Rockland 04841; 800-521-3939 in state; 207-596-2202 out-of-state.

Rockland to Vinalhaven: Year-round service between Rockland and Vinalhaven on the *Governor Curtis* (863-4421); 15 miles; crossing time: one hour and 15 minutes.

To North Haven: Year round on the *North Haven* (867-4441); 12.5 miles; crossing time: one hour and 10 minutes.

To Matinicus: Ferry service one day a month, call for schedule. On the *William Silsby* (596-2202); 23 miles; crossing time: two hours and 15 minutes.

This ferry carried passengers between the island of Vinalhaven and Rockland during the 18th century. Ferry service is still the island's most vital link to the mainland.

Courtesy of the Penobscot Marine Museum

Lincolnville to Isleboro: Year-round service on the *Margaret Chase Smith* (789-5611 or 734-6935); 3 miles; crossing time: 20 minutes.

Bass Harbor to Swans Island: Year-round service on the *Everett Libby* (526-4273); 6 miles; crossing time: 40 minutes.

To Frenchboro: Year-round service on the *Everett Libby* (244-3254); 8.25 miles; crossing time: 50 minutes.

Portland to Peaks, Great Chebeague; Long, Great and Little Diamond, and Cliff islands, with seasonal service to Bailey Island: Year-round service on the *Abenaki, Island Holiday, Island Romance, Machigonne II* by Casco Bay Lines, P.O. Box 4656 DTS, Portland 04112 (774-7871); 17 minutes to Peaks; 30 minutes to Long Island; one hour and 15 minutes to Chebeague. Ferry leaves Ferry Terminal at Commercial and Franklin streets. This is America's oldest ferry service.

Portland to Eagle Island: Leaves from Long Wharf daily between June 23 and Labor Day. Eagle Tours, 19 Pilot Point Rd., Cape Elizabeth 04107 (774-6098); 90-minute stopover on island.

Freeport to Eagle Island: Ferry service runs daily between Memorial and Labor days. Atlantic Seal Cruises, Main St., South Freeport 04078 (865-6112); one-hour stopover on island.

Portland to Yarmouth, Nova Scotia: Regular car and passenger service on the *Scotia Prince* from May through October with occasional "no-sail days." Prince of Fundy Cruises, P.O. Box 4216, Station A, Portland, 04101 (775- 5616 in Portland; 800-341-7540 in U.S.; 800-482-0955 in Maine; 800-565-7900 in Nova Scotia, New Brunswick, Prince Edward Island from May—Oct.; 902-742-6460 year-round in Canada); 11 hours. Leaves from the International Ferry Terminal, Commercial St., Portland. Children under 5 travel free. Vehicle and cabin rates extra. Tractor-trailer trucks often take this boat to save driving 850 miles. Once offshore you can gamble and shop duty free.

Cousins Island to Great Chebeague Island: Year-round service on the *Big Squaw* and *Islander;* Chebeague Transportation Co., Cumberland 04107 (846-

Monhegan Island's few trucks pick up passengers' gear from the ferry landing.

Emblidge

3700). No transient parking available at Cousins Island. Parking & shuttle bus service available from Cumberland Center.

Boothbay to Monhegan: Daily service Memorial Day to Columbus Day on the *Balmy Days II* with Capt. Box Campbell, P.O. Box 102, Boothbay 04538 (633-2284); one round trip per day. Leaves from Pier 8, Commercial St., Boothbay.

Port Clyde to Monhegan: Daily service from May through June on the *Laura B* with Capt. James Barstow, P.O. Box 238, Port Clyde 04855 (372-8848); one hour, 10 minutes.

New Harbor to Monhegan: Daily service Memorial Day through mid-September on the *Hardy III*, Capt. Vern Lewis, RR1, Box 530, Shore Rd., North Edgecomb 04556 (677-2026 or 882-7909). Reservations recommended.

Stonington to Isle au Haut: Four trips daily from June 15 through September 15 on the *Mink*, or *Miss Lizzie* with Capt. Herbert Aldrich, Stonington 04681 (367-5193); 45 minutes. Leaves from Atlantic Ave. Dock, Stonington.

Northeast Harbor to Sutton Island (on request), Great Cranberry Island and Islesford: Six trips daily late June through Labor Day on the *Sea Queen* and *Double B*, operated by Beal & Bunker, P.O. Box 33, Cranberry Isles 04625 (244-3575). Reduced schedule for remainder of year.

Bar Harbor to Yarmouth, Nova Scotia: Daily service June through September, three trips per week October to June on the *M.V. Bluenose*, operated by Marine Atlantic, 121 Eden St., Bar Harbor (288-3395; 800-341-7981, in continental U.S.); 6 hours. Leaves Marine Atlantic Ferry Terminal, Bar Harbor. Car and passenger ferry. Children under 5 travel free.

SHORTCUTS

Bottlenecks are common on the coast because there is one main thoroughfare, Rte. 1, that stretches the entire length. (I-95 follows the coast only between Kittery and Brunswick.) Rte. 1 in Maine is a two-lane highway, with few exceptions, and often it becomes packed.

Sometimes traffic jams are unavoidable. Freeport is intolerable on a rainy day. Shop, if you can, when the sun shines. Rte. 1 between Kennebunkport and Ogunquit is almost always busy. The Park Loop at Acadia National Park is packed during the summer and empty before Memorial Day and after Labor Day. (The loop closes at the first snowfall and reopens in late spring. Cross-country skiers "own" the loop during the winter.) If you want to travel through Bath on your way up coast, the slowdown at the Carlton Bridge is inevitable, particularly when workers change shifts at Bath Iron Works. (We give you a good alternate for this area, below.) The bridge over the Sheepscot River at Wiscasset is another trouble spot. Traffic here is often halted by a single, unyielding light.

Below are some shortcuts we've found. They are routes that will take you off the beaten track — and most of the time get you back on your way faster. If you don't want to miss the action, take Rte. 1 one way and the shortcut the other. Many of these shortcuts are just as scenic as, if not more than, more heavily trafficked routes.

SOUTH COAST

• To avoid downtown Ogunquit en route to Perkins Cove. As you travel north on Rte. 1 take a right onto Pine Hill Rd. just after Gerrity Lumber (on your left). Follow to Shore Rd. and take a left. You'll come out at Perkins Cove.

MIDCOAST

• To avoid bottlenecks at Carlton Bridge to the east of Bath, as well as the Wiscasset bridge. Take I-95 north to the Gardiner exit. Go east on Rte. 126 until you reach Rte. 32. Follow Rte. 32 south until you reach Rte. 1 in Waldoboro.

• To eliminate the heavily trafficked section of Rte. 1 through Rockland. Take Rte. 90 off Rte. 1 in West Warren. It leads you into Rockport, just south of Camden, and can save you up to 30 minuntes on a busy summer day.

EAST OF SCHOODIC

• To avoid the long jog in Rte. 1 through Hancock, Sullivan, Gouldsboro, Steuben and Milbridge. Take Rte. 182, 4 miles east of Ellsworth, to Cherryfield. It is a few miles shorter than Rte. 1 and the Rte. 1A section from Milbridge to Harrington and is faster and much less crowded. It winds through the hills and is one of the most scenic roads in New England.

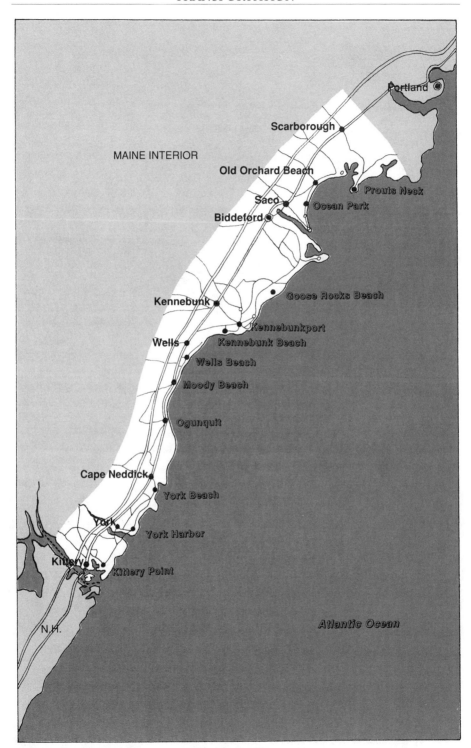

SOUTH COAST

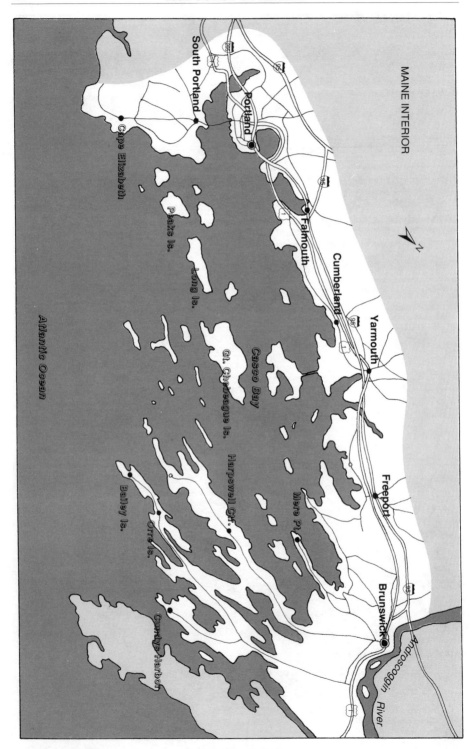

CASCO BAY

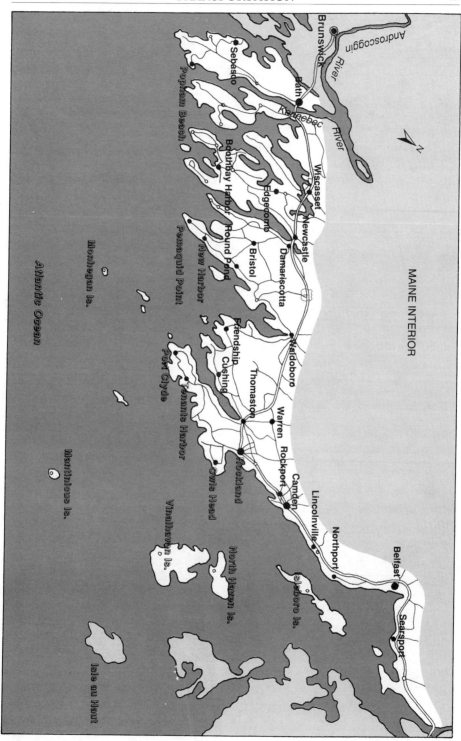

MIDCOAST

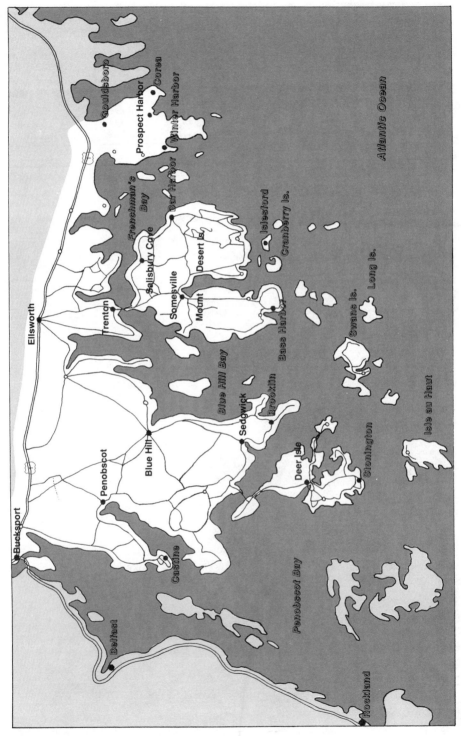

DOWN EAST/ACADIA

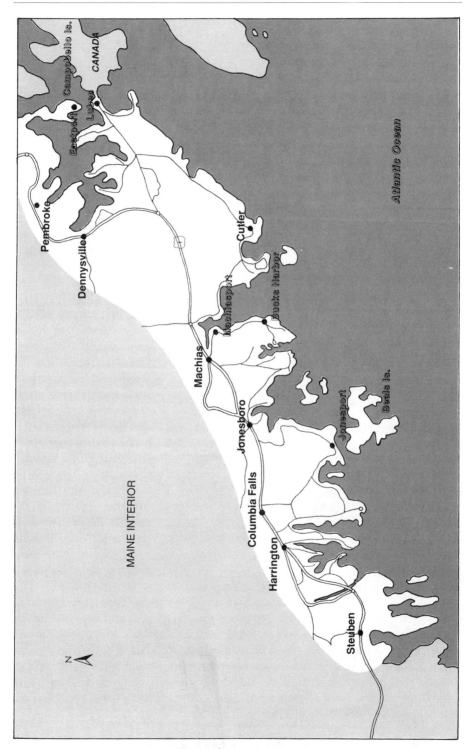

EAST OF SCHOODIC

CHAPTER THREE

Where Sea Captains Slept
LODGING

Samoset

The Samoset, Rockport, summer of 1917.

Romantic is the word that best describes the coast's lodging industry. Centuries of seagoing travelers made their homes here. Many of these grand houses have been turned into inns and bed and breakfasts and are now used by travelers who live in faraway places. There are so many of these stately homes with widow's walks and the wonderful carpentry of renowned Maine ships carpenters that all the sea lore can seem a bit passé to year-round and returning seasonal residents. A surprising number of these lodging houses are run by people from away — men and women who have visited the coast and found innkeeping a good opportunity to come back and enjoy it full time.

Equally romantic are the old summer resorts from the turn of the century, when Maine was discovered by prosperous New Yorkers and Bostonians. For the most part, these well-heeled places that still appeal to old money vacationers are expensive and spartan. To paraphrase local art critic Edgar Allen Beem, this is a place where above all — moderation and tradition — the hallmarks of Yankee pragmatism, are highly valued. Newer resorts, inns and bed and breakfasts often are not bound by these Yankee traditions and can be more lushly appointed and dedicated to good service.

The lodgings we have included in our survey represent places we either have stayed at, visited and toured or that have been recommended and written up by well-traveled friends and family. They are by no means the only places to stay on the coast (there are more than 300 inns and B&Bs in Bar Harbor alone), but a modest list of those places we know that provide a good resting place. Some of them, like the *Harbor Boat & Breakfast,* which operates out of Portland, offer unusual overnight experiences. Others are well situated for sightseeing and recreational opportunities. Some are quiet and beautiful enclaves where it might be worth staying for two or more nights to absorb all the peace the place has to offer. Several of the inns have restaurants. When possible, we have provided reviews of their dining rooms in the restaurant chapter. If we didn't eat there and the food is said to be good, we let you know.

For alternative listings, you can contact the *Maine Publicity Bureau* (P.O. Box 2300, Hallowell, ME 04347; 582-9300 in Maine; 800-533-9595 out-of-state and Canada). Every year they publish the *Guide to Inns & Bed & Breakfasts,* a list of inns and B&Bs by region. All of the listings are written and paid for by the owners, so you should take them with a grain of salt. The *Machias Bay Area Chamber of Commerce* (P.O. Box 606, Machias, ME 04654; 255-4402) distributes a pamphlet for 14 member inns and B&Bs in coastal Washington County. The *Maine Innkeepers Association Food & Lodging Guide,* with advertising from hotels, motels and inns throughout the state, is available at most tourist information centers, or from the association (305 Commercial St., Portland, ME 04101; 773-7670).

MAINE COAST LODGING NOTES

Rates

Rates generally increase close to Memorial Day and they are highest through the leaf season in mid- to late October. Special packages are often available for two or more nights stay, and frequently there are even better values during the off season. If breakfast and/or dinner is included with the price of a room, we do not alter the rate category, we just note that the room rate includes one or more meals.

Inexpensive	Up to $50
Moderate	$50 to $110
Expensive	$110 to $180
Very Expensive	$180 and up

These rates exclude required room taxes or service charges that may be added to your bill.

Credit Cards

AE — American Express	DC — Diner's Card
CB — Carte Blanche	MC — MasterCard
D — Discover Card	V — Visa

Minimum Stay   Many inns and B&Bs require a minimum stay of
                              two or more nights during the summer season. We
                              have noted minimum stays when possible, but it's
                              best to check when making room reservations.

Deposit/Cancellation   To reserve a room on the Maine coast, it is generally
                              necessary to make a deposit to cover the first night
                              of your stay — and some places may require up to
                              50 percent of the cost of the intended stay.
                              Cancellations often must be made at least seven to
                              10 days in advance, although some places require
                              only 24 hours notice. Check for the inn's specific
                              policy when you make reservations.

Handicap Access   At the printing of this book, the federal government
                              had just enacted a new law requiring businesses to
                              provide access to handicap persons. Many of the
                              inns and B&Bs in this book have yet to comply. In
                              most cases the lodgings that can guarantee at least
                              one room with access are in the minority, mostly
                              because these lodgings are often found in old
                              buildings renovated before the law was signed into
                              being. We have noted which of the businesses listed
                              have access.

Other Options   For information on camping, from tents to RVs, see
                              the section entitled "Camping" in the *Recreation*
                              chapter. If you plan to camp with an RV, be sure to
                              make reservations well in advance. If you plan on
                              tent camping, most of the national and state parks
                              and national forests campgrounds are available on
                              a first-come, first-serve basis, although some
                              advance reservations may be made for Acadia
                              National Park during the summer season.
                                  Another alternative for a stay in the Bar Harbor
                              area is the *American Youth Hostel* (Kennebec St., Box
                              32, Bar Harbor, ME 04609; 288-5587). Members may
                              find lodging there during the summer season for a
                              minimum fee. Reservations are suggested.

OFFSHORE LODGING

**HARBOR BOAT &
BREAKFAST**
Jeff and Beth Rand.
871-0208.
P.O. Box 10721, Portland
04104.
Seasonal.
Price: Moderate to Very
Expensive.
Credit Cards: None.

The Rands have found several boat owners interested in turning their boats into part-time floating B&Bs. Beth Rand got the idea while attending a wedding in Newport, Rhode Island. One of the guests offered to let them stay on his 61-foot Hatteras. Begun in 1991, they've enlisted sailboat and powerboat owners in four or five coastal towns, including a 46-foot riverboat in Kennebunkport and a 30-foot O'Day in Rockport. Some of the boats are dockside, others are kept at mooring. Some of the owners stay aboard. One — if the mood, the tide, and various other conditions are right — offers moonlight cruises. Others simply greet guests at the dock, show them to their quarters, then leave, returning next morning with a continental breakfast. Most stays are one or two nights. Children usually are welcome. Pets aren't. Neither, in most cases, are smokers.

LODGING — SOUTH COAST

Cape Elizabeth

Black point Inn. 800-258-0003

INN BY THE SEA
799-3134.
40 Bowery Beach Road,
Cape Elizabeth 04107.
Open all year.
Price: Expensive to Very
Expensive.
Credit Cards: MC, V,
AE.
Handicap Access: Partial.

This modern day weathered, shingled inn is not far from where Portland goes to the beach and comes to pick during strawberry season. It is a 43-suite complex, each suite featuring Chippendale furniture, TV and VCR packed away in a cherry armoire and terry-cloth robes in the closet. Many have ocean views. There are four cottages with rocking chairs on their porches. Amble down to Crescent Beach on the wooden walkway bordered by rose bushes. There are tennis courts, shuffleboard, a swimming pool and a restaurant — the Audubon, which looks out on Casco Bay and provides the mood for a romantic interlude. No pets. Smoking and non-smoking rooms.

The Kennebunks

CAPE ARUNDEL INN
Owner: Ann Fales.
967-2125.

Set on a hill with handsome trees and shrubberies, this forest-green-shingled inn makes the most of its aerie over the Atlantic. The common areas, dining room and guest rooms (seven at the inn,

P.O. Box 530A, Ocean Ave.
Kennebunkport 04046.
Open Memorial Day
weekend to Columbus
Day.
Price: Moderate to
Expensive.
Credit cards: AE, MC, V.
Handicap Access: Limited.

six at the motel, one in the carriage house) have dramatic panoramas of the sea. Curved windows and turrets add to the cache. Rooms are done in pale tones — white shag carpeting, cream spreads with dark wood antiques and reproductions. A few of the bathrooms are on the small side, but many have vintage sinks and clawfoot tubs. Country wicker and antiques fill the parlors, while the dining room leans toward early American. Not so the food, which is modern and inventive.

CAPTAIN LORD MANSION

Innkeepers: Bev Davis and
Rick Litchfield.
967-3141.
P.O. Box 800,
Kennebunkport 04046.
Corner of Pleasant and
Green sts.
Open all year.
Price: Expensive.
Credit cards: MC, V.
Handicap Access: Limited;
there are two ground-
floor rooms, wide
hallways and a ramp
entrance.

Seven generations of Lords lived in grand style here before this was made an inn. As inn lore goes, old Nathaniel Lord, the captain, built this stately home to keep his ships' carpenters busy during the British blockade in the War of 1812. Today it is an elegant stopping place in the historic district of this handsome seaside town. There are 16 bedrooms on three floors, 11 of them with working fireplaces. All are filled to the brim with lovely antiques, most from the Federalist period, oriental rugs and art. The beautifully restored woodwork and staircases are knockouts, thanks to the good handiwork of Captain Lord's employees. Breakfast is full and dignified, as suits this house: muesli, fresh fruit and yogurt for the healthminded; muffins, sweetbreads and occasionally fresh fruit pancakes or blintzes. They are more than willing to accommodate a guest's special diet with advance notice. Children over six. No pets. Smoking in guest rooms only.

ECONO LODGE

985-6100; out-of-state 800-
336-5634.
Rte. 1 south,
Kennebunk 04043.
Open all year.
Price: Inexpensive to
Moderate.
Credit cards: MC, V.
Handicap Access: Yes, but
call ahead during the
off-season.

Set against a backdrop of pines minutes away from downtown Kennebunkport, this Econo Lodge has more appeal than most chain motels. That's particularly appreciated in a town where lodging during the high season can be hard to come by and expensive. Wood balconies lend a rustic air to the low-slung brick-and-stucco building, and the rooms are, for the most part, tastefully done with ice blue carpeting, blue-and-pink floral spreads and coordinating prints. Color cable TV, phones, air conditioning and continental breakfast are among the perks, and there is an outdoor pool. Pets and smoking allowed.

GREEN HERON INN

Owners: Charles &
Elizabeth Reid.
967-3315.
P.O. Box 2578,
Kennebunkport 04046.
On Ocean Ave.
Open all year.
Price: Moderate.
Credit cards: None.

The old-fashioned rockers on the front porch say it all. Less than a mile from Dock Square, the Green Heron is a homey stop, just the thing for families. Rooms (there are ten of them plus a cottage with kitchenette) are cozy with pastel quilts, extra pillows, modern motel-style bathrooms, TV and air conditioning. Each sleeps four (there's a double plus a trundle). So what if the parlors are a mishmash of summerhouse wicker and hunting camp castoffs? The inn has many of the comforts of home — local and big city newspapers, books, jigsaw puzzles, cards and games. Breakfast is included with the room, and it's an elaborate one with homemade English muffins, buttermilk biscuits, vegetable frittatas, blueberry pancakes, orange French toast and Welsh rarebit.

→Yachtman (modern) → 967-2511

WHITE BARN INN

Owner: Laurie Bongiorno.
967-2321; Fax: 967-1100.
P.O. Box 560 C,
Kennebunkport 04046.
Beach St., off Rte. 9.
Open all year.
Price: Moderate to Very
Expensive.
Credit cards: AE, MC, V.

Beach house Inn.
967-3850

It's hard to imagine this as a boardinghouse in 1800. It's too grand. Lush landscaping, antiques and English country floral fabrics. Fresh flowers, robes and comfortable beds are a given in the 18 rooms; seven suites also have fireplaces, sitting areas, marble baths with whirlpools and TV. The parlor, with its claret walls, elegant wing chairs and garden views, is an ideal spot for an aperitif. And the restaurant is arguably the best (and most expensive) in town. Clever items like lamb chops with eggplant ravioli and halibut with fennel and leeks are served in a flower-filled, candlelit barn. Don't be fooled by the vintage "Harness Repairing" signs. Jackets are suggested for dinner. Also lavish is the "country continental" breakfast, included in the tariff along with afternoon tea (dinner is separate). Special off-season packages with dinner are available.

THE WOODEN GOOSE INN

Innkeepers: Jerry Rippetoe
and Anthony Sienicki.
363-5673.
P.O. Box 195,
Cape Neddick 03902.
Closed in January.
Price: Moderate to
Expensive.
Credit Cards: None.

This warm six-bedroom inn envelopes you. It gives you the cozy feeling that comes from being at your grandmother's house, although it is not likely the average grandmother had such an eye for detail and color. Handsome antiques, exquisite fabrics, elegant furnishings against a backdrop of interesting, rich colors like persimmon, dark teal and sage. Yes, it's beautiful here, but anyone who stays here will admit that breakfast is really the thing. If you choose, you can be awakened in the morning by a light knock on the door, with a tray bearing tea and coffee left behind. Or you can roam to the dining room for a rich, inventive breakfast that takes the innkeepers five and a half hours to prepare —lobster quiche, poached pears with Grand Marnier custard sauce, potato pancakes with poached eggs and Hollandaise sauce, date bread and orange-pineapple muffins. An equally extravagant tea is served every afternoon, where you may be offered paté, homemade tarts and other baked wonders. We know innkeepers in the area who not only tell their guests to stay here, but when they have a chance, go themselves. Only open a few years, Rippetoe and Sienicki, the owners of The Wooden Goose, don't advertise. They don't have to. No smoking in the inn.

Kittery

GUNDALOW INN
Innkeepers: Cevia and
  George Rosol.
439-4040.
6 Water St., Kittery 03904.
Open all year.
Price: Moderate.
Credit Cards: MC, V and
  personal checks.
Handicap Access: Yes.

He was an electrical engineer. She was a publicist and editor. In 1990 the Rosols found a brick Victorian just across the Piscataqua Memorial Bridge after a long search for "the perfect house." There was a barn next door and they bought that, too. They renovated both with the help of local craftsmen. Now the two buildings connect via the kitchen, in which you might see tomatoes broiling as you pass by. The dining room has views of the river. The six well-appointed guest rooms have private baths with lovely restored bathroom fixtures. Everywhere there are magazines and books. We recommend breakfast on the patio — if the weather's good. You can watch boats on the river from the porch. There's a crisp, professional manner to this inn, which is inviting, yet respectful of the guests' privacy. No pets, children under 16 or smoking.

Ogunquit Area

THE CLIFF HOUSE
Innkeepers: The Weare
  family.
361-1000.
P.O. Box 2274,
  Ogunquit 03907.
Bald Head Cliff (follow
  Shore Rd.).
Open: End of March to
  mid-Dec.

The landscape here is the stuff Mary Shelley would have died for. A 100-foot rocky cliff, pounding surf, an occasional fog. The resort itself is thoroughly modern (the newest portion of it, "Cliffscape," opened in 1990), and the view from within is equally dramatic. From the lobby, the line of sight leads down past a shiny black grand piano to thick safety plate windows and out to water breaking against Bald Head Cliff. There are more than 150 guest rooms and every one has a picture window and deck. The service is everything you would expect of an enterprise on this scale. The ocean too cold for your taste? There is an indoor,

Price: Moderate to Very
Expensive.
Credit Cards: V, MC, AE.
Handicap Access: All
public areas and some
rooms.

heated pool as well as a game room, an exercise room, a sauna and whirlpool. This place can be a bit self-contained — as if you were on a passenger liner. There is a dress code in the dining room. No pets. Some non-smoking rooms. Special packages are available.

HARTWELL HOUSE

Innkeepers: Alec and
Renee Adams.
646-7210.
P.O. Box 393, 118 Shore Rd.,
Ogunquit 03907.
Open all year.
Price: Expensive.
Credit Cards: V, MC, AE.
Handicap Access: Yes.

With 16 rooms in its two houses, Hartwell House is among the largest B&Bs in Ogunquit. Modeled after the English country inns of Europe, it is also one of the most elegant. In keeping with the theme, they serve a lovely "European" tea every day at 4:30. The rooms are large, full of light and carefully decorated and furnished with Early American or English antiques. All are equipped with air conditioning and have private baths, and many of the rooms have decks, patios or balconies and views of the water. Several extremely large suites include a kitchen and a living area and are good for families or groups traveling together. Unlike many of the town's inns, the Hartwell has a good bit of property. Its two buildings flank Shore Rd., and this assures privacy and plenty of greenery and gardens to enjoy. No TV or telephone in the rooms. No pets. No smoking.

OLD VILLAGE INN

Innkeeper: Benjamin J.
Lawlor.
646-7088.
30 Main St.,
Ogunquit 03907.
Open all year.
Price: Moderate to Very
Expensive.
Credit Cards: AE, MC, V.

The three-story Victorian has six spacious suites, all with private baths and high ceilings that reflect a 19th-century heritage. They also have air conditioning — a rarity in most small Maine inns — and cable television, something that's not so rare. The inn's downtown location gives guests the opportunity to stroll to shops, galleries and the beach. There's a trolley that makes a stop near the inn and will carry you to Ogunquit's high spots. A continental breakfast is provided. The inn also serves a full breakfast and dinner, but there are better dining options in town.

THE TRELLIS HOUSE

Innkeeper: Tom Greene.
646-7909.
P.O. Box 2229,
2 Beachmere Pl.,
Ogunquit 03907.

The Trellis House is the sort of place that becomes familiar quickly, where guests feel at home soon after arriving. Originally a summer cottage, the gray-shingled house with the large screened porch looks friendly, comfortable and homey. Inside, the rooms are filled with a mixture of antiques and collectibles. A fireplace in the living

Open: Mid-May to
  mid-Oct.
Price: Moderate.
Credit Cards: MC, V.
Handicap Access: Limited.

room encourages conversation and mingling, and there are many private nooks in the house. There are six guest rooms, including a two-room suite, all with private baths. There is also a carriage house near the main house that is perfect for couples or families traveling together, which contains a kitchen, bath and a deck. It is handicapped accessible, although the main house is not. Best of all, the Trellis House is within walking distance of the village, the beach, Perkins Cove and the Marginal Way. So there's no worry about where to park while doing the rounds.

Old Orchard Beach

**THE ATLANTIC
  BIRCHES INN**
Innkeepers: Dan and
  Cyndi Bolduc.
934-5295.
P.O. Box 334, 20 Portland
  Ave., Old Orchard
  Beach 04064.
Open all year; Sept. to
  Apr. only by reservation.
Price: Inexpensive to
  Moderate.
Credit Cards: V, MC,
  AE, D.

She's like a dignified, unassuming old lady, out of place among her younger, more updated counterparts — dozens of five-room motels that sprang up in Old Orchard Beach during the '60s. For those who care more about charm than a private bath, and more about homeyness than having a TV in the room, the Atlantic Birches may be the place to stay. It is one of Old Orchard Beach's two B&Bs (the other, the Carriage House, is next door). Dan and Cyndi Bolduc, the young couple who bought the Atlantic Birches three years ago, are responsible for the new rating. They have done a lot of facelifting and remodeling of the Victorian house, built in 1910 and located on a tree-lined street — a rarity for lodging places in this town, where asphalt predominates. Visitors can sit back on the big porch, read or watch passersby coming and going from nearby Old Orchard Street, the town's main strip. The rooms have flowered wallpaper, oriental rugs and a smattering of antique touches. Given the opportunity, the Bolducs' gregarious young son helps out with breakfast: fresh-baked muffins, fruit salad, cereals and juices served every morning in the dining room. Children are welcomed here. Smoking isn't. Those who insist on a private bathroom and phone, be consoled: one room offers both.

THE BEACHFRONT
934-7434.
Walnut St., Old Orchard
  Beach 04064.
Open all year.
Price: Moderate to
  Expensive.
Credit Cards: D, MC, V.

If you have wanted to get as close to the beach as possible, the Beachfront is a good choice. The beach is out the front door. All seven miles of it. The Beachfront is modern and big — 24 units altogether — and it has all the stuff to make a longer stay comfortable. The one- and two-bedroom units all have color cable TV and modern bathrooms. All of the rooms have kitchenettes, so handy when you've got kids running around. And every room has a view of the beach. Also, they are open year round, a rarity in this summer town.

Scarborough

BLACK POINT INN
883-4126.
Prouts Neck,
  Scarborough 04074.
Open May to Nov.
Price: Very Expensive.
Credit Cards: V, MC.

1-800 258 0300

The Black Point Inn is a place to give the driver a rest for a few days. Located between two sandy beaches on a wooded peninsula south of Portland, it is an elegant combination of luxurious resort and the kind of 19th-century decor and VIP service that makes you feel you're staying in a wealthy friend's summer home. Fresh flowers daily, antique furniture, plenty to occupy you, plenty of space to relax. You can beachcomb on Ferry Beach; wander through the balsams where Winslow Homer painted (his studio is still here); relax and read on the long veranda or in one of several welcoming living rooms (most TV-free) with fine old furniture and deeply comfortable chairs, a piano, shelves of old inn books and games and tables available for bridge or chess. Or you can be active. There's an indoor pool and fitness center; an outdoor heated pool; a putting green and shuffleboard; downstairs billiards and ping pong — and often movies. Golf and tennis are nearby (and additional), as is the Prout's Neck Yacht Club. Of course, you can opt for the simplest of vigorous pleasures and swim in the lovely, shallow sand-bottom waters of the bay right out front. The inn also has music and dancing every night in the bar. The 80 bedrooms are large, many have an ocean view; some rooms have a sleeping porch. The steepish prices include two excellent meals with plenty of choice. Lunch is available by the outdoor pool on fine days. Dinner tends to be dressy.

THE BREAKERS
Innkeeper: Rodney
  Laughton
883-4820.
2 Bayview Ave.,
  Scarborough 04074

It's big and not particularly pretty, but chances are you'll love it because the setting and the view are superb. The Breakers — in Maine — is not the rococo mansion you may have seen in Newport. This one is a nondescript four-story affair perched on the edge of the broad, flat, sweeping beach at Scarborough. From almost any of the 15 rooms in the house you'll see and hear the ocean. At low tide this beach is a huge playing

Open: Apr.-June 15 and
  Labor Day to Oct. 31 —
  B&B; June 15-Labor Day
  — weekly only.
Price: Moderate.
Credit Cards: None;
  checks accepted.

field for kids, dogs, kite flyers, and fishermen. Rooms at the inn are furnished vaguely a la 1950s, and breakfast on the glassed-in porch has that just-like-your-Mom-made-it-style. This place is fun.

The Breakers in Scarborough reflects on itself at low tide.

Emblidge

The Yorks

**DOCKSIDE GUEST
    QUARTERS**
Innkeepers: Harriet and
  David Lusty.
363-2868.
Harris Island, Box 205,
  York 03909.
Just off Rte. 103.
Open: Memorial Day
  through early
  November and
  weekends in May.
Price: Moderate.
Credit Cards: V, MC,
  personal and traveler
  checks accepted.

"No swimming pool," says Betty Chase, the bookkeeper, "but you can go to the beach." This hideaway compound offers Yankee austerity and million dollar views. Harris Island is actually a peninsula that sticks out into York Harbor with the Dockside taking up the better half. Vacationers tend to come back with their families year after year. The Dockside Restaurant is a short walk. People living aboard their boats sometimes move here for the winter. There's a shuffleboard court, croquet and a sandbox. There are five guest bedrooms in the main house, an elegant white clapboard summer cottage with black shutters. Most have a bath, a porch or direct access to the level, well-kept lawn. The four cottages are clean, neat and '50s-looking. Some have apartments suitable for two to four people. Others are studios for two or three. All have private baths and private decks. Pets allowed; one per building.

EDWARDS' HARBORSIDE INN

Innkeeper: Jay Edwards.
Manager: Julie Young.
363-3037.
P.O. Box 866,
  York Harbor 03911.
Stage Neck Rd. just off
  Rte. 1A.
Open all year.
Price: Expensive to Very
  Expensive.
Credit Cards: MC, V (with
  3% service charge
  added). Personal and
  traveler's checks
  accepted.

Come by boat and tie up at the pier. Take advantage of fishing rods made available to guests. This three-story, turn-of-the-century inn, all sprawling and multi-gabled, looks like a mass of sails in a brisk wind. Inside the house is immaculately kept, open, airy and quiet and opens onto a great stairway. Most of the 10 rooms have a view, TV and air conditioning. Some have a shared bath; others, including the suites, have private baths. All are furnished simply and elegantly. Out front, the well-tended lawn runs down to the water or Little Harbor Beach. Breakfast is continental, and a nice feature is afternoon wine and cheese, a great relaxer after a hard day at the beach. During the winter, they offer Gourmet Cooking Class Get-Away Weekends, taught by New England chef Bonnie Barnes. Children 10 or older. No pets. No smoking.

SCOTLAND BRIDGE INN

Innkeepers: Sylvia S. B.
  and Dick Jansen.
363-4432.
One Scotland Bridge Rd.,
  York 03909.
Open May–Oct.
Price: Moderate.
Credit Cards: MC, V for a
  $5 fee; cash or check
  preferred.

"It's a little different," says Sylvia Jansen, a tall, country-elegant woman. About two miles west of I-95, this rambling yellow 19th-century farmhouse may be the only inn in Maine that provides kimonos. There are three rooms, which share a bath and a two-room suite with private bath. All are stocked with highboys and comfortable beds. There's also a fine collection of chairs on the porch for rocking chair activities, and breakfast that is apt to be served on Wedgwood, sterling silver and cut glass. There also is an herbal English garden (hers) and a putting green (his). They don't accept pets, and children only "if they are very well-behaved." The York River is a short walk away. In the winter, cross-country skiers make use of the surrounding trails.

LODGING — CASCO BAY

Brunswick & the Harpswells

Add this time

CAPTAIN DANIEL STONE INN

Manager: Martha August.
725-9898.

The Captain Daniel Stone Inn mixes old and new to appealing effect. The "old" is the Federal-style home from which the inn gets its name (Capt. Daniel Stone owned it). The "new" refers to the wings that have been added in recent years. Rooms

10 Water St.,
   Brunswick 04011.
Off Rte. 1.
Price: Moderate to
   Expensive.
Credit Cards: AE, DC,
   MC, V.
Handicap Access: Yes.

and suites have modern conveniences like color TV, VCRs and cassette players. Furnishings are period reproductions. No two of the 25 rooms are alike. Some are done in pine, others in mahogany. Several have whirlpool baths and brass beds. The inn also has a popular restaurant, the Narcissa Stone (named for the captain's daughter) and serves lunch and dinner, in the summer on an outdoor verandah. A lavish continental breakfast buffet is included in the price of the room.

THE HARPSWELL INN
Innkeepers: Susan and Bill
   Menz.
833-5509.
141 Lookout Point Rd.,
   South Harpswell 04079.
Open all year.
Price: Moderate.
Credit Cards: MC, V with
   5 percent surcharge;
   personal checks.
Handicap Access: Partial.

A shipbuilder built this home to house and feed himself, his family and the raft of shipwrights busily building boats not far from his door. It's a beautiful old home with white clapboards, black shutters and more windows than anybody would ever want to clean. Susan and Bill Menz moved here recently from Houston. Bill had gone to Bowdoin. The other night Susan said she cried looking across Middle Bay at sunset. The downstairs is filled with furniture they've picked up in their travels to China and Europe. There are 12 large bedrooms, two with private bath. The Menzes are still in the process of naming them. There's the Bowdoin room, of course. And there's soon to be a Texas room. "We have told our Texas friends to send us a steer head," says Susan. There are also three rooms in the cottage. Breakfast may include quiche, homemade muffins and French toast. Pets on approval. Kids over eight. Smoking on the porch.

Casco Islands

CHEBEAGUE INN
864-5155.
Box 492, South Rd.,
   Chebeague Island 04017.
Open: Mid-May to
   mid-Sept.
Price: Moderate.
Credit Cards: AE, MC, V.

On a gently sloping hill overlooking Casco Bay, the Chebeague Inn is the sort of old-style seaside hotel that's fast becoming extinct. The 21 rooms — some are on the small side — are simply done in pale tones. Many have ocean views, as does the dining room, which serves breakfast (included with the room rate), lunch and dinner (See *Restaurants and Food Purveyors*, Chapter Five). While there's a public golf course right next door, beaches nearby and plenty of spots on the island to walk or bike to, more sedentary types will set up camp on the expansive porch with its cane-backed rocking chairs. There's also a comfortable living room with loungers and a stone fireplace should the weather turn chilly. Chebeague Island is a 15-minute ferry ride from Cousin's Island and an hour's ride from Portland.

Freeport, So. Freeport

ATLANTIC SEAL BED & BREAKFAST
Innkeepers: Captain Thomas and Gaila Ring.
865-6112.
Main Street, Box 146, South Freeport 04078.
Open all year.
Price: Moderate to Expensive.
Credit Cards: Personal checks.
Handicap Access: Limited.

The village of South Freeport sits on the water; so does the Atlantic Seal. It has since the mid-19th century. The Rings are from here. Gaila's husband, Tom, a tugboat captain who has worked around the world, grew up in this old Cape, and generations of his family have gone to sea and returned with furniture. The house is filled with Ring family treasures, including wonderful seascapes. The three rooms, all named after ships, have pumpkin pine floors, hand-hooked rugs and beds with homemade quilts. One comes with a private whirlpool bath. Another has a window seat overlooking the harbor. Each has a private bathroom. Breakfast is served on Sunday-best blue Camilla Spode with a silver setting. "I figure you can't take it to the grave," she says. The meal itself can include lobster omelets or something called "stuffed" French toast, and the mahogany dining table it's served at has been all over the world on a sailing vessel. Gaila and Tom also offer sea cruises out to the neighboring islands and a short course on how to lobster. No smoking. No pets.

The elegant and intimate Atlantic Seal Bed & Breakfast.

Atlantic Seal

THE BAGLEY HOUSE
Innkeeper: Sigurd Knudsen, Jr.
865-6566 or 800-765-1772 out-of-state.
RR3, Box 269C, Rte.136, Freeport 04032.

If you're not that interested in being right on top of the shopping district, Sigurd's home is a fascinating place to stop. Six miles out of town, it's the oldest house in the village of Durham. It's near where L. L. Bean offers kayak and canoe lessons as part of their Outdoor Discovery Program. Sig's filled

Open all year.
Price: Moderate.
Credit Cards: MC, V, AE, D, personal checks.

it with Eskimo spears, dolls and other artifacts acquired during 10 years in Alaska. If you want to see what one of Maine's famed Friendship sloops looks like up close, he's got one out back. Begun in 1770 and completed in 1772, the home originally served as an inn. One of the rooms has two rope beds covered at one time with corn husks, but not now. He also has three beds built by Chris Becksvoort, who used to work for Thomas Moser, and whom a number of people consider a better furniture maker. Becksvoort, a neighbor, has added a small circle in the center of the headboard of his pencil-post bed, called an argument settler in the days when travelers rented half a bed. There are five rooms, all with private baths and all with individual thermostats. There is very little carpeting. Sigurd prefers to show off the wide plank pine flooring. There's a full breakfast served in the kitchen around an 8-foot baker's table: yogurt, granola, homemade muffins and possibly the proprietor's "decadent French toast," made from croissants and liquors, or nasturtium omelets in season. "Only the Californians don't bat an eye," he says. Out back there's miles of hiking or cross-country skiing. All kids "with well behaved parents." No pets, although there are two labradors in residence. No smoking.

HARRASEEKET INN
Manager: Nancy Gray
865-9377 or 800-342-6423
out-of-state.

With 540 rooms and suites, the Harraseeket Inn hardly qualifies as a small country hostelry. But this is Freeport, and everything here is on a grand scale. Right on the village's main drag, this elegant black-shuttered inn is really a series of con-

Michael Loomis

The Harraseeket Inn, comprised of old and new buildings, is luxurious throughout.

162 Main St.,
    Freeport 04032.
Exit 20 off I-95.
Open all year.
Price: Moderate to Very
    Expensive.
Credit Cards: AE, D, DC,
    En Route (a Canadian
    card), MC, V.

necting buildings. The newest was built in 1989; the other two in 1798 and 1850. Many of the rooms have luxe features like fireplaces, jacuzzis, steam baths and canopied beds. All have air conditioning and cable TV and are done in tasteful muted florals. The elegant and spacious parlor has cushioned wing chairs and couches and is accented with gleaming old silver and dark wood antiques — very much like the drawing room of a country estate. The dining room is one of the best in Maine (See *Restaurants and Food Purveyors*, Chapter Five) and there is a more casual tavern as well. Breakfast is included with the room rate, as well as afternoon tea and hors d'oeuvres. No pets.

**ISAAC RANDALL
    HOUSE**
Innkeepers: Shannon and
    Synba Ryan.
865-9295.
5 Independence Dr.,
    Freeport 04032.
Open all year.
Price: Inexpensive to
    Moderate.
Credit Cards: MC, V.
Handicap Access: Partial.

Just down the block from the shopping district, descendants of Mayflower passengers built this farmhouse, which later served as a stop on the Underground Railway and a speakeasy during Prohibition. Today it retains most of its original flavor. The caboose out on the back five acres is there because the previous owner liked trains. The new owners — he's a psychologist, she worked in day care — love their new job. The eight rooms, six with private bath, share an upstairs sitting room — adults can rent VCR tapes on the house — and a common-area kitchen, stocked with cheese, crackers and soft drinks. Travelers on a tight budget can cook dinner here. The Ryans enjoy families, have volunteered to babysit on occasion and most of the rooms are designed with families in mind. There's a Honeymoon Suite with a kingsize wicker bed; and a Southwestern Room with exposed beams, prints of New Mexico and an antique copper captain's tub in the bathroom — something male visitors seem to take to. They subscribe to a classy selection of magazines and leave coffee table books in all the rooms. A full kitchen breakfast is served in shifts of nine. Guests watch while he cooks — homemade breads, granola and six days a week something different from the griddle. She handles the money. There's also a pond out back. In the winter they encourage people to bring skates. The caboose may be toured anytime. Pets allowed in two of the rooms. No smoking.

Portland

INN ON CARLETON
Innkeeper: Phil and Sue
    Cox.
775-1910.

This is a lovely, airy bed and breakfast in a stately Victorian-style brick townhouse that is within walking distance of nearly all of Portland's sights. There are seven guest rooms on the second and

46 Carleton St.,
   Portland 04102.
Open year round.
Price: Inexpensive to
   Moderate.
Credit Cards: V, MC, D.

third floors, all informally decorated with antiques and old furniture and fine firm beds. Three of the larger rooms have private baths; one of those is a mere postage stamp and guests marvel at the feat that it fits both a toilet and a shower. Don't worry, you can apply makeup and shave at the ample sink in the room. The shared baths are all roomy and have clawfoot tubs. A full breakfast is served in the formal and inviting dining room. The comfortable sitting room is decorated in country wicker, and the teapot there is always on. After dinner in town, stroll along the Western Prom, just down the street. It's a good relaxer before settling in for the night. Children are welcome. No smoking; no pets, although there is a resident cat.

THE POMEGRANATE INN
Innkeepers: Isabel and
   Alan Smiles.
772-1006; out-of-state 800-
   356-0408.
49 Neal St.,
   Portland 04102.
Open all year.
Price: Moderate to
   Expensive.
Credit Cards: MC, V, AE.

Near Portland's Western Prom, this stuccoed Georgian looks proper from the outside, but one step over the threshold and the visitor is likely to be left breathless. Isabel Smiles was an antiques dealer and interior designer before she and her husband turned their efforts to innkeeping. She has created an entertaining, offbeat small inn that always offers the visitor an eyeful. Handpainted walls and a striking collection of paintings, antiques and collectibles — some of them downright unnerving.

Michael Loomis

The Pomegranate, with contemporary hand-painted walls and its striking collection of antiques, is one of Maine's most unusual inns.

There are seven rooms, each decorated differently and each with a bath. The lovely and quiet room over the garage is actually a small apartment with a kitchen for travelers who might want to cook their own dinner or merely make their own coffee or tea. In the morning, Alan serves up a full breakfast —which friends and family all tell us is a great starter for a big day.

PORTLAND REGENCY
Manager: Anne
  Derepentigny.
800-727-3436 or 774-4200.
20 Milk St., Portland
  04101.
Open all year.
Price: Moderate to
  Expensive.
Credit Cards: AE, D, DC,
  MC, V.
Handicap Access: Yes.

Right in the heart of the Old Port, a lively enclave of restored Victorian townhouses, boutiques, antique shops and restaurants, the Portland Regency has a lot of charm for what used to be an old armory. A brick-paved circular drive, marble floors in the lobby and parlors with Oriental rugs and antiques give this turn-of-the-century, block-long brick building an aura of luxury. The 95 rooms, some of them a little cramped, are done in antique reproductions and muted florals in gray, peach and green. Several have four-poster beds and standing mirrors. There's also a restaurant, lounge and health club on the premises.

WEST END INN
Innkeepers: Hilary and
  Tom Jacobs.
772-1377.
146 Pine St.,
  Portland 04102.
Open all year.
Price: Moderate.
Credit Cards: AE, V.

A tiny inn tucked in a quiet side street, this is a gem. New Zealander Hilary Jacobs loves flowers, and during the summer her city garden overflows with bright colors; and in all seasons she fills the house with fresh-cut flowers. She and her husband, a retired businessman from New York, bought and renovated the house a few years ago. There are three guest rooms, each with its own modern and spacious bath, decorated in soft pastel florals. The shelves of the dining room are lined with a fine collection of old teapots and teacups — tea and homebaked chocolate chip cookies often are served in the next room — a true sitting room with a comfortable, overstuffed sofa and chairs. The Jacobs serve a full breakfast — usually French toast, pancakes or waffles and homemade muffins and sweet breads. Book well in advance during the busy season (May through Oct.). The inn fills up quickly. No children, smoking or pets allowed.

LODGING — MIDCOAST

Bath

THE INN AT BATH
Innkeepers: Tara Ana
  Finley and Nicholas
  Bayard.
443-4294.
969 Washington St.,
  Bath 04530.
Open all year.
Price: Moderate to
  Expensive.
Credit Cards: MC, V, AE.
Handicap Access: Partial.

"I like to talk," says innkeeper Nicholas Bayard, who in a former life was a Wall Street investment banker. Likely he will hold forth on everything from investment tips to the changeable Maine weather. This old house was built in 1830, and one of its most striking characteristics is its twin parlors (an architectural trademark in private homes up here), along with a marvelous marble fireplace, some nice antiques and family pieces. There are five guest rooms, all with private bath, and one suite. Our favorite was the River Room, formerly a hayloft in the attached barn, which now has exposed old wood beams and a woodburning fireplace to take the chill off an autumn evening. Breakfast in the dining room includes eggs and bacon or granola and baked sweet muffins. The inn is set in the heart of Bath's well-worn historic district — which we like for its being somewhat rough around the edges. Smoking in the parlor.

Belfast

HIRAM ALDEN INN
Innkeepers: Jim and Jackie
  Lovejoy.
338-2151.
19 Church St.,
  Belfast 04915.
Open all year.
Price: Inexpensive.
Credit Cards: None;
  personal and traveler's
  checks accepted.
Handicap Access: Limited
  to two bedrooms on first
  floor, with doorways
  that may be narrow.

This was one of Belfast's first B&Bs and today is still run by its original owners. The fine old Greek Revival sits in the thick of this culturally lively town — a young Camden waiting to happen. There are eight rooms, two on the first floor. All share baths, although some rooms have marble-top sinks. Downstairs there are ornate tin ceilings and a beautiful, hand-carved cherry curved staircase. A full breakfast is served in the dining room — and in July and August often includes raspberries straight from the garden. Children are welcome. Check first about pets. Smoking, "if necessary," is limited to the parlor.

**PENOBSCOT
MEADOWS**
Innkeepers: Dini and
  Bernie Chapnick.
338-5320.
Rte.1, Belfast 04915.

Bernie Chapnick still consults for the State Department and often is just back from Nicaragua, Laos or a dozen countries in between. He and his wife Dini run a lovely gray-blue shingled inn and restaurant on 5.5 acres on Penobscot Bay. There

Open all year.
Price: Moderate.
Credit Cards: V, MC, D.

is a path that leads down to "what Mainers laughingly refer to as a beach," says Bernie. There are seven comfortable guest rooms, all with private bath, handmade quilts and handpainted furniture. Dinner here is excellent (see *Restaurants and Food Purveyors,* Chapter Five), and the wine list is very good. Breakfast is likewise good — try the locally made granola. Smoking is permitted, and they say, "We'd rather see pets than children."

Boothbay Harbor Area

FIVE GABLES INN
Innkeepers: Ellen and Paul
  Morissette.
633-4551.
Murray Hill Rd.,
  East Boothbay 04544.
Open: Mid-May through
  mid-Nov.
Price: Moderate to
  Expensive.
Credit Cards: MC, V.

Recently restored, this 125-year-old cream-colored inn sits halfway up a hill and overlooks Linekin Bay. All 15 rooms come with private bath and water view; five have working fireplaces. Airy, clean, cozy, this inn serves as a retreat in an otherwise busy part of the coast. Flowerbeds and rocking chairs on the porch. Smoking is allowed on the verandah and in the garden. No pets. Children over 12 welcome.

**NEWAGEN SEASIDE
  INN**
Innkeeper: Heidi Larsen.
633-5242; out-of-state 800-
  654-5242.
P.O. Box 68,
  Cape Newagen 04552.
Open mid-May through
  Sept.
Price: Moderate to
  Expensive.
Credit Cards: MC, V;
  personal and traveler's
  checks accepted.

Pronounced "new wagon," this resort inn sits on 85 acres at the southern tip of Southport Island six miles from Boothbay Harbor. The inn retains a '40s look and feel — that green-and-white-cabins-and-the-main-house-tennis-in-the-pines atmosphere that makes you think of Bing or Bob on the set of a favorite old movie. Almost any good day in the season you can hear that quiet, comforting *pock pock* of the ball being batted back and forth. On inclement days you can hear the foghorn — one magazine tells of a guest complaining about the sound of one nearby. He said if it wasn't turned off he was leaving. (One person's romantic is another's nightmare.) Most of the 22 rooms in the main inn have an ocean view; all have private baths. There are several cottages, most rented out seasons in advance. During the day you have a choice of activities — tennis, horseshoes, badminton, volleyball, rowboats, fishing, swimming in the saltwater pool or heated freshwater pool. The dining room serves all three meals. No pets.

SPRUCE POINT INN
Innkeeper: Angelo
  Digiulian.
633-4152 or 800-553-0289
  out-of-state.
Boothbay Harbor 04538.
Open: Late May to mid-
  Oct.
Price: Expensive.
Credit Cards: AE, MC, V.
Handicap Access: Yes.

From a hunting lodge to a boarding house to an inn for the last 40 years, this grand old resort set on 16 acres at water's edge recently changed hands. The '60s look has been tossed out and replaced with more traditional style — a crisp coat of white paint, green trim and inside lots of varnished wood, plenty of flowers and brass fixtures. The Kennedy clan used to stay here. These days people drive in, sail in and even helicopter in. Every room here has a private bath and many have a deck and views, although views are best from the second-floor rooms in the main house. There is also a complex of cottages, each with two or three bedrooms and a living area. Many guests come for two to four weeks, although more and more for two or three days. Nevertheless the inn offers a full roster of events — lobster bakes, boat trips from its dock, tennis, and both fresh- and saltwater pools and regular musical entertainment — to keep even the longest-term guests entertained. Breakfast and dinner are included in the rates, and breakfast is full and includes "whatever you want," says Digiulian. No pets, but they will recommend a kennel. Smoking is limited.

SQUIRE TARBOX INN
Innkeepers: Karen and Bill
  Mitman.
882-7693.
RR 2, Box 620, Rte. 144,
  Westport Island 04578.
Open: mid-May through
  late Oct.
Price: Moderate.
Credit Cards: None.

Karen and Bill Mitman met while working at the Copley Plaza Hotel in Boston, and although this handsome, beautifully kept farmhouse inn with its pastoral setting may seem charmingly rustic, there is nothing less than polished about the service. The main house has wide colonial floorboards, an interesting mix of antiques, and four guest rooms with private baths and working fireplaces; the barn has seven romantically removed bedrooms and bath. The barn dates from 1763 and includes comfortable seating and a woodstove. The food, served in a simple paneled and brick dining room with fireplace, is excellent (breakfast and dinner are included). Beyond hospitality and good food, the primary products here are distinctive goats' milk cheeses —the inn and its restaurant (see *Restaurants and Food Purveyors*, Chapter Five) operate in the midst of a working farm complete with its own herd of purebred Nubian goats. No pets; no children under 12.

Camden

MAINE STAY
Innkeepers: Peter and
 Donny Smith and
 Diana Robson.
236-9636.
22 High St. (Rte. 1),
 Camden 04843.
Open all year.
Price: Moderate
Credit Cards: MC, V

You might want to plan your arrival here for late spring. During the fall, the Smiths and Donny's identical twin sister Diana Robson plant more than 1000 bulbs on the grounds of this early 18th-century farmhouse that sits on two acres in the heart of Camden's historic district. There are four bedrooms, each with a modern, private bath, and four with shared bath in the house and its attached carriage house. Out back there is a majestic four-story barn. Peter Smith is a retired navy pilot, and the house is full of things they've picked up on their travels — including a *tonsu*, a 300-year-old Samurai warrior's chest. There's a television room with a VCR, two parlors, each with a fireplace with matches on the mantel and wood and paper ready to be burned when you want. Every morning, breakfast is cooked on an old Queen Atlantic black stove and served on Spode china at a long pine farm table. Usually it's "something eggy one day, something not the next," says Donny. (The breakfast menus have been fed into the computer. If you were here two years ago, they can tell you what was served that day and you can have it again or try something different.) No smoking. Children eight and older. No pets.

NORUMBEGA
Innkeeper: Kathleen Keefe.
236-4646.
61 High St.,
 Camden 04843.
Open all year.
Price: Expensive to Very
 Expensive.
Credit Cards: AE, MC, V.

The Norumbega is a stone castle on a hill by the sea that was built about a century ago. Since it opened as an inn a few years back it has become a favorite of honeymooners — perhaps because of its brooding, romantic presence enhanced by Victorian antiques scattered everywhere on its lovely birds-eye maple floors. Altogether there are 13 guest rooms, including the recently added penthouse. (It's really the attic done over into a luxe suite. It offers the best views in the house; it is also the most expensive room at the inn — and perhaps in the entire state.) Most of the rooms have private baths. Almost all the beds are king-sized. The Warwick and the Kensington rooms have fireplaces and impressive views. The library is just that — a haven

The Norumbega, with its brooding castle-by-the-sea looks, is a favorite among honeymooners.

Michael Loomis

for the literary traveler. Outside there are some stately elms and well-kept gardens. This may not be for everyone — but it certainly is impressive.

THE OWL AND THE TURTLE
Innkeepers: The Conrads.
236-9014 or 236-8759.
P.O. Box 1265, 8 Bay View,
    Camden 04843.
Open all year.

A bed & breakfast and bookstore, right on the harbor in beautiful downtown Camden. For some, it couldn't get much better. Bob and Lee Martin recently bought the bookstore from the Conrads, who keep the three rooms upstairs. Each room comes with bath or shower, mountain or har-

Each of the Owl & Turtle's three rooms has a view of the water and the promise of plenty of bedtime reading.

Owl & Turtle

♦ OWL & TURTLE ♦
Bookshop ♦♦♦ Guest Rooms

Price: Moderate.
Credit Cards: MC, V or
 personal check.

bor view. And there's always something to read. Breakfast includes homemade muffins. No smoking and no pets.

WHITEHALL INN
Innkeepers: The Dewing
 family.
236-3391.
52 High St.,
 Camden 04843.
Open May to October.
Price: Expensive.
Credit Cards: None.

Poet Edna St. Vincent Millay once worked and read in this fine white Greek Revival sea captain's home overlooking the harbor. There are 41 wicker decorated guest rooms, some in two houses across the street, done in colonial colors, many with private bath. This has been a favorite retreat for repeat summer vacationers since 1901. It's a great place to sit on the porch and rock away the day. Full breakfast and dinner is included for the price of the room. Children welcome. No pets.

Damariscotta, Newcastle

THE NEWCASTLE INN
Innkeepers: Ted and Chris
 Sprague.
563-5685; 800-832-8669
 out-of-state.
River Rd.,
 Newcastle 04553.
Open all year.
Price: Moderate.
Credit Cards: MC, V.

"The hardest employee to keep is the chef," says Chris Sprague, one reason why she finally decided to see if she could cook the breakfasts and five-course dinners herself. Her efforts have paid off — especially with her philosophy of allowing desserts like bread-and-butter pudding and pies for breakfast. Everything at the inn is well organized. There are 15 guest rooms, all with private bath; nine are in the main house and six in the carriage house. In several you can lie in your pencil-post bed and stare out at the Damariscotta River. The common room, with its stenciled floor, fireplace and high- backed antique wing chairs, is a great place to relax with fellow guests. There's also a sunporch with comfortable lawn chairs and a view of the river. No small children, pets or smokers. Price usually includes dinner — check to make sure the dining room is open. People also come here to cross-country ski.

Monhegan

THE TRAILING YEW
Innkeeper: Josephine
 Davis Day.
596-0440.
Monhegan Island 04852.
Open mid-May to
 mid-Oct.
Price: Moderate.
Credit Cards: None

Spartan and yet delightful is this almost-one-of-a-kind inn located a short walk from the ferry landing on what is arguably Maine's most beautiful offshore island. A cluster of unassuming, white clapboard buildings around a central lawn, where pre-dinner horseshoe games are de riguer, is the whole affair. Rooms are clean and well kept but not memorable. Minimal electric lighting is provided by generator to most rooms through part of the day and evening; then it's the charm of oil lamps and candles. Family-style meals are robust if not gourmet, and mingling with fellow guests is a diner's delight. Highly recommended for those who eschew standard motels.

Pemaquid Peninsula

THE BRADLEY INN
Innkeepers: Bill and Cathy
  Tracy.
677-2105
Rte. 130, HC 61 Box 361,
  Pemaquid Point,
  New Harbor 04554.
Open all year.
Price: Moderate.
Credit Cards: AE, MC, V.

Built more than 100 years ago as an inn, the building was "literally gutted" by the Tracys, who increased its size, brought it up to the standards of the modern leisure traveler and filled it with nautical pictures and charts and huge ship models. There are 12 rooms, all with private bath. There's also a cottage across the croquet court. From the top floor, the cathedral-ceilinged rooms look out onto John's Bay, and garden clubs often come to lunch and admire the flowers, which are tended five hours a day. Bill, who grew up just down the road in Christmas Cove and for a while lived in Colorado, is especially proud of the pub's granite-topped bar around which a mix of guests and local residents often gather. No smoking in the rooms or above the first floor.

GOSNOLD ARMS
Owners: The Phinney
  Family.
Summer 677-3727;
  winter 407-575-9549.
HC 61, Box 161,
  New Harbor 04554.
Open: May to Nov.
Price: Moderate.
Credit Cards: MC, V.

The Gosnold Arms is the type of old Maine inn that people like to visit again and again. In its first incarnation this was a saltwater farm. It has also served as a summer boarding house for Smith College students (it still has a Please No Men Permitted Upstairs sign), and it's easy to imagine the exuberant voices of Smith women ringing in the hallways and across the inn's green lawn. The Gosnold sits at the entrance to New Harbor, not far from the splendid Pemaquid Point and its lovely lighthouse. There are accommodations for 40 to 50 guests (every room has its own bath) spread out among the farmhouse, the three-story barn and 10 separate cottages. One of the cottages is a former steamboat freight office; another is a steamboat cabin. The dining room seats 80 — or you can take your meal on the porch and watch as working and pleasure boats pass by. Dinner is real Yankee fare — fresh seafood, beef and homemade desserts. We haven't eaten here, but with this view, you almost can't lose.

Rockland & Rockport

**NAVIGATOR MOTOR
  INN**
594-2131.

If you've missed the last boat for Vinalhaven, this is the place. It sits right across the street from the Maine State Ferry Terminal. The electric red/brown

520 Main St.,
    Rockland 04841.
Open all year.
Price: Moderate.
Credit Cards: MC,V,
    AE, D.
Handicap Access: Yes.

wall-to-wall in our room was a little hard to take, the TV a little beat up and the bed a little soft. The bathroom was spotless and comforting. There was plenty of hot water with good water pressure. We also didn't lack for Eurogel and clean white towels. Afterwards, it didn't take long to fall asleep. We don't recommend the restaurant, but the Brown Bag and the Captain's Table are nearby (see *Restaurants and Food Purveyors*, Chapter Five).

THE SAMOSET RESORT
594-2511; 800-341-1650
    out-of-state.
Waldo Ave., off Rte. 1,
    Rockport 04856.
Open all year.
Price: Expensive.
Credit Cards: AE, DC,
    MC, V.
Handicap Access: Yes.

This is one of the places where Mainers like to stay — quite possibly because the resort offers so much for a population that tends to be physically active. Ten kilometers of great cross-country skiing in the winter; golf in the summer on an 18-hole course called the "Pebble Beach of the East" by *Golf Traveler* magazine. Year round there is tennis (they have indoor and outdoor courts), racquetball, indoor and outdoor pools, bicycles, basketball, fitness room with Nautilus, croquet, badminton, volleyball and, the sport of presidents, horseshoes. How do they fit all this in? The resort sits on an ample 230 acres that stretches to the water. While everything's deluxe, including the rooms, off-season package deals make it affordable for everyone. Although the resort was established more than 100 years ago, the rooms are decorated in modern day hotel and built to give you a good night's sleep after a hard day at play. There is a good restaurant on the premises called Marcel's, or you can venture into Rockport, Rockland or Camden to give yourself a break from all that activity. No pets.

Set on 230 acres, the Samoset is a great resort for those who prefer an active holiday.

Samoset

Searsport / Stockton Springs

THE CARRIAGE HOUSE INN
Innkeepers: Brad and
  Cathy Bradbury.
548-2289.
Rte. 1, Searsport 04974.
Open all year.
Price: Moderate.
Credit Cards: MC, V

Set back from the main road, this beautifully restored 1874 Victorian has its own ghost. Capt. John McGilvery, the sea captain who built the house, is seen every now and then wandering through. Beyond the ghost, there's plenty of history to contemplate here. Maine artist Waldo Pierce once made this his summer retreat, and his friend Ernest Hemingway used to visit once in a while. Innkeeper Brad Bradbury now sells antiques out of Pierce's old studio. Whether for the ghost, the painter or the excellent condition of this fine old Victorian, it was put on the National Register in 1983. The four guest rooms are large, comfortable and have private baths. There is an open porch, and the grounds are nicely landscaped. This is a restful place, a good staging ground for day trips to the Blue Hill peninsula or Mount Desert Island. Smoking is permitted downstairs. There are pets in residence.

THE HICHBORN INN
Innkeepers: Nancy and
  Bruce Suppes.
567-4183.
Church St.,
  Stockton Springs 04981.
Open all year.
Price: Inexpensive to
  Moderate.
Credit Cards: None;
  travelers and personal
  checks accepted.

It is quiet around this carefully restored former shipbuilder's house that is on the National Register of Historic Places. With high ceilings, handsome Victorian furniture, fireplaces, down quilts and fresh-ground coffee, this is a wonderful home base for those exploring nearby Fort Point State Park (a great spot for biking), antiquing in the as of yet undiscovered Stockton Springs or a nice quiet stop outside busy Mount Desert Island. The inn is small. There are three guest rooms with private and shared baths and views of Stockton Harbor. You can have breakfast in your room, or venture downstairs for Belgian waffles with real maple syrup or "Dutch babies" — eggy, oven-baked pancakes that guests fill with fresh fruit in season or the Suppes' homemade raspberry jam. There is no smoking. "Well mannered" school-age children are welcome. No pets, although there are two Maine Coon cats in residence (they are not allowed in guest rooms).

THE WILLIAM & MARY INN
Innkeepers: William and
  Mary Sweet.
548-2190.
Rte. 1, Searsport.
Open all year.

In 1774 Capt. Perry Pendleton sailed into town and built a log cabin just across the street from what is now the William and Mary Inn. More than 50 years later, the captain's granddaughter, Prudence, moved into this elegant home on a hill just two miles northeast of Searsport center. The inn is

Price: Inexpensive to
  Moderate.
Credit Cards: None;
  personal and traveler's
  checks accepted.

named for its owners — former history teacher Bill and Mary Sweet. They recently have redone the house to emphasize its architectural features — including the wonderful six-on-six windows. There are three guest rooms with pencil-post beds and reproduction wallpapers; each has its own bath tucked into former closets. Breakfast every morning is served in a style befitting this elegant New England home at the Chippendale table in the dining room.

The William & Mary Inn sits high on a knoll overlooking Penobscot Bay.

William & Mary Inn

Vinalhaven

THE FOX ISLAND INN
Innkeeper: Gail
  Reinertson.
863-2122.
Carver St., Vinalhaven.
Open June through Sept.
Price: Moderate.

This once was an island home; now it is a small village inn that offers guests a homelike setting. Open only during the summer months, there are several lovely, clean single and double rooms with shared bath and a recently restored three-room suite with a private bath. Gail serves breakfast and lets guests use the kitchen — a nice option for picnickers and those made hungry by the sea air.

Waldoboro

ROARING LION
Innkeepers: Bill and Robin
  Branigan.
832-4038.
P.O. Box 756, 995 Main St.,
  Waldoboro 04572.
Open all year.

In a town that's world famous for sauerkraut and sausage, this inn is an anomaly. It has built a reputation for catering to vegetarians and other people on special diets. Built at the turn of the century, this was originally a tourist home that once refused to give breakfast to traveling salesmen. There are four rooms at the inn. One has a private

At the Roaring Lion the owners cater to travelers on special diets — lo-cal, vegetarian and macrobiotic.

The Roaring Lion

Price: Inexpensive to
 Moderate.
Credit Cards: None.

bath and a queen-sized bed; two have double beds and one has twin beds. One of the double-bed rooms has a fireplace. Downstairs there are four tables in the dining room, and every morning there they serve fresh coffeecake, muffins and other homemade breads to their guests, all with healthy sides of homemade jams and jellies. Ask for the sourdough pancakes — made from sourdough starter nurtured for more than 22 years. The Branigans are big on gardening, and homegrown flowers are everywhere. No pets or smoking. Children of all ages are welcome.

LODGING — DOWN EAST/ACADIA

Blue Hill Peninsula

THE BLUE HILL INN
Innkeepers: Mary and Don
 Hartley.
374-2844.
P.O. Box 403, Rte. 177,
 Blue Hill 04614.
Open all year.
Price: Moderate to
 Expensive.
Credit Cards: MC, V.
Handicap Access: Limited;
 there are three small
 steps leading into the
 inn and several ground-
 floor rooms.

This place is no newcomer to innkeeping; this lovely old clapboard and brick building framed by stately elms and handsome gardens has been an inn since 1840 (before that it was a private residence). It is, in fact, the oldest continuously operating inn in the state and, like much of the rest of Blue Hill, is listed on the National Register of Historic Places. There are 11 guest rooms, all furnished with period antiques, many with fireplaces. Every one has a private bath. You might as well plan for the whole works while staying here. Dinner (see *Restaurants & Food Purveyors*, Chapter Five) is so good you will regret it if you don't eat here at least once while you're in town. Besides, dinner is included except during the week in the winter. Breakfast and hors d'oeuvres are included and served year round. There is a rate that does not include dinner.

THE CASTINE INN
Innkeepers: Mark and
  Margaret Hodesh.
326-4365.
P.O. Box 41 Main St.,
  Castine 04421
Open May through
  October.
Price: Moderate.
Credit Cards: V, MC.

Bright, airy and welcoming, the Castine Inn is the more affordable of two inns in Castine, and it offers all a visitor could want by way of lodgings in this stunning seaside town — a fine restaurant, harbor views from many of the rooms and a perfect location. Perched half-way up the main street that ascends from the town's bustling port, the inn is a good example of the many late-Victorian structures that grace this historic area. There are plenty of spots that beckon you to relax after a busy day — on the lovely front porch with its flowers and rocking chairs; out back in the gardens; or inside in the sitting room with a wood-burning fireplace. Contemporary and older oil paintings of seascapes and harbor views hang on every wall. The inn's pub is popular among the locals. It's a good place to meet a captain from one of the many windjammers that drop anchor in the port and to have a nightcap before retiring. No pets, children under five.

PENTAGOET INN
326-8616.
P.O. Box 4, Main St.,
  Castine 04421
Open May to October.
Price: Expensive.
Credit Cards: MC, V.

Most towns are lucky to have one good inn. Castine is blessed with two. The Pentagoet, a lovely three-story Victorian, sits right across the street from the Castine Inn and right down the street from the water. There are 15 rooms in the main building and an older colonial. There are turrets, balconies, tea rose prints and a flower-decked porch with rockers. Friends tell us this is a great place to eat. After dinner, you can digest in the sitting room, the book-lined music room with its velvet uphol-stered chairs and Bosendorfer upright. During the summer the Millers frequently arrange chamber music programs preceding dinner. *Pentagoet* is Old Breton for "on a hill lined with trees leading to the water," an apt description of a restful inn. Dinner and a full breakfast are included.

JOHN PETERS INN
Innkeepers: Rick and
  Barbara Seeger.
374-2116.
P.O. Box 916, East Blue
  Hill Rd., Blue Hill 04614.

Just a mile out of Blue Hill village, the John Peters is on a sparsely inhabited peninsula known as Peters Point. The inn, built in 1810, is on the National Historic Register. Some changes have occurred to the main building, such as the addition of porches,

Open: May to Oct.
Price: Moderate to
    Expensive.
Credit Cards: MC, V.

but the original structure remains intact and possesses a great deal of romantic charm. It has eight rooms in the main house and six in the carriage house, many with fireplaces, all with warm, country furnishings. Several of the rooms have a view of the bay. Some have outside decks; all have private baths. Four have kitchens. Breakfast is a special occasion at the inn. It always includes fresh crabmeat or lobster prepared in various ways, including the Seegers' lobster omelette. For those guests who can tear themselves away from the comfort of the inn, there are a sailboat and canoe available. The inn sits in a lovely field that rolls down to the tidal waters of Blue Hill Bay. No smoking allowed.

Deer Isle and Stonington

**THE CAPTAIN'S
    QUARTERS INN &
    MOTEL**
367-2420.
P.O. Box 83, Main St.,
    Stonington 04681.
Open all year.
Price: Inexpensive to
    Moderate.
Credit Cards: AE, MC, V.

Stonington is a town known for its rough edges, and in that milieu, the Captain's Quarters is perfect. A rambling string of loosely connected waterfront structures, no two of the 18 rooms are the same, although they are all furnished in well-worn comfort. The motel sits right on the water, and several of the rooms have decks with views of Isle au Haut Bay; some have a fireplace; and a few have access to a kitchen. From here it's an easy walk to the Isle au Haut ferry. One acquaintance calls it "rustic," and adds, "but we liked it."

PILGRIM'S INN
Innkeepers: Jean and Dud
    Hendrick.
348-6615.
Deer Isle 04627.
Open: Mid-May to
    late Oct.
Price: Expensive.
Credit Cards: None.

There are 13 wide pine-floored guest rooms in this 18th-century National Register house about 15 minutes drive from Stonington. Eight have private baths and all are furnished with antiques and Laura Ashley fabrics. There are two parlors where you can read before the fire until hors d'oeurves are served and people gather for dinner, served in what once was a goat barn. The food is good, country inn fare. Breakfast may include homemade granola, cheddar omelets, or pancakes. Breakfast and dinner included. Children discouraged.

Hancock

LE DOMAINE
Owner: Nicole Purslow.
422-3395.
Rte. 1, Hancock, 04640 .

As one might guess from the name, Le Domaine is less a New England inn and more an *auberge*. The handsome black-shuttered red facade and lush landscaping give the place a definitely European

Open: May to Nov.
Price: Expensive.
Credit Cards: AE, MC, V.

feel. Stepping inside only enhances the sensation. From the small parlor with its floral settees and tiny bar to the handsome dining room dominated at one end by a huge walk-in fireplace, the inn has the look of a Provençal hideaway. The seven rooms are divided between the inn and a more modern annex adjoining at the rear that overlooks the grounds. Though the rooms at the inn are smaller, all are stylishly done with good Italian reading lamps, small libraries, crisp new linens, lounge chairs and lovely modern baths. Several also have porches or terraces. Breakfast, included with the room rate, can be had in the room or on the terrace. It's a French-American hybrid — croissants, homemade granola, yogurt cream, fresh fruit and honey from the inn's own hives. The inn's restaurant, with an extensive wine list and excellent cuisine, is among the finest in all of Maine. Dinner is included in the room rate.

Isle au Haut

THE KEEPER'S HOUSE
Innkeepers: Jeff and Judi
 Burke.
367-2261.
P.O. Box 26,
 Isle au Haut 04645.
Open May through Oct.
Price: Very Expensive.
Credit Cards: None;
 personal checks
 accepted.

Isle au Haut is the best kept secret of Acadia National Park, and the Keeper's House is a wonderful place to enjoy this national treasure. Guests ride the mail boat from Stonington — the innkeepers ask you to either plan to amuse yourself all day on the island shore and trails or take the later boat. The stone cottage used to be the home of the lighthouse keeper before it was converted to an inn in 1986, and today it and a small cottage nearby are furnished with antiques and comfortable beds with down comforters for cool island evenings. There's very little electricity — just enough to run the Burkes' Cuisinart as they prepare dinner. You eat and relax after dinner in candlelight. There is one kerosene lantern in the common room for reading, but usually there's too much talk among guests to truly concentrate. The room rate may seem steep, but it does include an exquisite dinner cooked by Ms. Burke (bring your own wine and don't expect red meat), as well as a hearty breakfast and a bag lunch to take with you as you explore the island the next day. Be sure to make your reservations early. Aside from the park lean-tos, this is the only lodging on the island and fills up quite rapidly during July and August. If you're lucky enough to find room at the inn in late August, look for the wild blueberries and raspberries that grow in abundance on the island.

Mount Desert Island

ASTICOU INN
276-3344.
Northeast Harbor 04662.

The Asticou Inn is in the low key, wealthy summer town of Northeast Harbor, and it has all sorts of charms —simple furnishings, courteous

Open: Mid-June to
mid-Sept.
Price: Expensive.
Credit Cards: MC, V.

bellmen, ties and jackets required at dinner, un-adorned, locally caught halibut, and Grapenut pudding for dessert. It is a sage and weathered-looking place — with 50 rooms it looks like a over-grown summer cottage that is set in the middle of beautiful, well-groomed lawns and gorgeous gardens. Guests are welcome to the heated pool and the inn's tennis court. Rates in the summer include breakfast and dinner. No pets. No children under six. The inn's Cranberry Lodge and cottages are open April to January.

INN AT CANOE POINT
Owner: Don Johnson.
288-9511.
P.O. Box 216, off Rte. 3 in
Hull's Cove 04644.
Open all year.
Price: Moderate to
Expensive.
Credit Cards: None.

Closeted away in the garret room of the Inn at Canoe Point, one is apt to feel like the heroine of a Brontë novel. Despite its Tudor trappings and the pounding surf below, the five rooms are stylishly modern. Lots of pillows, sleek subdued fabrics, white walls and beds as comfortable as the one at home. Down in the parlor, the look is polished as well — dark wood floors, a flickering fireplace, handsome chairs. In summer, a substantial and delicious breakfast is served on the porch: homemade blueberry pancakes, quiches, muffins. Set in a wooded area, the inn has a commanding view of Frenchman Bay, and exploring the rocky outcropping is a favored pastime among guests. Though the feeling is remote, Bar Harbor is minutes away.

Inn at Canoe Point

The Inn at Canoe Point on the shore of Frenchman Bay in Hulls Cove is a quiet spot on busy Mount Desert Island.

LINDENWOOD INN
Owner: James King.
244-5335.
Box 1328, Southwest
Harbor 04679.
Open all year.
Price: Moderate.

Sitting on the deck of the little cottage here it's hard to believe that in August as many as 9,000 cars a day are touring the Park Loop Rd., not far away. That's probably why acquaintances of ours have been here twice for what could be called their "annual interlude." This turn of the century sea captain's home with its sweeping porches has seven

Credit Cards: None; cash, personal and traveler's checks accepted.

guest rooms in the main house, many with harbor views, and a guest cottage. There's a harpsichord and a fireplace in the dining room and possibly cinnamon blueberry pancakes for breakfast. There's also a small cottage —just right for two —with a kitchen, a living room with ocean views, its own deck and, need we say it again, plenty of privacy. No children under 12 in the inn; no children under six in the cottage. No pets. No smoking.

Schoodic Peninsula

OCEANSIDE MEADOWS B & B INN
Managers: Marge and
  Norman Babineau.
963-5557.
Rte. 195,
  Prospect Harbor 04669.
Open all year.
Price: Inexpensive to
  Moderate.
Credit Cards: DC, MC, V.

The Massachusetts transplants who manage this 19th-century home, which comes with a lovely private cove and beach, are the people who make you feel comfortable. Before long you find yourself seated on the kitchen floor listening to stories about their most interesting visitors — sailors and pilots who on occasion carry Norman off on auxiliary adventures. Others are about couples or families from all over the world who may find themselves stranded here in a storm and spontaneously decide to stay on for weeks, taking over Marge's kitchen. They'll also tell you countless local points of interest, many that aren't on the map — like how famed Maine historian Louise Dickinson Rich used to summer right next door. Argos, our dog, took right to snooping around the place and was encouraged. There are seven guest rooms, one of them a suite, and two rooms that are adjoining (the suite has a private bath, the remaining rooms share). All are immaculate and have nice hard beds. During the summer the sound of the surf is a great lullaby. Have the pancakes in the morning, but don't have the syrup (it's counterfeit). Well-behaved children and amiable dogs are welcome. No smoking inside the inn.

THE SUNSET HOUSE
Owners: Kathy and Carl
  Johnson.
963-7156.
Rte. 186,
  West Gouldsboro 04607.
Open year round.
Price: Moderate.
Credit Cards: MC, V.

This family-run bed and breakfast offers ocean views from the front bedrooms and views of a freshwater pond and an old millstream from the rear bedrooms. The seven rooms are small and cozy, and most beds have crocheted coverlets like your grandmother used to make. The breakfasts are heartwarming: raisin French toast from fresh homebaked bread; freshly cured bacon; sourdough waffles; and if you're lucky enough to visit in the wintertime you may be asked to stay for a homestyle dinner cooked by Carl, who is an executive chef during the summer at a big deal restaurant in nearby Bar Harbor. No pets are allowed. There are two cats in residence. The Johnson family also keeps goats. No smoking. Bikers take note: the Sunset House is located near the 27-mile bike trail through the Acadia region.

Swans Island

JEANNIE'S PLACE B&B
Innkeepers: Llewellyn and
Jeannie Joyce.
526-4116.
Box 125, Swans Island off
Bar Harbor 04685.
Open all year.
Price: Inexpensive.
Credit Cards: None.

A 45-minute ferry ride from Bass Harbor on Mount Desert Island, this gabled home has three available rooms, all with double beds that share a single bath. Two rooms overlook Burnt Coat Harbor, so named, "because I guess somebody burnt their coat there. At least that's how the story goes," says Jeannie in an accent thick enough to block fog. The look is plain, homey and clean, and everyone is treated as part of the family. "They can chit-chat or watch TV. They're not restricted. They don't have to stay in their rooms." There's also a cabin she prefers to rent by the week. There's a full breakfast for those who want it that includes homemade bread and muffins, cereal, eggs and bacon. No smoking, drinking or pets allowed. Kids welcome.

LODGING — EAST OF SCHOODIC

Dennysville

LINCOLN HOUSE COUNTRY INN
Innkeepers: Mary Carol
and Jerry Haggerty.
726-3953.
Rte. 86 and Rte. 1,
Dennysville 04628.
Open all year.
Price: Moderate to
Expensive.
Credit Cards: V, MC, AE.

T he lemon-yellow Georgian-style inn lords over the surrounding rural landscape from a dramatic hillside perch above the Dennys River. Mary Carol and Jerry Haggerty, a professional carpenter and antique restorer (who worked at the Smithsonian), bought the 200-year old home during the mid-1970s, and have fashioned it into an immaculate and handsome showcase for antique lovers and history buffs. Many of the original features of the National Register home are still intact.

Lincoln House

Built in the late 1700s as a private home, the Lincoln House is now a handsome six-room inn.

The inn has six rooms with shared baths. A couple of years ago, the owners bought and restored the MacLauchlan House across the river. That inn has five rooms with private baths. Both are a favorite stop for birders, who often roam the adjoining 100 wooded acres on beautifully groomed trails that become ski trails in winter — although Jerry says he's about the only one who skis them. A stay at the inn includes a full country gourmet dinner and full breakfast. During the summer season, visitors can relax after dinner, in the eponymous-named Woodshed Pub, a picturesque and rustic counterpart to the inn's manicured rooms and dining room. No pets; no children under 10; moderate smoking allowed.

East Machias

RIVERSIDE BED & BREAKFAST
Owners: Carol and Tom Paul.
255-4134.
Rte. 1, East Machias 04630.
Open all year.
Price: Moderate.
Credit Cards: MC, V.

As we walked in the side door of this pretty, intimate 1820 cape-style sea captain's home, shortbread cookies were coming out of the oven. Carol was in the middle of preparations for Friday night dinner for the public dining room downstairs. The lodging house, which overlooks the Machias River, is a civilized resting place in a busy town. Three bedrooms with a single shared bath are small but elegantly appointed with antique furniture and old linens collected over the years by the Pauls, who used to own an antiques store in Newport, Rhode Island (they now have a shop in the barn next to the house). The prix-fixe dinner here, friends tell us, is one of the best and tastiest bargains Down East.

Eastport

TODD HOUSE
Owner: Ruth McInnis.
853-2328.
Water St., Todd's Head, Eastport 04631.
Open year round.
Price: Inexpensive to Moderate.
Credit Cards: None.
Handicapped Access: Rooms available.

After a career in Portland teaching and collecting antiques, Ruth McInnis returned home to Eastport where she bought and restored this classic Cape farmhouse, which is now on the National Register of Historic Places. It was built during the Revolutionary War on the banks of the Passamaquoddy Bay. The owner gladly will take you on a tour, asking advice on her latest antique purchase or giving insight into the town's workings. The six rooms vary greatly in feel: one has a working fireplace; several are bedecked with antiques, old books about the coast and brimming with historical significance; others are strictly modern with queen-size beds, TVs, private modern baths and kitchenettes. A simple, but ample, breakfast is served in the common room: cranberry muffins, cereal and some very welcome fresh fruit. Ms. McInnis does not accept cards, and there are no cash machines in town. She told us we could mail her the money, which we did. Children and pets are welcome.

WESTON HOUSE
Owners: Jett and John
  Peterson.
853-2907.
26 Boynton St.,
  Eastport 04631.
Open all year.
Price: Inexpensive to
  Moderate.
Credit Cards: None.

The Weston House is a civilized place. The formal parlor, with comfortable sofas and wing chairs, odd lamps, and a dish of pistachios on the coffee table, is the perfect place to curl up with a book as the afternoon wanes. There's also a cheerful back room for watching TV. Breakfast, served in the handsome dining room, is a gourmet affair—pancakes with fruit syrup, fresh baked breads and whatever else Jett Peterson — a prodigious cook — is experimenting with these days (Mrs. Peterson will also pack box lunches and make dinner on request). Five comfortable guest rooms are furnished with handsome antiques and fabrics in floral and calico prints; some have fireplaces and four-poster beds as well.

Lubec

**PEACOCK HOUSE BED
& BREAKFAST INN**
Owners: Chet and Veda
  Childs.
733-2403.
27 Summer St., Lubec 04652.
Open: May to October.
Price: Inexpensive to
  Moderate.
Credit Cards: MC, V.

From the outside, the Peacock House looks like any one of hundreds of old sea captain's homes. The white clapboard house sits on a quiet corner near the far end of Lubec's main street. Step over the threshold and you find yourself at a crossroads where Texas meets New England. The bed and breakfast is named for five generations of the Peacock family who once lived there. It was converted to a lodging house by two Southerners — Chet and Veda Childs — who with their grown daughter serve up expansive breakfasts of homemade Texas-size muffins, blueberry crepes or "rum-runners" French toast. Seven small to large rooms are decorated with a mix of comfortable, modern and reproduction furniture and have either a private or shared bath. The smallest, the Captain's Cabin, is a cozy single named for Capt. William Trott, who built the house for his bride in 1860. The largest — the Margaret Chase Smith — is named after the Maine senator who was a friend and frequent guest at the home. Some rooms have cable TV. Pets are not allowed, although the owners have a friendly dog. No smoking.

**MOONRAKER BED &
BREAKFAST**
Owners: Bill and Ingrid
  Handrahan.
546-2191.
Rte. 1 (Main St.),
  Milbridge 04658.
Open year round.
Price: Inexpensive.
Credit Cards: MC, V.

This spotless, well-kept B & B is named for roving sailors who navigated beautiful clipper ships. The Victorian house overlooks the Narraguagas River and Bay, and most of the rooms on the second and third floors have lovely ocean views. All five are decorated with handsome mahogany furniture and have shared bathrooms. In summer, breakfast is continental: homemade muffins, fresh fruit and cereal. In cooler weather, the Handrahans promise a "heartier bill of fare" to help get the engines running. This is a good stopping place en route to locations further Down East and is only 30-plus miles from Ellsworth and Bar Harbor. You can climb a ladder to the cupola, which offers great views of the water and countryside. No pets or smoking allowed.

CHAPTER FOUR

What To See, What To Do
CULTURE

On the 26th of December, 1950, on the evening of freezing cold and in the almost polar silence of Mount Desert Island, off the Atlantic shore, I was striving to live again through the smothering heat of a day in July, in the year 138 in Baiae, to feel the weight of a sheet on weary, heavy limbs, and to catch the barely perceptible sound of that tideless sea as from time to time it reached a man whose whole attention was concentrated upon other murmurs, those of his approaching death. I tried to go as far as the last sip of water, the last spasm of pain, the last image in his mind. Now the emperor had but to die.

WoodenBoat

—Marguerite Yourcenar,
*Reflections on the
Composition of
Memoirs of Hadrian*

The Maine coast has long attracted artists and writers like Brussels-born author Marguerite Yourcenar, who in the latter part of her life made her home on Mount Desert Island. Many found the coast a place from which they could advance their art and gather their inspiration. Others found it a good place to look out at the tabula rasa that is the Atlantic Ocean stretching eastward to Europe, with everything filtered through a hard, cool northern light. For several, the Maine coast has been a great place to get away from the hectic pace of New York or Boston for a few months every summer—and just

At WoodenBoat School in Brooklin, students learn to build traditional wooden craft including canoes, Friendship sloops and other small boats that have been made in Maine for centuries.

close enough to their rich patrons' summer homes to make the stay profitable.
The earliest painters to record life in Maine were itinerant limners or portraitists

The earliest painters to record life in Maine were itinerant limners or
portraitists who traveled the roads between Boston, Portsmouth, Kittery and
points north. They painted portraits of ships' captains, merchants and their
families. The true boom in Maine painting came with the arrival of the summer
artists. The first were from the Hudson River and Luminist movements. They
were at once transfixed by the coast's rugged beauty and the quality of its
sunlight. In 1844, Thomas Cole came to Bar Harbor and Mount Desert Island
in search of a picturesque reality to idealize. Cole found a virtual Eden, and
he kept coming back, often bringing with him fellow painters, including his
premier student, Frederic Church. His style, which became the cornerstone of
the Hudson River School, became popular with his wealthy patrons, as did the
idealized works of Fitz Hugh Lane, the leader of the Luminist movement, who
first painted Mount Desert Island four years later.

Painters, sculptors, musicians, poets and writers all have found the coast a
place to concentrate on their art. Edgar Allen Beem, a local art critic, has
described the attraction of Maine for artists who have always been "mavericks
and loners seeking privacy and freedom from influence." The coast, he writes,
offers "a sense of authenticity that occurs only when nature and culture are in
right relation with each other." That relation has become an elusive balance in
most other parts of America these days.

During the late 1800s, Winslow Homer painted at Prouts Neck, a 112-acre
point of land stretching into the Gulf of Maine south of Portland (his mother
was born in Bucksport). Realists Robert Henri, Rockwell Kent and George
Bellows painted on Monhegan during the early 20th century. Soon after the
turn of the century, painter Charles Woodbury and modernist Hamilton Easter
Field established two competing and sometimes fueding painting schools at
Perkins Cove in Ogunquit. Their presence drew other artists there through the
mid-1900s, including Alfred Stieglitz, Georgia O'Keeffe, Maurice Stern and
Stefan Hirsch. Walter Kuhn, one of the greatest American painters of the 20th
century, made his home in Ogunquit, too, although he kept himself aloof from
the sometimes raucous antics of the local art colony.

Sculptor Louise Nevelson lived near Rockland for many years. Andrew
Wyeth painted his famous canvas *Christina's World* on the site of an old farm
near Cushing. In 1991, the Olson family, who owned the three-story farmhouse
with gray weathered clapboards, donated the saltwater farm on Hawthorne
Point Rd. to the Farnsworth Museum in Rockland. Neil Welliver, whose
landscapes hang in the Metropolitan Museum of Art and Museum of Modern
Art in Manhattan, has a farm in Lincolnville, northeast of Camden.

Essayist and author E. B. White summered on the Blue Hill peninsula and
found inspiration for his famous children's story, *Charlotte's Web*, at the Blue Hill
Fair, now almost 100 years old. Before him, there were a long line of American
authors who wrote in and about the coast. Henry David Thoreau contemplated
nature here; Harriet Beecher Stowe (whose husband taught at Bowdoin College

in Brunswick) wrote *Orr's Island* here; Sarah Orne Jewett, who was born and lived much of her life in South Berwick, wrote her fine novel, *Country of the Pointed Firs*, in Maine.

Edna St. Vincent Millay was born at 198 Broadway in Rockland (the house, a private residence, still stands) and spent much of her childhood in Camden, the subject of many of her poems. For one long and painful year, novelist Jean Stafford (*The Mountain Lion*) and her husband, poet Robert Lowell, lived in Damariscotta Mills. Their marriage hit the rocks there. Later Stafford wrote *An Influx of Poets*, about poets and their quarrelling wives and mistresses who came to visit them during their short residence. Author and environmental activist Rachel Carson, who summered in the South Coast, found Maine a wonderful laboratory for her study of the environment. She wrote *At the Edge of the Sea* here.

Today there are dozens of artists and writers who live here year round, many lured by the relatively low cost of living compared with the exorbitant rents in art centers to the south. A thriving crafts community is centered near the Haystack Mountain School of Crafts in Deer Isle, and a talented group of photographers live in the midcoast region stretching from Bath to Rockland. Novelist Anne River Siddons summers near Blue Hill. Gay activist and author John Preston writes from Portland.

The result of all this artistic activity throughout the years is a public that has a deep and healthy appreciation for the visual and spoken arts. In this chapter we have tried to give you an idea of the people and organizations that give shape to the coast's cultural community. Still it has not been possible to list every historic site and arts organization. For a more complete listing for the area you plan to visit, contact the chamber of commerce for that region (See T*ourist Information*, Chapter Eight).

ARCHITECTURE

T he earliest buildings built by Europeans making their homes on the coast are believed to have been turf and thatch huts similar to those in England of the same period. It is thought that soon after settlers began using the abundant local forests. Few examples of the wood structures built by European settlers prior to 1760 remain. Farmhouses, forts and other early buildings were the victims of the ongoing French and Indian Wars, which lasted from 1675 to 1763. One exception is the **Old Stone Gaol** in York, a stone building built in 1653. The old jailhouse is now a museum and is the oldest stone building still in use in the United States.

Wood continued to be the most popular building material throughout the several architectural periods. Brick became popular in Portland after two fires, in 1775 and 1866, tore through streets lined with wooden structures. Native granite, quarried inland and on several islands off the coast, was primarily used for decorative facades.

Machias today is an historical center of the coast. The first naval battle of the American Revolution was fought near here.

Roy Zalesky

The earliest surviving wood-built houses are similar to those found to the south in New Hampshire and Massachusetts. The design focused on a central chimney and entranceway. A parlor and a dining room usually flanked the entranceway. The kitchen was situated at the rear of the chimney with a small room to either side filling out the basic rectangular shape of the building. Upstairs there were two main bed chambers at the front of the house and two smaller rooms to the rear. Many of the old houses were expanded throughout the years with rooms and a covered walkway connecting to a barn at the back of the house. Outside the houses were finished clapboards (a few were built from brick), and the earliest houses were devoid of outside decoration.

Many examples of the Federal and Georgian styles have survived and seem to have been the preferred architecture for well-to-do residents during the late 1700s and early 1800s. The Greek Revival took hold of Maine during the mid-1800s at a time when the coast was experiencing a great influx of wealth from the shipbuilding and shipping trade. Many of the newly wealthy were ships' captains, and their houses that line the coast are rich with elegant woodworking and flying staircases. A good example of the Greek Revival is the **Sarah Orne Jewett House** in South Berwick. The Gothic Revival movement was not as popular, although there are several fine examples that have survived. In Brunswick, there are two Gothic Revival churches: the **First Parish Church** is the more ornate of the two; **St. Paul's** is a more austere example of the trend. In Kennebunk, the **Wedding Cake House** is perhaps the state's most conspicuous example of the Gothic. Portland is home to the state's most outstanding example of the Italianate phase of the Gothic Revival. The **Victorian Mansion**, also known as the Morse-Libby House, was built in 1859 and is rich in Italian detail.

After the Civil War, the coast became a summer playground for wealthy Bostonians and New Yorkers. Thus the predominate style of architecture during the late 1800s was the grand "cottage," summer homes that were the size of small mansions back at home. Boston architect William R. Emerson made a great impact with the cottages he designed for wealthy patrons on Mount Desert Island — rambling wooden shingled buildings with large airy rooms that also incorporated native granite and stone. Portland architect John Calvin Stevens expanded on Emerson's principles and lined streets throughout the state with stately shingled cottages for both summer and year-round residents.

Since the mid-1600s, the predominant trend in coastal architecture has been simplicity and practicality. That is still seen in the small lobster and fishing shacks that seem to grow out of the rocks and have changed little during the past 100 years: the new *Maine Maritime Museum* in Bath, I.M. Pei's *Portland Art Museum,* and perhaps the most famous home in Maine, the *Olson house* in Cushing. It was made so by artist Andrew Wyeth in his painting *Christina's World.*

For architecture buffs, there is a state inventory of Maine architecture on file at the architectural archives at Colby College in Lewiston. Several chambers of commerce, including the Greater Portland, Wiscasset and Belfast, offer maps for self-guided walking tours of local historic buildings. Many of these annotated maps are available at state tourism offices (see *Tourist Information,* Chapter Eight). An excellent guide for those in making a driving survey of the coastal architecture is *Maine: A Guide "Downeast,"* published in 1970 by the Maine League of Historical Societies and Museums. Although the book is out of print, it is available in the Maine collections of most local libraries.

FILM

Film on the coast can mean everything from foreign and art films shown in funky old opera houses to full-blown Hollywood extravaganzas playing the screen at the neighborhood multiplex. There's the *Leavitt Theatre* in Ogunquit that has shown first-run movies on their big screen since 1923. There's also the *Movies at Exchange Street* in Portland, which offers a steady repertory of old classics, art and foreign films for dedicated movieholics and the *Opera House Theatre* in Stonington, a bonafide old opera house that has been restored and now shows first-run movies.

Movies are important to people on the coast. A while back, the *Nickelodeon,* one of two downtown movie houses in Portland, threatened to move west to the mall. There was an uproar from citizens who felt the theater was an important part of the city's cultural scene. Civic leaders convinced the theater to keep its doors open by providing the owners free rent. That's how the Nickelodeon became Portland's second movie house to show foreign films.

South Coast

Cines 8 (282-5995; 5 Points Shopping Center, Biddeford).
Leavitt Theatre (646-3123; Rte. 1, 40 Main St., Ogunquit).
Ogunquit Square Theatre (646-5151; Shore Rd., Ogunquit).
York Beach Cinema (363-2074; 6 Beach St., York Beach).

Casco Bay

Cinema City (729-0116; Cooks Corner Shopping Center, Brunswick).
Evening Star Cinema (729-5486; Tontine Mall, Brunswick).
The Movies at Exchange Street (772-9600; 10 Exchange St., Portland).
Nickelodeon Cinema (772-9751; Temple & Middle sts., Portland).
Hoyts Cinema 8 (879-1511; Clarks Pond Pkwy., So. Portland).
Maine Mall Cinema (774-1022; Maine Mall Rd., So. Portland).

Midcoast

The Colonial Twin Cinemas (338-1930; 121 High St., Belfast).
Harbor Light Cinema (633-3799; Harbor Village Shopping Center, Boothbay Harbor).
Bay View Street Cinema (236-8722; Bay View St., Camden).
Strand Cinema (594-7266; 339 Main St., Rockland).

Down East / Acadia

Criterion Theatre (288-3441; 35 Cottage St., Bar Harbor).
Maine Coast Mall Cinemas (667-3251; Maine Coast Mall, Ellsworth).
The Grand (667-9500; Main St., Ellsworth).
Opera House Theatre (367-5161; Main St., Stonington).

East of Schoodic

The Milbridge Theater (546-2038; Main St., Milbridge).

GALLERIES

Many of the best galleries on the coast are the commercial ones we have listed in *Shopping* (Chapter Seven). There is a first-class small permanent collection at the Payson Gallery in Westbrook, and several community-oriented galleries on the coast offer a good view of locally produced art during their regularly changing exhibits.

Casco Bay

Joan Whitney Payson Gallery of Art (797-9546; 716 Stevens Ave., Westbrook College, Westbrook). Remember the stir caused when a Japanese company bought Van Gogh's *Irises*? The painting had been part of this collection, and there are still several great works on display here, including those by Van Gogh, Picasso, Degas, Homer and Winslow (what self-respecting Maine collection would be without the latter two). This is a gem of a gallery housed in a small but beautiful building.

Baxter Gallery (775-5152; Portland School of Art, 619 Congress St., Portland). Work by the faculty of this small but powerful art school, plus frequent shows of students' work. This is a good place to find out what's on the mind and in the eye of young artists everywhere. Check out the handsome stone facade on the building, tucked into the woodwork of a busy city street.

Midcoast

Round Top Center for the Arts (563-1507; Business Rte. 1, Damariscotta). This young but growing center offers shows of area artists in its Main Gallery, including an annual exhibit of its members' work. They also offer alternative looks at the arts with exhibits of quilting and other crafts. Each show is accompanied by a lecture open to the public.

GARDENS & GARDEN TOURS

W inters on the coast are long. The growing season is short, and the soil, although rocky, is rich. It's no wonder that summer and-year round residents here take so much pride in their gardens. The rusticators who settled summer coastal communities were renowned for their green thumbs, and their gardens often stretched for acres to the sea. These days, the *fin de siecle* show gardens of Bar Harbor, some of which required as many as 40 full-time gardeners, are gone.

The Thuya Gardens, a public paradise that is open to what historian and summer resident Samuel Eliot Morrison calls the "habitues of the motel and the Acadia National Park camp and trailer grounds" will give you an idea of what those grand plots fashioned after the great gardens of England were like. *The New York Times* described Thuya Gardens as an "accidentally available private retreat left over from another time."

In addition to the public gardens listed below, there are several annual garden tours no self-respecting garden lover would miss. *Waldoboro* hosts a yearly community garden tour in early July. For information call 832-5555. Annually garden watchers line up for the *Coastal Garden Tour* that takes in gardens from Bath to Wiscasset (443-3471). That tour takes place the first week of July. *The Camden Open House & Garden Tour* takes place every year during mid-July (call 236-4404 for information). For further information about regional garden tours, call the chamber of commerce for the area you plan to visit (see *Tourist Information*, Chapter Eight).

Azalea Gardens (Rte. 3 and 198, Northeast Harbor, Mount Desert Island). Twenty different varieties of azaleas. They bloom in June. The rest of the year, the garden features native plants and trees and a Japanese sand garden. Open 7 a.m.-9 p.m. daily.

The Black House (Surry Rd., 1/2 mi. off Rte. 1, Ellsworth) The formal gardens to the rear of this historic mansion weren't planted until 1903, about 100 years after construction of the house. Following a period of disrepair, the grounds and gardens have been returned to their original state.

Hamilton House (Vaughan's Ln., S. Berwick). Overlooking the Pisquataqua River, these are some of the most beautiful grounds in Southern Maine. Open dawn to dusk from June to mid-Oct.

Merryspring (Conway Rd. off Rte. 1, on the Camden-Rockport town line). A 66-acre nature park with an herb garden, a lily garden, a 10-acre arboretum

and more cultivated wonders. Guided tours are available. Open dawn to
dusk year round.

Nickels-Sortwell House (Federal and Main Sts., Wiscasset). A 1920s garden
that is still in the process of restoration, but well worth the visit. June-Sept.
30, noon-5 p.m.

Thuya Gardens at Asticou Terraces (Rte. 3, Northeast Harbor on Mount Desert
Island). A formal English garden filled with country flowers — zinnias,
dahlias, plume poppies, goatsbeards, monkshood. The garden was founded
by Joseph Henry Curtis, a Boston landscape architect who summered in
Northeast Harbor from 1880 to 1928. 7-7 daily.

The Wild Gardens of Acadia (Rte. 3, Sieur de Monts Spring entrance, Mount
Desert Island). Maintained by the Bar Harbor Garden Club, this is an
exquisite collection of native plants. Open year round.

HISTORIC BUILDINGS & SITES

Andre the seal, honorary Harbormaster of Rockport Harbor, is dead, but
his stone image continues to guard the harbor. Harry Goodridge found
Andre when he was a young pup; he raised and trained the seal, who became
a local celebrity. The entire state mourned when Andre died in 1986, and his
statue is one of the coast's most unusual historic markers.

There are hundreds of historic homes and sites that date from Maine's
earliest days as part of the Massachusetts Bay colony and are open to the
public. Many of them are the product of the boom times the maritime industry
experienced in the late 18th and early 19th centuries. Below, we provide an
abbreviated list of notable ones, as well as forts and other coastal history hot
spots. Many of these charge a nominal fee for admission (between $1 and $5);
others are open to the public free of charge. We've also tried to list the ones
with public phones.

Courtesy of Penobscot Marine Museum

*Capt. Frank Irving Pendleton (1848-1915) in an Asian
costume he brought back from his sea travels. Capt. Pendleton
was one of many sea captains who made their homes in
Searsport during the age of the windjammer.*

If you are a truly serious history buff, check in with the *Maine Historical Society* (774-1822; 485 Congress St., Portland 04101); the *Maine Historic Preservation Commission* (289-2133; 55 Capitol St., Augusta 04330); or the *Society for the Preservation of New England Antiquities* (603-436-3205; 141 Cambridge St., Boston, MA 02114). The last will provide you with a free visitors' guide to their historic homes in Maine if you send a self-addressed, postage paid envelope (you'll need two first-class stamps).

South Coast

FORT McCLARY
693-6231.
Rte. 103 (Kittery Point Rd.), Kittery Pt.
Season: May 30–Oct. 1.

The granite fortification that dates back to 1715 saw strategic duty during the Revolutionary War, the War of 1812, the Civil War and the Spanish-American War. The fort was named for Andrew McClary, a local soldier who died at the Battle of Bunker Hill.

J. David Bohl

Overlooking the Pisquataqua River, the Hamilton House has beautiful grounds and gardens.

HAMILTON HOUSE
603-436-3205.
Vaughan's Ln., S. Berwick.
Season: June–Oct. 15; tours at noon, 1, 2, 3, 4 on Tues., Thurs., Sat., Sun.; grounds open dawn till dusk year round.

First built for a wealthy merchant during the 18th century, then altered by Boston residents Emily Tyson and her daughter Elise in 1898 to use as a summer home. The two women, friends of author Sarah Orne Jewett, outfitted it in grand Colonial Revival style. Several of the younger Tyson's period photographs are on view, testament to the civilized coastal summer life they enjoyed. The gardens and grounds are lovely, and many visit just to picnic in warm weather or cross-country ski in winter.

OLD YORK HISTORICAL SOCIETY
363-4974.
Lindsay Rd. and Rte. 1A, Old York.
Season: Mid-June–Sept. 30.
Nominal admission.

A "living history" museum that includes six period village buildings including: the Old Gaol (1720), the oldest public building still in use; the Emerson-Wilcox House (1740); the Elizabeth Perkins house (1731); the Jefferds Tavern (1750); the Old Schoolhouse; and the John Hancock Wharf and Warehouse. A good representation of the life and commerce of an 18th-century seaside town. Demonstrations of cooking and maritime crafts; displays of period furniture, china and glass, and the only complete set of the American crewel work in existence (at the Emerson-Wilcox House).

NOTT HOUSE
967-2513.
Main St., Kennebunkport.
Season: Open mid-June through mid-Oct., Wed.–Fri. 1–4.

A lso known as "White Columns," this beautiful Greek Revival home dates to 1853. It still retains many of its original features and furnishings including wallpapers, carpets and furniture.

LADY PEPPERELL HOUSE
Kittery Pt.
Season: Summer: 1–4
Admission charged.

T he 1760 Georgian home of Sir William Pepperell's widow (Sir William led colonial forces at the definitive battle at Louisburg on Cape Breton and was given a baronet for his success). The house contains period furnishings and several family portraits — including a portrait of Jane Pepperell, the first painting to be associated with Maine — as well as a good collection of fans and dishes.

SAYWARD-WHEELER HOUSE
603-436-3205.
79 Barrell Ln., York Harbor.
Season: June–mid-Oct., Wed.–Sun. noon-5.
Nominal Fee.

J. David Bohl

The Sayward-Wheeler house is typical of the lifestyle in Maine in the 18th century.

The mansion was built in 1718 and later enlarged and remodeled for civic leader Jonathan Sayward who was well known during the Revolution for his Tory sympathies. The owner was wealthy but frugal, and with its small, modest rooms and good, locally made woodwork and furniture, this well-preserved home provides a realistic view of a typical Mainer's lifestyle during the 18th century. The house also has a good collection of Chippendale and Queen Anne furniture, family portraits and china brought back as booty from the successful skirmish with the French at Louisburg in 1745.

SARAH ORNE JEWETT HOUSE
603-436-3205.
5 Portland St., S. Berwick.
Season: June 1–Oct. 15,
Tues.,Thurs., Sat., Sun.
noon–5
Nominal admission.

This is the home in which Ms. Jewett spent much of her life, and her room remains today as it was when she lived there. Beyond the literary connections, the house itself is an attractive mid-Georgian structure that has been restored to reflect the sophisticated mix of family heirlooms and arts and crafts pieces that Jewett and her sister used in their decoration.

Writer Sarah Orne Jewett's home in South Berwick. Jewett is the author of Country of the Pointed Firs, *an entertaining chronicle of life on the coast during the late 1800s.*

Maine Historic Preservation Commission

Casco Bay

JOSHUA L. CHAMBERLAIN HOUSE
729-6606.
226 Main St., Brunswick.
Season: June–Aug., Tues.–
Sat. 1–4; by appointment
during the rest of the year.

An 1825 house that was once occupied by the former governor of Maine and president of nearby Bowdoin College. Several rooms have been restored and are on view, as well as a collection of Chamberlain's Civil War memorabilia.

FIRST MEETINGHOUSE
721-8950.
Rte. 123, Harpswell
Center.
Season: July and Aug.,
Sun. 2-4 and by
appointment.
No charge.

Constructed in 1757, this is Maine's oldest meetinghouse, and its earliest congregations included what residents called "praying Indians." The building is still in general use as a town office and is an excellent example of early church architecture.

NEAL DOW MEMORIAL
714 Congress St., Portland.
Open year round, Mon.–
Fri., 11–4.

Neal Dow was a Quaker who was a leader in social reform during the 19th century. The memorial is the home he and his wife, Maria Cornelia Durant Maynard, built in 1829. Dow was an outspoken advocate for temperance, an abolitionist, Civil War general, two-time mayor of Portland and candidate for the U.S. presidency on the Prohibition Party ticket. His home, now managed by the Maine Women's Christian Temperance Union, is on the National Register of Historical Places.

ADMIRAL ROBERT E.
  PEARY HOME
693-6231.
Eagle Island, Casco Bay.
Season: June–Labor Day;
  accessible by boat.
No charge.

Construction of this handsome summer home began five years before Peary discovered the North Pole. The restored home features many striking design elements, including three quartz and fieldstone fireplaces. There are nature trails and a public pier where tour boats and visiting sailors can tie up.

PORTLAND
  OBSERVATORY
774-5561.
138 Congress St., Portland.
Season: Memorial Day to
  Labor Day.
Nominal fee.

Built in 1807, this is the last remaining signal tower on the eastern seaboard. The architecture is clunkily elegant — with heavy timbers forming a hexagonal tower that narrows at the top.

SKOLFIELD-WHITTIER
  HOUSE
729-6606.
161 Park Row, Brunswick.
Season: June–Aug., Tues.–
  Fri. 10–4; Sat. 1–4.

Three generations of prominent Brunswickians resided in this handsome 17-room home. They were doctors, mariners and educators, and the house remains pretty much as it was when they last lived here in 1925.

VICTORIA MANSION
772-4841.
109 Danforth St., Portland.

Also known as the Morse-Libby House, the imposing brownstone Italianate villa built for Ruggles Sylvester Morse looks as if it were a set for an episode of *The Addams Family*. Morse was a hotelier between 1858-60, and much of this small man-

Season: June–Sept., Tues.–
Sat. 10–4; Sun. 1-4. Open
by appointment the rest
of the year.
Nominal admission.

sion is packed with lavish, hotel-sized Victorian details. The house is still in the process of being restored, but is well worth visiting for its seven hand-carved Italian marble fireplaces and mantels alone. Our favorites are the "Turkish" room, where the gentlemen gathered to smoke, and the collection of Confederacy memorabilia (Morse was a Southern sympathizer).

**WADSWORTH-
LONGFELLOW
HOUSE**
774-1822.
485 Congress St., Portland.
Season: June through mid-
Oct., 10–4; tours on the
hour.
Nominal fee.

This is the boyhood home of poet Henry Wadsworth Longfellow. Built in 1785 by Henry's grandfather, Gen. Peleg Wadsworth, it is the oldest brick house in Portland, and today contains family artifacts and furnishings dating from 1750 to 1900. This is reported to be the most visited historic home in the state, but don't worry about lines. During warm weather the shaded garden is a wonderful place for a picnic.

Midcoast

**BOOTHBAY REGION
HISTORICAL
SOCIETY**
633-3462.
Elizabeth Reed House.
70 Oak St., Boothbay
Harbor.
Season: July–Aug., Wed.,
Fri., Sat. 10–4; rest of the
year Sat. 10–2.

An excellent collection of period photographs depicting the region's daily activities, including fishing, ice cutting, lumbering, farming, shipping and shipbuilding. Plus early fishing gear, shipwrights tools and navigation instruments.

CASTLE TUCKER
882-7364.
Lee and High sts.,
Wiscasset.
Season: July–Aug., Tues.–
Sat. 11–4; June 15-30 and
Sept. by appointment.
Nominal admission.

The coast is rich with boom-and-bust stories, and Castle Tucker is a perfect example. In 1807 Judge Silas Lee decided to build himself a "great house" on the hill overlooking Wiscasset Harbor, and nothing stopped him, not even his bank account. By the time of his death seven years later he had so heavily mortgaged the house that it became the property of his three neighbors. It was bought in 1958 by Capt. Richard Tucker, a third-generation mariner. Today the house is still owned by the Tucker family. It has original Victorian furniture, kitchen and wallpapers and a handsome elliptical staircase.

**COLONEL BLACK
    MANSION**
Rte. 172 (Surry Rd.), one
    quarter mi. off Rte. 1,
    Ellsworth.
Season: June—mid-Oct.,
    weekdays 10–4:30.

John Black's father-in-law and employer was a member of George Washington's staff during the Revolutionary War, and although this stately brick Georgian mansion dates to 1802, stories and knickknacks connected to the house go further back. The grounds and gardens (laid out in 1902) are gorgeous. Inside, there is an intriguing mix of Jacobean, Queen Anne, Chippendale, Sheraton and Hepplewhite furniture, Waterford and Sandwich glass and Canton and Spode china — all used by Black and his descendants.

Maine Historic Preservation Commission

The 1802 Georgian facade of the Black Mansion near Ellsworth. The house is a museum open to the public, and the grounds, laid out in 1902, are a lovely example of a Maine summer garden.

FORT WILLIAM HENRY
Pemaquid Peninsula.
Nominal fee.

The fort was a hot spot before and during the French and Indian Wars and changed hands — and names — several times. Fort Pemaquid (1632) was looted by pirates; the later Fort Charles was captured by the French in 1689; Fort William Henry, believed to be New England's first stone fortification, was captured by the Baron de Castine; Fort Frederic was built from the ruins of Fort William Henry in 1729. What you see today is an impressive replica of the fort in addition to the authentic Old Fort House built in 1729. The Old Burial Ground, just down the road from here, has graves dating to 1695. Also nearby is an archaeological excavation of the Pemaquid settlement established in the 1620s. A museum with artifacts from the dig is nearby.

**PARSON FISHER
    HOUSE**
374-2459.
Blue Hill .
Season: Open July through
    mid-September.

House built in 1814 by Jonathan Fisher, the town's first settled minister. Fisher was a man of many avocations — farmer, missionary, scientist, mathematician, portrait and landscape painter and poet among others. His house is full of the fruits of his labors, including his paintings, furniture, manuscripts and other unusual memorabilia.

FORT EDGECOMB
Right off Rte. 1 just past
Wiscasset Bridge,
Edgecomb.
Free.

The restored fort with an octagonal, two-story blockhouse was first built in 1808 to protect the port of Wiscasset from its vantage point overlooking the Sheepscot River. Great place for a picnic.

FORT KNOX
469-7719.
Rte. 174 off Rte. 1 just east
of Stockton Springs.
Nominal fee.

Looking west across the Penobscot River from Bucksport, this great granite fort looks like a medieval castle. It was built in 1844 as a defense against the British during the Aroostook War. In 1842, U. S. troops tromped north to meet British troops in New Brunswick; the "war" reached a negotiated settlement after some tense posturing on both sides. Today, the fort is the state's most complete historical military structure. It was constructed of granite mined from nearby Mount Waldo and named for the first U. S. Secretary of War, who was from the territory that eventually became the state of Maine.

Tom Hindman

A historical re-enactment at Fort Knox near Stockton Springs. The fort was built in 1842 to defend the coast from a threatened invasion by the British.

MONTPELIER
354-8062.
Rtes. 1 and 131,
  Thomaston.
May 30–Labor Day.

A replica of the 1795 house built by Gen. Henry Knox and his wife Lucy Flucker. Knox served in President George Washington's cabinet as Secretary of War. Tour guides in period costumes lead tours through the reconstructed mansion furnished with much of the original furniture.

**NICKELS-SORTWELL
  HOUSE**
882-6218.
Federal and Main sts.
  (Rte. 1), Wiscasset.
Season: June 1–Sept. 30,
  Wed.–Sun.; tours at
  noon, 1, 2, 3, 4.
Nominal fee.

B uilt in 1807 for Capt. William Nickels, a shipmaster in the lumber trade, this elegant Federal mansion also did service as a hotel during the 19th century. The furnishings are Colonial Revival style. Don't miss the beautiful elliptical stairway, and the wooden inlay work on the facade of the house. The gardens are currently being restored to their 1920 design.

The Nickels-Sortwell House.

Society for the Preservation of New England Antiquities

OLD CONWAY HOUSE
236-2257.
Conway Rd., Camden.
Season: July 1–Labor Day:
Tues.–Sun. 1–5.

T he Camden-Rockport Historical Society has restored this old farmhouse, which offers an authentic picture of farm life during the 1700s. There is a blacksmith shop on the premises and a small historical museum.

**OLD GERMAN
  MEETING HOUSE**
832-7742.

T his meetinghouse, which has a spectacular wineglass pulpit and striking, unpainted square-benched pews, was built in 1772 by the Ger-

Rte. 32, Waldoboro.
Season: June–Aug., daily
  1–4.
Free.

**ST. PATRICK'S
  CHURCH**
563-3240.
Academy Hill Rd.,
  Newcastle.
Open year round 9 a.m.–
  sundown.

**WALDOBOROUGH
  HISTORICAL
  SOCIETY**
832-5135
Rte. 220, just south of
  Rte. 1, Waldoboro.
Season: July & Aug., daily
  1–4:30.
Admission free.

Down East / Acadia

THE WILSON MUSEUM
Perkins St., Castine.
Season: Late May–Sept.,
  Tues.–Sun. 2–6.
Admission free.

East of Schoodic

BURNHAM TAVERN
255-4432.
Main St., Machias.
Season: June, July, Aug.,
  9–5; winter by
  appointment.
Nominal admission.

man families that settled the town 24 years earlier. The church was built on the eastern bank of the Medomak River, but later was moved to its current location.

T he oldest surviving Catholic church in New England, St. Patrick's was dedicated in 1808 and served a small group of Catholics who had immigrated from Ireland. The early Federal-style church was designed by architect Nicholas Codd and built from locally fired bricks. The pews and colored glass window date from 1896, but mass has been served continually from the altar since 1808.

T his is three buildings — a schoolhouse, a barn and a small museum — in addition to an 1819 pound where stray livestock were impounded. The barn houses displays of old toys, period clothing, china and glass, as well as a library and a reconstructed 19th-century kitchen and Victorian-style bedroom.

T his is really a series of several historic houses and commercial buildings, including a working blacksmith shop, the Hearse House (with 100-year-old summer and winter hearses) and the pre-Revolutionary John Perkins House (admission is charged here). The Wilson is home to a collection of prehistoric artifacts from North and South America, Europe and Africa that stress man's development of tools from the Paleolithic to the Bronze and Iron ages. It also has a collection of ship models, rocks and minerals and an 1805 kitchen exhibit.

R evolutionary War aficionados will appreciate the importance of this 1770 gambrel-roofed tavern, the oldest building in the U. S. east of the Penobscot River. This was where local leaders met and planned the first naval battle of the war in which Machias patriots aboard the schooner *Unity* captured the British schooner *Margaretta*. The building also served as a hospital during the war and a meeting place for local Masons.

RUGGLES HOUSE
483-4637.
Just off Rte. 1, Columbia Falls.
Season: June–mid-Oct., weekdays 9:30–4:30; Sun. 11–4:30.

Judge Thomas Ruggles did it all; he was a lumber dealer, a store owner, the local postmaster, captain of the local militia and a judge of the Court of Sessions. His house, designed by Massachusetts architect Aaron Sherman and built in 1818, befits a man of his many talents and high standing in society. The "flying" staircase is a marvel. So is the hand-carved woodwork, which took an English woodworker three years with a very sharp penknife to complete.

LIBRARIES

South Coast

Dyer Library (283-3861; 371 Main St., Saco). Part of the York Institute Museum since 1976, the Dyer is home to genealogical materials, city records and manuscripts of local interest.

Historical Society of Wells & Ogunquit (646-4775; Rte. 1, Wells). A collection of manuscripts and genealogies pertaining to the two towns and their early residents.

Ogunquit Memorial Library (646-9024; Shore Rd., Ogunquit). Nannie Connarroe built the library in 1897 as a memorial to her late husband George M. Connarroe. It is on the National Register of Historical Places.

Rice Public Library (439-1553; 8 Wentworth St., Kittery). Housed in its original 1888 building, the Rice has an extensive collection of Maine books and historical materials on Kittery.

Casco Bay

Maine Historical Society Library (774-1822; 485 Congress St., Portland). More than 60,000 monographs and serials published after 1497, including the state's most comprehensive collection of historical documents and printed materials. Open Tues.-Fri. 10–4, and the second Sat. of every month 9–5.

Museum of Yarmouth History Merrill Memorial Library (846-6259; Yarmouth). Two galleries of changing exhibitions and historical collections. Open Sept.–June: Tues.–Sat. from 10–5, and July–August: weekdays from 10–5.

Portland Public Library (871-1700; 5 Monument Sq., Portland). One of the largest libraries in the state. The Portland Room houses an excellent Maine collection, including old children's books. Mon., Wed., Fri. 9–6; Tues., Thurs. noon–9; Sat. 9–5.

Salt Documentary Archive (761-0660; 19 Pine St., Portland). Collection of photographs and taped recorded interviews detailing the way of life of people in Maine. Home of *Salt* magazine.

Midcoast

Bagaduce Music Lending Library (374-5454; Greene's Hill, Blue Hill). A music resource with a collection more than 500,000 items. Open year round: Tues., Wed., Fri. from 10–3, or by appointment.

Farnsworth Art Museum Library (596-6457; 19 Elm St., Rockland). A collection of art reference materials, including books, magazines and videotapes in the Greek Revival library. Call for library hours.

Maine Crafts Association (348-9943; 6 Dow Rd., Deer Isle). The group has put together an impressive collection of books and periodicals for craftspersons. Members' portfolios are also on file.

Stephen Phillips Memorial Library (548-2529; Church Street, Searsport). Part of the Penobscot Marine Museum. Open April–Oct., Mon.–Fri. 9–4; Nov.–March 8:30–3:30.

Southport Memorial Library (633-2741; Cape Newagen). Home of one of the largest butterfly collections in the country. July–Aug., Tues., Thurs., Sat. 1–4 and Tues. evenings 7–9; winter hours Tues. and Sat. 1–4; Tues. evenings 7–9.

Down East / Acadia

Jesup Memorial Library (288-4245; 34 Mount Desert St., Bar Harbor). An interesting collection of historical records from the island's past, including old hotel registers and scrapbooks, some with photos of the island before the 1947 fire. The library is open mid-June through Oct., Mon.–Sat. 1–4 and Wed. 7–9, and by appointment during the winter. Closed holidays.

LIGHTHOUSES

L ighthouse keepers are no more. Most of the lighthouses in the country have been automated. The historic, whitewashed lighthouse at *Goat Island*, near George Bush's Kennebunkport summer home, was automated in 1990 as a cost-saving measure by the government. With the lightkeeper retired, the island now serves as an air-sea command center that can warn the Secret Service if a plane is headed toward Walker Point — that's the huge, black, constantly whirling radar beacon that stands next to the old lighthouse.

All told, there are 60 lighthouses along the coast of Maine (we've listed some of the more prominent ones below). Each is filled with legends of shipwrecks, ghosts, drownings and rescues. Some now serve as museums, youth hostels or bed and breakfasts.

Today, there are societies dedicated to the restoration and preservation of these symbols of our maritime heritage. *The Lighthouse Preservation Society* (508-281-6336, Rockport, MA 01966 and the *United States Lighthouse Society* (415-362-7255; 244 Kearny St., Fifth Floor, San Francisco, CA 94108).

If you'd like to tour some of the unaccessible lighthouses in the midcoast region, *Acadia Air* out of Bar Harbor Airport offers a lighthouse flight. For information call the airline, 667-5534. If you want to view the inaccessible light-houses way Down East, you can sign up for a lighthouse cruise with **Capts. Barna and John Norton** (497-5933; RR#1. Box 990, West Jonesport 04649-9704). If you'd like to spend the night in a lighthouse, try the **Keepers House** in Isle au Haut (see *Lodging*, Chapter Three). If you'd like to learn more about light-houses, visit the **Shore Village Museum** in Rockland (see "Museums," below). It has one of the largest collections of lighthouse material in the country.

Tom Hindman

The Egg Rock Light in Frenchman Bay was built in 1890 and is an active lighthouse that is now automated. It can be seen from the Bluenose, *the ferry from Bar Harbor.*

Casco Bay

Portland Head Light (Shore Rd., S. Portland), constructed in 1791 at the order of President George Washington, is the oldest on the East Coast.

Midcoast

As far as Maine lighthouses go, the **Grindle Point Light**, built in 1935, is young. Today the building on Isleboro houses the Sailor's Memorial Museum. It is open mid-June through August.

The **Marshall Point Light** (1895) in Port Clyde is home to a collection of lighthouse memorabilia. It is open weekend afternoons in May, September and October, and Tuesday through Sunday afternoons in June, July and August.

The keeper's house at the *Monhegan Island Light* (1824) is now a museum that contains exhibits of the island's native plants, wildlife and Native American artifacts.

The *Owls Head Light* sits on a park called the the U. S. Lighthouse Reservation. The light was built in 1826, and although it is only 26 ft. high, it can be seen from 16 miles at sea.

The *Pemaquid Lighthouse Park* (Lighthouse Rd., Pemaquid Point) is a good place to relax for a picnic. The lighthouse was built in 1827, and the keeper's house has been converted to an art gallery and museum featuring exhibits about saltwater fishing.

You can walk on the breakwater 7/8 mi. to the *Rockland Lighthouse* (take Rte. 1 north to Waldo Ave. and Samoset Rd.). A favorite fishing spot is at the end of the breakwater under the lighthouse.

East of Schoodic

The brashly striped light at *West Quoddy Head* in Lubec sits at the easternmost point in the U. S. It was built in 1807 and was featured on a 1990 U. S. Postal Service stamp commemorating the 100th anniversary of the Coast Guard.

Tom Hindman

The Pumpkin Island Light in Penobscot Bay is near Deer Isle. Built in 1854, it is visible from the air but hard to see from land.

MUSEUMS

There are more than 115 registered museums in Maine, and it is estimated there are more than 300 if you count all the small private collections of painting, sculpture, memorabilia, ephemera and historical bric-a-brac that are put on display here. Here is a list of a few museums on the coast.

South Coast

AUTO MUSEUM AT WELLS
646-9064.

Once a private collection, now a nonprofit car-lovers' organization, this museum has a collection of more than 70 gas-, steam- and electric-

Rte. 1, Wells.
Season: mid-June–mid-
  Sept., daily 10 a.m.
Free.

powered automobiles that have been restored. Stanley Steamers, Rolls Royces, Fords and motorcycles, license plates, bicycles, antique toys and nickelodeons, this is an entertaining look at our motoring past among other things. Particularly fun are rides in one of the museum's Model T's.

BRICK STORE MUSEUM
985-4802.
117 Main St., Kennebunk.
Season: Open year round,
  Tues.–Sat. 10–4:30, Wed.
  until 8 p.m.
Donations.

T his museum that tells the story of Kennebunk began as a small collection of artifacts on display in the town's old general store. These days it encompasses an entire block and runs changing exhibits that tell about the region's maritime and social history. The museum offers tours pointing out the town's architectural highlights, June–Oct., Wed. at 10 and Fri. at 1.

**KITTERY HISTORICAL
  AND NAVAL MUSEUM**
439-3080.
Roger Rd. (Rte 236 off
  Rte. 1), Kittery.
Season: June–Oct.,
  weekdays 10–4, or by
  appointment.
Admission: $2 adults; $1
  children; those under
  seven free.

K ittery is Maine's oldest town, and this relatively young museum (1976) commemorates the burg's history as a shipbuilding town. There is a 12-foot model of the *Ranger*, John Paul Jones' ship that had its keel laid here. There are other exhibits about the accomplishments of the local naval yard, the first U. S. shipyard and the one responsible for the building of several Civil War ships, as well as the country's first submarine.

MAINE AQUARIUM
284-4511 (recorded
  message).
Rte. 1 (2 mi. north of exit
  2B on Maine Turnpike),
  Saco.
Season: June 15–Sept. 15,
  daily 9–9; Sept. 16–
  June 1, 9–5.
Admission: $6.50 adults;
  $5.50 seniors; $4.50
  children 5 to 12 years;
  $2.50 children 2 to 4
  years.

S harks! Penquins! Seals! Live sea animals from the world over are on display in this zoo of underwater creatures. Aquatic animals from the Gulf of Maine, and a "touchable" tidepool full of seashore plants and animals for the young ones (summer only).

**MUSEUM OF ART OF
  OGUNQUIT**
646-4909.
Shore Road, Ogunquit.

B uilt by the painter Henry Strater, the museum houses a good collection of 20th-century American artists who came here to scramble over the rocks, soak up the summer sun and, of course,

Season: July 1–Labor Day;
daily 10:30–5.
Free.

**SEASHORE TROLLEY
MUSEUM**
967-2800.
Log Cabin Rd.,
Kennebunkport.
Season: Summer daily 10–
5 with sunset rides 7–9;
winter by appointment.

**YORK INSTITUTE
MUSEUM**
282-3031.
371 Main St., Saco.
Season: May–Oct., Tues.–
Fri. 1- 4, Thurs. until 8;
Nov.–April, Tues.–
Wed. 1–6, Thurs. 1-8;
July–Aug.: Sat. 1-4.
Free.

Casco Bay

**BOWDOIN COLLEGE
MUSEUM OF ART**
725-3275.
Walker Building, Bowdoin
College, Brunswick.
Open year round. Tues.–
Sat. 10–5; Sun. 2–5.
Closed Mondays and
national holidays.
Free.

DESERT OF MAINE
865-6962.
95 Desert Rd. (just off Rte.
1 and I-95), Freeport.
Season: mid-May—mid-
Oct., daily 9—dusk.

paint and sculpt. Works on view are by Walt Kuhn, Marsden Hartley, Rockwell Kent and others.

B ack when mass transportation was fashionable, handsome trolleys like the ones on display here carried passengers almost everywhere. If you made your connections right, you could trolley all the way from Washington, D. C., to Portland. This museum has the world's largest and oldest collection — more than 100 vintage cars from Biddeford, Saco, San Francisco, Nagasaki and Rome. It also operates a two-mile stretch of track for daily trolley rides and a streetcar workshop where visitors can see a trolley restoration in process. Call or write them for a list of special streetcar events sponsored by the museum throughout the year.

E xhibits of paintings, textiles, household items and furnishings of several periods in American history, including Colonial, Federal and Colonial Revival. The adjoining gallery hosts changing art exhibits, and the library has an excellent Maine history collection.

A beautiful Greek Revival building houses the museum's permanent collections including ancient Mediterranean art and European and American paintings, sculpture, drawings, prints and photos. Of special interest are the selection of Colonial and Federal portraits and paintings by Winslow Homer, John Sloan and Rockwell Kent. The museum also regularly features changing art exhibits.

T he first chapter in the history of this geologic oddity occurred during the Ice Age, when glaciers deposited sand and minerals. During the late 1700s and early 1800s a family of farmers came, clearcut the land, grew crops, grazed their animals and failed to use good farming techniques that could have prevented erosion of the thin layer of topsoil. What remains is a genuine sand desert smack in the

Admission: $4.75 adults;
  $4 seniors; $3.50 ages 13
  to 16; $2.50 ages 6-12;
  children under 6 free.

**PEARY-MacMILLAN
  ARCTIC MUSEUM**
725-3416.
Hubbard Hall, Bowdoin
  College, Brunswick.
Open year round: Tues.–
  Sat. 10–5; Sun. 2-5.
Guided tours available
  during the academic
  year; call to schedule.

**PORTLAND MUSEUM
  OF ART**
773-2787.
619 Congress Ave.,
  Portland.
Open year round, Tues.–
  Sat. 10–5; Thurs. until
  9; Sun. noon–5.
Admission: $3.50; $2.50
  seniors and students; $1
  youths; children under
  12 free.

Midcoast

**BOOTHBAY RAILWAY
  VILLAGE**
633-4727.
Rte. 27, Boothbay.
Season: Mid-June to
  Columbus Day, daily
  9:30–5.

**BULL MOOSE
  RAILROAD**
338-2931.
11 Water St. off City
  Landing, Belfast.

middle of coastal Maine, a favorite local tourist attraction since the mid-1930s. Walking and coach tours available. Gift shop, picnic grounds and campground on the premises.

A dmirals Robert E. Peary and Donald B. MacMillan were both graduates of Bowdoin College, and this museum commemorates their joint explorations. Peary was the first man to reach the North Pole on April 6, 1909; MacMillan was Peary's chief assistant on that expedition. Exhibits include the log and a sledge from the 1909 expedition, as well as displays of Inuit art and artifacts from Labrador and Greenland that MacMillan gathered on subsequent expeditions to the north.

M aine's oldest public museum resides in an impressive granite and brick structure designed by I. M. Pei. Inside exhibit space is open and airy, much like space Pei designed for the East Wing of the National Gallery of Art in Washington, D. C. The permanent collection includes a worthwhile selection of American and European art, including paintings by Van Gogh, Picasso, Degas and many Winslow Homers (he painted and lived part of the year at Prouts Neck, about 15 minutes from the museum) and a significant holding of Colonial and Federal portraits. The museum also is temporary home to visiting exhibitions. On Saturday mornings, the doors are opened free of charge.

T hey have recreated a quaint New England village and its transportation system on eight acres here. There are more than 60 vehicles on display, including a steam locomotive, which for 15 minutes carries you back to a simpler time on 1.5 miles of narrow-gauge track. A doll museum is on the premises.

T he Belfast & Moosehead Lake Railroad (nicknamed "Bull Moose") was founded in 1867 to carry lumber from inland Maine to the coast. That plan was short-circuited only a few years later when B&ML RR decided to hook up with the Maine Central Railroad just 33 miles inland. These days, the

Season: June—mid-Oct., several one-hour runs a day. Call for schedule. Admission charged.

line is operated by the City of Belfast and its mixed freight and passenger runs are shorter. Visitors are invited to ride the rails for a one-hour excursion along the coast several times a day.

FARNSWORTH MUSEUM
596-6457.
19 Elm St. (off Rte. 1), Rockland.
Season: Year round daily 10–5; Sun. 1–5. Closed most legal holidays and Mon. Oct.–May.
Admission: $3 adults; $2 students and those over 65; children under 12 free.

When Rockland resident Lucy Copeland Farnsworth died in 1935, she left $1.3 million and instructions that the money be used to build a library and a one-room art museum. With a little finagling the Farnsworth legacy grew to one of the best regional collections in the country. The home of this collection is almost as outstanding as the paintings themselves, a well kept complex with the museum, an excellent art library and the Farnsworth Homestead (1850), a gorgeous Greek Revival home with original high-Victorian furnishing and decor. The focus of the museum's permanent collection is on American art, mostly that painted in New England, and includes work by the Wyeths (N. C., Andrew and Jamie), Winslow Homer, John Marin, Fitz Hugh Lane, Edward Hopper, Neil Welliver and sculptor Louise Nevelson.

FRIENDSHIP MUSEUM
Rte. 220 and Martin's Pond Rd., Friendship.
Open Mon.–Sat. noon–5.
Donations welcome.

A one-room brick schoolhouse dedicated to the history of the Friendship sloop.

OLD LINCOLN COUNTY JAIL & MUSEUM
882-6817.
Rte. 218, Wiscasset.
Season: July and Aug., Tues.—Sat. 11—4:30.

An unusual view of life in the 19th century. Visitors can peruse prisoners' cells with original graffiti. The jail was built in 1811, has granite walls 41 inches thick and saw service as recently as 1953. Inside the jailor's house there is a display of early American tools, costumes, artifacts and changing exhibits about local history.

MAINE MARITIME MUSEUM
443-1316.
243 Washington St., Bath.

With an abundance of interpretive and hands-on exhibits, ships you can climb aboard and a museum-sponsored narrated cruise along the waterfront, this is a great museum for visitors of every age. The core of the museum is the Percy & Small Shipyard (open late spring through late fall), the

Open year round 9:30–5
except Thanksgiving,
Christmas and New
Year's Day.
Admission: $6 adults;
$2.50 children 6 to 15.

only surviving shipyard in the country where large wooden sailing ships were built at the turn of the century. It is also home to the *Sherman Zwicker*, a Grand Banks fishing schooner, visiting historic craft that stop in during the warm months and an apprentice shop where young boatbuilders are taught the craft of bygone days (weekdays only).

MUSICAL WONDERHOUSE
882-7163.
18 High St., Wiscasset.
Season: Memorial Day–
Oct. 15, daily 10–5.
Admission: $8 adults; $5
for seniors and children
under 12. Informal tour
included.

Danilo Konvalinka owns hundreds of restored music boxes and musical instruments and has put them on display in his Greek Revival ship captain's home. Many are works of art and are capable of playing complicated songs with a wide range of notes. Some date from 1750. There are pocket boxes and floor models. He also keeps player pianos and other mechanical musical treasures. Reportedly he keeps his entrance fee high because he doesn't need the traffic. He also buys, sells and repairs music boxes.

OWLS HEAD TRANSPORTATION MUSEUM
594-4418.
Rte. 73, Owls Head.
Season: Winter hours,
weekdays 10–4, Sat.
and Sun. 11–3; daily
10–5 in summer.
Nominal entrance fee.

An interesting collection of pioneer aircraft, automobiles, engines, motorcycles, bicycles and carriages — almost anything that moves. The museum has guided tours of these conveyances, all of which are run from time to time. Some planes and vehicles operated on weekends.

PENOBSCOT MARINE MUSEUM
548-2529.
Church St., Searsport.
Admission: $4 adults;
$3.50 senior citizens;
$1.50 children 7-15.

At the height of the shipping industry in Maine during the 19th century, 10 percent of America's deepwater shipmasters lived in Searsport. They brought mementos of the world back to this pretty little town. The museum, consisting of nine buildings restored or converted to individually themed galleries, is a terrific place to spend the day. It is home to one of the largest collections of marine paintings in the state, including ship portraits commissioned and painted in the ports of Europe and China. The Old Town Hall is devoted to the description of the great Down Easters, the square-rigged vessels built in Maine during the late 1800s.

The museum sponsors annual events, concerts, lectures and readings by Maine authors. Call for a current schedule.

The Penobscot Marine Museum

The Penobscot Marine Museum is housed in several period buildings in Searsport, which during the 1800s was a lively port and home to hundreds of ships' captains. The museum has one of the largest collections of marine paintings in the world.

SHORE VILLAGE MUSEUM
594-4950.
104 Limerock St., Rockland.
Season: June–mid-Oct., daily 10–4.
Free.

This small museum situated on an old Rockland street is crammed with an odd assortment of historical materials: the world's largest selection of lighthouse paraphernalia and Coast Guard memorabilia; uniforms, weapons and papers concerning the local men who fought in the Civil War; and the Llewella Mills collection of 34 dolls dressed in period costumes from the Middle Ages to the Gay '90s.

Down East/Acadia

ROBERT ABBE MUSEUM OF STONE AGE ANTIQUITIES
288-3519.
Rte. 3 near Sieur de Monts Spring, Acadia National Park.
Season: Spring and fall, 10–4; summer, 9–5.
Nominal fee.

This impressive small museum houses a record of Maine's native inhabitants of 11,000 years ago to now. Stone tools, baskets, musical instruments and ornaments — some as old as 5,000 years — and a canoe made from a single piece of birch bark are among the items that have been brought together from the Frenchman Bay and Mount Desert Island area. During the summer weekends members of the Micmac, Maleseet, Passamaquoddy and Penobscot tribes demonstrate Native American art such as basket and jewelry making.

**WENDELL GILLEY
MUSEUM OF BIRD
CARVING**
244-7555.
Herrick Rd. and Main St.
(Rte. 102), Southwest
Harbor.
Season: Closed at the end
of January for the
winter. Call for museum
hours.
Admission: $3 adults; $1
children; free to members.

Wendell Gilley was a plumber until he decided to quit and devote himself to his hobby full time. He carved birds, more than 10,000 of them. Beautiful specimens of airborne nature — wooden eagles, chickadees, ducks, owls and tiny lyrical songbirds. His birds are in full feather and on view here.

**JACKSON
LABORATORY**
288-3371.
600 Main St., Bar Harbor.
Season: Mid-June–Aug.,
Tues. and Thurs. 1–2.
Call for exact hours and
dates.
No charge.

The Jackson Laboratory was founded in 1929, and since that time has made a name for itself in the world of mammalian genetic research. Currently the laboratory performs research on such varied human maladies as cancer, AIDS, allergies, diabetes, reproductive disorders, aging and transplantation rejection. It also raises more than 1,300 genetically unique laboratory mice and sells them to research scientists around the world. They offer a one-hour lecture and multimedia presentation describing the lab's mission and ongoing research every Tuesday and Thursday.

**M.D.I. BIOLOGICAL
LABORATORY**
288-5339.
Old Bar Harbor Rd., Rte. 3
(northwest of Bar
Harbor), Salisbury Cove.
Season: June 20–Aug.,
Wed. only, 1:30.
No charge.

M.D.I. is a laboratory that conducts research in marine organisms. While most of their work is confined to animals that live in the sea, it has many implications for human health and the environment. Once a week the lab provides the public an opportunity to see what they do during a lecture, tour and video presentation.

**MOUNT DESERT
ISLAND HISTORICAL
SOCIETY**
Rte. 102, Somesville,
Mount Desert Island.
Season: July and Aug.,
Sun. and Wed. 2–5.
Donations welcome.

Bric-a-brac and other interesting stuff from Mount Desert's past including period clothing, furniture, early household items, sleigh bells, guns from the Revolutionary War days and old pewter. Tools from the wool, grist, saw, tannery and barrel stave mills that were operated nearby. Kids will want to see Dr. Nehemiah Kittredge's tooth extractor. It will make them cringe.

**MOUNT DESERT
OCEANARIUM**
288-5005.
Three locations: Rte. 3,
Thomas Bay, Bar
Harbor; One Harbor
Place, Bar Harbor; and
Clark Point Rd.,
Southwest Harbor.
Season: All three mid-
May–Oct., 9–5, later in
July and Aug.
Nominal admission.

These three museums are fun stops for any aquatic-minded tourist, particularly younger ones. The Thomas Bay branch is home to some happy harbor seals, and the Maine Lobster Museum, where a licensed lobster fisherman will take you aboard a real lobster boat and answer your questions about the crusty crustaceans (they also offer a guided walk through Thomas Bay Marsh). The branch at One Harbor Place in downtown Bar Harbor has a working lobster hatchery where you can see between 5,000 and 10,000 tiny lobsters being raised for future release in the Gulf of Maine. The Southwest Harbor Oceanarium, located right next to the Coast Guard base, has 20 tanks filled with resident Maine sea life, a touch tank and an audio-visual exhibit where you can hear whale "songs."

**NATURAL HISTORY
MUSEUM**
288-5015.
College of the Atlantic, 105
Eden St., just north of
Bar Harbor.
Season: Mid-June–Aug.,
daily 9–5.
Adults $2.50; children ages
3-12 $.50; senior citizens
$1.50.

In earlier times this was a lovely granite summer cottage, known as the Turrets. Today it is a museum that offers an environmental perspective on Mount Desert Island. On display are interpretive exhibits about more than 50 species of island animals, plants and trees. Every day at 11 a.m., there is a free program open to all visitors; and the museum hosts weekly evening lectures on topics regarding the native populations of the island from Native Americans to seabirds and coyotes. Call for a schedule of events.

**PERRY'S TROPICAL
NUT HOUSE**
338-1630.
Rte. 1, Belfast.
Season: daily 9-7.
Free.

Founded in the mid-20s, this famous tourist trap houses an oddball's collection of nuts, seashells and worn stuffed animals including the remains of P. T. Barnum's circus animals and a water buffalo reportedly shot by President Teddy Roosevelt. There are also nuts for sale (the kind you eat) and store-made fudge. In other words, there is something here for the whole family.

STATE OF MAINE
326-4311.
Castine.
Season: July and Aug., 9–
12 and 1–4.
Free.

This is the training ship for students at nearby Maine Maritime Academy.

East of Schoodic

**SARDINE VILLAGE
    MUSEUM**
733-2822.
Rte. 189, Lubec.
Season: Mid-June–mid-
    Oct., Tues.–Sat. 1-5.
Nominal fee.

Years ago when people ate sardines like potato chips, Lubec was the sardine capital of the world. These days consumption is down, and the area has only a couple of canning plants still operating. This museum tells the story of the rise and fall of the Maine sardine and has interesting exhibits, including original processing equipment.

**WAPONAHKI MUSEUM
    AND RESOURCE
    CENTER**
853-4001.
Pleasant Point Indian
    Reservation, Perry.
Open Mon.–Fri., 9–11, 1–4.

The Passamaquoddy Indians were among the tribes that once inhabited Maine shores during the summer. After Europeans settled the coast, their numbers diminished. In 1822 there were 379 Passamaquoddy. Today there are more than 2,000. This museum offers a glimpse of their rich culture through the implements they fashioned from nature —graceful birch bark canoes, handsome ash baskets, snowshoes, clothing and arrowheads. Also on exhibit are photographs that document life on the reservation in the past and present. The museum is a repository for a growing collection of books, tapes, dictionaries and reference books, all of which serve to preserve the Passamaquoddy language. Classes in the tribe's new written language are taught here.

Near the Coast

Both of these museums are near enough to the coast and worthwhile enough for a half-day excursion.

SHAKER MUSEUM
Sabbathday Lake, Rte. 26,
    Poland Spring.
Season: Memorial Day—
    Columbus Day, 10—
    4:30. Closed Sundays.
Nominal admission.

A small community of Shakers still live and work here today, tending their gardens, drying herbs and preserving their heritage. The view from this historic hillside religious community is breathtaking. Once inside the small, spare buildings on the compound, you begin to understand why the Shakers' simple, elegant style of dress and furniture is so popular even today. Shaker furniture, tools, textiles, tin, woodenware and folk art are on display, and if you like you can sign up for a guided walking tour of the village.

**ROOSEVELT
    CAMPOBELLO PARK**
Campobello Island, New
    Brunswick.
Free.

Just a stone's throw from Lubec sits the island summer home of former U. S. President Franklin D. Roosevelt. Although on Canadian soil, the historic site is maintained jointly by the U. S. and Canada and the only auto route to the island is via the international bridge at Lubec (a ferry provides access on the Canadian side). The house recently has been restored and contains many of the Roosevelt family's original furnishings.

MUSIC

Music is a passion on the coast. Small chamber groups like the *Portland String Quartet*, amateur opera companies such as the *Surry Opera Company* in Surry, and blues and rock and roll bands like the *Red Light Revue* out of South Portland make sure there's a program of good music year round.

During the past century and a half the coast has been home to many musicians as well. American composer and Harvard professor Walter Piston (1894-1976) was born in Rockland. French-born conductor Pierre Monteux (1875-1964) once made his home in Hancock, a small hamlet outside of Bar Harbor. Although he led world-class orchestras in Boston, Paris and San Francisco, he took great pride in being named chief of Hancock's Volunteer Fire Department. Today Hancock hosts a music festival named for him. Portland is home to the famed Kotzschmar Memorial Organ at the City Hall Auditorium. Citizens are working to have the organ, which is dusted off for periodic recitals, fully restored to its former glory.

Harps, dulcimers, brass quintets, jazz quartets — the coast is home to dozens of musical groups and festivals every year. Below we've listed some of the larger and better-known musical organizations on the coast. But be warned, there are many more. For a comprehensive schedule of musical events for the area you plan to visit, contact the local chamber of commerce (see *Information, Chapter Eight*).

Casco Bay

CUMBERLAND COUNTY CIVIC CENTER
775-3458.
1 Civic Center Sq. (at the corner of Spring and Center sts.), Portland.
Open year round.
Tickets: $6–$35, depending on event.

The acoustics aren't great, but that doesn't daunt folks who travel from way Down East and the far northern reaches of the state to hear good music. Folk, rock, heavy metal plus the occasional circus, ice show or traveling Broadway hit play here.

PORTLAND CONCERT ASSOCIATION
772-8630 or 800-639-2707
262 Cumberland Ave., Portland.
Season: fall–spring.
Tickets: $10–$40.

Every year this group books a range of traveling talent from perennial favorites like the Canadian Brass Ensemble or the Flying Karamazov Brothers to world class performers like Isaac Stern and the New York City Opera Company. Concerts are held at the Portland City Hall Auditorium.

PORTLAND STRING QUARTET
761-1522.
Ticket information: P.O. Box 11, Portland 04112; performances at the Charles A. Dana Auditorium, Maine Medical Center, 22 Bramhall St., Portland.
Season: Sept.–May.
Tickets: $7–$10.

T his is one of the few classical quartets to endure a quarter of a century rehearsing, touring and performing together without a single change in personnel. The result is a mature sound that can take on the most difficult work and play it beautifully. The group's music is an impeccably performed mix of classic and new chamber works commissioned for the group. When this talented quartet isn't on the road, they perform at an auditorium at the Maine Medical Center.

PORTLAND SYMPHONY ORCHESTRA
773-8191 or 800-639-2309.
30 Myrtle St. off Congress, Portland.
Concerts throughout the year.

P ortland is the smallest city in the U.S. to have a full-time symphony orchestra, and local audiences are extremely appreciative. The symphony, under conductor and music director Toshiyuki Shimada, performs the classics and pops most of the year in the Portland City Hall Auditorium just down the street from their offices. During the summer, they take to the outdoors with a series of concerts at beautiful Fort Williams Park in Cape Elizabeth.

Courtesy Portland Symphony Orchestra

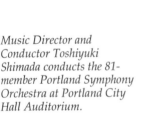

Music Director and Conductor Toshiyuki Shimada conducts the 81-member Portland Symphony Orchestra at Portland City Hall Auditorium.

Midcoast

BAY CHAMBER CONCERTS
236-2832 or 236-0860.
P.O. Box 191, Camden 04843.
Season: Winter series Oct.–May; summer series July & Aug.
Tickets: $5–$15.

T his group has brought music to midcoast Maine for more than 30 years. The summer season runs from mid-July through August, and includes twice weekly lectures and concerts with the Vermeer Quartet and guest artists. The organization also promotes the music of young performers with a $10,000 piano competition and its Next Generation program in August. During the winter the group sponsors monthly classical and jazz concerts by world-renowned artists. All concerts take place at the renovated Rockport Opera House.

ROUND TOP CENTER FOR THE ARTS
563-1507.
Bus. Rte. 1, Damariscotta.
Open year round.
Tickets: $6–$10 for music and theater events; $2.50 and up for craft and art shows.

The Round Top was a dairy farm in a former life. They still make and sell 30 flavors of the best-loved ice cream in the county (they import the milk). Since 1987 their main product is music, theater, arts and crafts taught and put on display. Business has been so good they can hardly restore and convert the old farm's buildings fast enough to accommodate the growth. During the warm weather many of their concerts, children's and adults' plays, art and crafts shows, lectures and workshops are staged outside. Come winter, activities move indoors. One of their most popular events is the annual concert by the Portland Symphony Orchestra during late July or early August. Nearly 3,000 people come every year to picnic and hear the music under the stars.

Down East/Acadia

COMPOSERS STRING QUARTET
Mount Desert Island.
Every Tuesday in the summer.

Since the late '60s the Composers String Quartet, a resident ensemble, has celebrated the works of Haydn, Schumann, Brahms and Bartok as well as other classical and contemporary composers.

SURRY OPERA COMPANY
667-9551.
Surry 04684.
Season: Call for schedule.

Walter Nowick founded this small, amateur opera company in 1984 with high aims — "to promote beautiful music and work toward peace through people-to-people experiences." During the summer of 1991 the group hosted a festival of Russian opera with the Leningrad Amateur Opera Company.

East of Schoodic

STAGE FRONT: THE ARTS DOWNEAST
255-3313.
9 O'Brien Ave., Machias.
Season: mid-Sept.–April.
Tickets: $4–$6.

Folk music from Bolivia, gospel, jazz, classical and country music. For 13 years Stage Front has been bringing a broad spectrum of music to the Performing Arts Center at the University of Maine, Machias. The group also sponsors theater and dance performances.

MACHIAS BAY CHAMBER CONCERTS
255-3168 or 255-3889.

This group has brought classical chamber music to Machias for almost a quarter of a century. Many of the same instrumental groups that play in Rockport's Bay Chamber series play here in the

P.O. Box 332, Machias 04654
Season: July & Aug.
Tickets: $7 adults, $4 children.

Machias Congregational Church, which is known for its excellent acoustics. The series of six concerts begins on the first Tuesday evening after July 4.

SEASONAL MUSIC EVENTS

Annual Bar Harbor Music Festival (212-222-1026; 288-5744 after July 1; locations throughout Bar Harbor). This series of classical, jazz and pops concerts, with an emphasis on young and upcoming talent, celebrated its 25th year in 1991. Mid-July–mid-August.

Annual Bluegrass Festival (725-6009; Thomas Point Beach, Brunswick). Country music with a twang. September.

Annual Rockport Folk Festival (594-1041; Rockport Opera House). For more than two decades top folk singers have collected here in mid-July.

Annual Downeast Jazz Festival (Samoset Resort, Rockport). Jazz greats gather every August.

Lincoln Arts Festival (633-2353; contact the Boothbay Harbor Region Chamber of Commerce). An annual festival of choral and classical music performances by American musicians held in various locations throughout Lincoln County.

The Arcady Music Festival (288-3151; Mount Desert Island High School). Guest artists perform throughout the summer every Monday and Tuesday.

Festival of Traditional Sea Music (443-1316; Maine Maritime Museum, Bath). Concerts & workshops featuring sea chanties & maritime music traditions. Late May–early June.

Downeast Dulcimer & Harp Festival (288-5653; Agamont Park & Congregational Church, Bar Harbor). Song sharing, workshops and concerts featuring these traditional American instruments. Early July.

NIGHTLIFE

South Coast

Shelley's (284-9283; 23 Lincoln St., Biddeford). Karaoke Madness, Budball, ladies' night, last year they did a Beatles retrospective; pool, darts, and naturally, proper dress.

Port Gardens Pub (967-3358; Ocean Ave., Kennebunkport). A place for Bush watchers to relax.

Norton's Sports Bar and Music Club (439-7892; 518 Rte. 1, Kittery/York). Wednesday it's Laser Karaoke with Paula. The rest of the week it's groups like Heavens to Murgatroid and Lost Dog.

Soho's (934-4524; 43 West Grand Ave., Old Orchard Beach). Monday night football, locals' night, ladies' night, pizza night, and, now, recession night.

Casco Bay

Cafe No (772-8114; 20 Danforth St., Portland). Live jazz seven nights a week. Good Middle Eastern food.

Planets (828-0112; 27 Forest Ave., Portland). Open till 1 a.m., with fuel until 11 p.m., for the after-theater, after-club crowd.

Raoul's Roadside Attraction (775-2494 or 773-6886; Forest Ave., 1.5 mi. from exit 6B, I-295, Portland). Bands play rock, country, pop. More listening than dancing.

T-Birds (773-8040; 126 N. Boyd St., Portland). DJ and live music for dancing.

Zootz (773-8187; 31 Forest Ave., Portland). Club where there's more dancing than listening to regional and touring acts. DJ plays eclectic selection.

Midcoast

The Blue Goose (338-3003; Rte 1, Northport).

Downeast/Acadia

Left Bank Bakery & Cafe (374-2201; Rte. 172, Blue Hill). In addition to serving a great meal (breakfast, lunch and dinner), these guys serve up good music — Mose Allison, Peggy Seeger, Aztec Two Step, Paul Geremia and others. Music starts at 8 p.m.

SEASONAL EVENTS

South Coast

Harvestfest (363-4422; York). An old-fashioned New England harvest festival with old-timey entertainment including oxcart races, apple bobbing and a big-time tug of war. Mid-October.

Laudholm Trust Nature Crafts Festival (646-4521; Wells Reserve at Laudholm Farm, Wells). Juried crafts show by artists and craftspeople. Early September.

La Kermesse-Franco Americaine Festival (Contact La Kermesse-Franco Americaine Society, P.O. Box 289, Biddeford 04005; St. Louis Field, Biddeford). Food, entertainment, cultural displays documenting the French-American heritage in Southern Maine. Mid- to late June.

Saco Sidewalk Art Festival (282-6169; Main St., Saco). More than 90 national artists display and sell their work. Mid-June.

Roy Zalesky

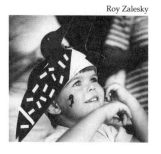

A young celebrant at one of the many small summer festivals on the Maine coast.

Casco Bay

Apple Cider Day & Bird Seed Sale (781-2330; Maine Audubon Society, 118 U.S. Rte. 1, Falmouth). For bird lovers. Mid-October.

Cumberland County Fair (829-4182; Cumberland Fairgrounds, Cumberland). Livestock, rides, agricultural and cooking competitions. Mid- to late September.

Deering Oaks Family Festival (772-2811; Deering Oaks Park, Portland). Food booths, arts & crafts, music, children's programs. Mid- to late August.

Maine Festival (772-9012; Thomas Point Beach, Brunswick). More than 600 artists and craftsmen on site. Folk Arts Village highlighting music and crafts traditional to Maine, plus bands and performers from other parts of the country. Early August.

Maine Highland Games (582-2243; Thomas Point Beach, Brunswick). People of Scottish ancestry show their colors. Bagpipe bands, highland dancing, food, border-collie demonstrations and clan exhibits. Mid-August.

Old Port Festival (772-6828; Old Port, Portland). Weekend street festival with music, sidewalk art, food and more. Early June.

Winter Festival (772-2811; downtown & Deering Oaks Park, Portland). Snow & ice sculpture, torchlight ice-skating, pancake breakfast, chicken BBQ, discounts at some area businesses. Early February.

World's Largest Garage Sale (828-6666; Cumberland County Civic Center, Portland). Every year coastal residents clean out their garages for charity around the end of May or early June.

Yarmouth Clam Festival (846-3984; Main St., Yarmouth). Entertainment, crafts, bike race, midway and, of course, clams. Mid-July.

Midcoast

Arts & Crafts Festival (236-4404; Public Library, Bok Amphitheater, Camden). Crafters from all over show and sell their work. Mid-July.

Damariscotta River Oyster Festival (563-8340; Damariscotta). Grab some fresh lemons and enjoy. Mid-July.

Fall Foliage Festival (633-4727; Boothbay Railway Museum, Boothbay Harbor). Leaves, music, crafts, food and fun for the family. Mid-October.

Fishermen's Festival (633-4008; Boothbay Harbor). Miss Shrimp Contest, lobsterboat races, chowder contest and other great fisherman things, all to benefit the Fishermen's Memorial Fund. Late April.

Maine Poets Festival (for information write to Institute for Advanced Thinking, 22 Salmond St., Belfast 04915). Early July.

Military Aviation Airshow (594-4418; Transportation Museum, Owls Head). Fly-bys and demonstrations of armed forces aircraft. Late June.

Rockland Maine Lobster Festival (596-0376; Public Landing, Rockland). Just about everything to do with lobster, including lots to eat. Early August.

Rockport Maine Storytellers Festival (743-0757; Rockport Opera House, Rockport). Tales of Down East told by the pros. Late June.

Winter Carnival (338-2151; Belfast). Fun in the cold weather. Mid-February.

Down East/Acadia

Blue Hill Fair (374-9976; East Blue Hill). This fair was the inspiration for E.B. White's children's classic *Charlotte's Web*. Late August to early September.

Tom Hindman

Relaxing at the Blue Hill Fair, which has been held every year at summer's end for almost a century, and was the inspiration for Charlotte's Web.

The Mainescape Garden Center Annual Scarecrow Contest (374-2833; Blue Hill). Scarecrows are on display in "Scarecrowland" through most of October and depart after the voting around Halloween.

East of Schoodic

Blueberry Festival (255-4402; Centre & Main sts., Machias). Fish fry, parade, 5-mile blueberry run — all to celebrate the wild blueberry harvest. Mid-August.

Indian Day Celebration (853-2551; Pleasant Point Reservation, Rte. 190, Perry). Witness ceremonial dancing, match-lighting and ash-pounding contests. Eat moose, bear, muskrat, rabbit, porpoise or seal. Passamaquoddy crafts and jewelry; canoe races and horseshoe-throwing competitions, plus Warrior Run and Miss Passamaquoddy pageant. Early August.

Tom Hindman

A ceremonial dance at the annual Indian Day Celebration in Perry; a chance for visitors to experience a mix of old and new customs of the Passamaquoddy tribe.

Harvest Fair (853-4161; Fire House, Perry). Who's got the best quilts, crafts, vegetables and fruits around? Find out at this traditional autumn competition. Early October.

July 4 and Old Home Days (853-4644; Eastport). Every year this small fishing town of 2,000 quadruples in size when everyone who has ever lived here comes to celebrate the easternmost 4th in the country. Great parade. Make sure to make your lodging reservations early.

Salmon Festival (853-4644; Eastport). All you can eat, tours of the salmon pens from the water and codfish relays. First Sunday after Labor Day.

THEATER

The arts continue to thrive Down East. A new theater is being established in Machias on the top floor of the Howard's Men's Shop. According to store owner Wayne Mallar, the new theater, to be called The Rubicon, will focus on community productions. The inaugural offering will be a mystery entitled Catch Me If You Can.

The Downeast Coastal Press, Oct. 1, 1991

Theater in coastal Maine is generally an unpretentious experience. Patrons often arrive in jeans and Bean boots and depart with a good dose of Shakespeare, Fugard, Mamet or Pinter. The play is the thing. Here are some of the more established companies on the coast. Call to find out their season schedules, times and ticket prices.

South Coast

City Theater (282-0849; 205 Main St., Biddeford).

Actors Theatre of Maine (646-5151; during the spring and fall at the Ogunquit Square Theater, Shore Rd., Ogunquit).

Ogunquit Playhouse (646-5511; Rte. 1, Ogunquit). For 60 summers they have presented musicals and comedies with big-name performers.

Vintage Repertory Company (828-4654; Jordan Hall, Temple Ave., Ocean Park, Old Orchard).

Casco Bay

Maine State Music Theatre (725-8769; Pickard Theater, Bowdoin College, Brunswick). Topnotch musicals with resident professional talent who for more than 30 years have belted out great show tunes.

Young People's Theater (729-8584; 14 School St., Brunswick). Dramas, contemporary plays, summer theater. Classes.

Freeport Community Players (865-6041; Freeport High School, Freeport). Young community theater group that presents three shows annually — in the spring, summer and winter. Visiting performers welcome to audition.

Mad Horse Theater (797-3338; 955 Forest Ave., Portland). Musical comedies, dramas in the round.

Paula Newsome as Billie Holiday in Lady Day at Emerson's Bar & Grill *at Portland Stage Company.*

David A. Rodgers,
Courtesy of Portland Stage Company

Portland Stage Company (774-0465; 25A Forest Ave. Portland). Solid local company that often brings actors up from Boston and New York for bigger roles.

Midcoast

Studio Theater (442-8455; Center for the Arts at the Chocolate Church, 804 Washington St., Bath).

Iron Horse Dinner Theater (338-2931; 11 Water St. off City Landing, Belfast). Actually, it's dinner, theater and a train ride.

Belfast Opera House Management (338-5777; 59 Church St., Belfast).

Boothbay Dinner Theatre (633-6186; McKown Hill, Boothbay Harbor). Broadway musicals and dinner. Summer.

Boothbay Playhouse and Theatreside Restaurant (633-7601; Rte. 27, Boothbay). Musicals served with dinner. Summer.

Camden Civic Theatre (236-4866; Camden Opera House, Rte. 1, Camden). Musicals.

Lincoln County Community Theater & Orchestra (563-5532; P.O. Box 601, Newcastle). Drama, comedies and music.

Down East/Acadia

The New Surry Theatre (374-5057; performances in the Blue Hill Town Hall or the Ellsworth City Hall). Since 1972 these folks have been producing fine summer repertory theater — usually a selection of comedy, musical comedy and drama — performed by students at the New Surry Acting School. Season Mid-June to mid-August, plus occasional productions during other seasons.

Cold Comfort Summer Theater (326-4311 or 469-3131; several locations throughout Castine). Comedies, dramas and other summertime fare.

Acadia Repertory Theater (244-7260; Masonic Hall, Rte. 102, Somesville, Mount Desert Island). Modern comedies and dramas every summer for more than 20 years.

East of Schoodic

Eastport Arts Center (Dana and Water sts., Eastport).

Down River Theater Company (255-4244; Machias Grange Hall, Elm St., Machias). Musical theater from *South Pacific* to *Chicago*. Summer.

SCHOOLS

What is culture, anyhow? We raise the question because maybe this section on schools merits an answer. Here you will find schools not only for painters and musicians but also schools for fly fishermen and ocean navigators.

L. L. Bean Outdoor Discovery Program (865-3111; Casco St., Freeport). An interesting series of low-cost lessons that cover everything from cross-country skiing (on weekends beginning in January) and fly fishing to orienteering and emergency wilderness medicine. The program also offers free evening lectures on topics ranging from survival in the Maine woods to making soap, tanning hides, paddling sea kayaks, building fly rods and cooking small game.

Center for Creative Imaging (236-2333; P.O. Box 1348, 51 Mechanic St., Camden 04843). Eastman Kodak founded this state-of-the-art educational and experimental facility that offers week-long workshops in the use of Macintosh computers for magazine and book publishing. Their specialty is study of the digital manipulation of photographic images. School operates year round.

Kodak's Imaging Center, which opened in 1991, is part of a thriving art, design and business community that has sprung up in Camden during the past two decades.

Michael Loomis

Haystack Mountain School of Crafts (348-2306; P.O. Box 518 Deer Isle 04627). One of the foremost craft schools in the country, Haystack offers one-, two- and three-week sessions for artists and craftspersons working in a variety of media. Evening lectures and seminars by faculty and visiting artists are open to the public. Public tours are offered weekdays at 1 from June to August.

Courtesy of Outward Bound

Learning how to pull together on one of Outward Bound's pulling boats.

Hurricane Island Outward Bound School (594-5548 or 800-341-1744 out-of- state; Mechanic St., Rockland). Courses lasting 5 to 26 days are offered on

Hurricane Island in Penobscot Bay, May to October. There are sessions for every age and both sexes; they focus on sailing, rock climbing, and outdoor problem-solving. Prices are a bit steep. An international program begun in Wales, OB challenges participants to do things they never thought they could and then push themselves just a little further. For details, write Box 429, Rockland 04841.

Kneisel Hall School for String and Ensemble Music (374-2811; Blue Hill). Summer school for chamber musicians.

Landing School of Boat Building and Design (985-7976; River Rd., Arundel). Learn how to build your own sailing craft in their program that runs the months from September to June.

Maine Coast Art Workshops (P.O. Box 236, Port Clyde 04855). Throughout the summer five-day workshops with recognized artists are held here on the St. George peninsula, taking advantage of the surrounding natural setting. Fourteen workshops to choose from; tuition is about $200.

Maine Photographic Workshop (236-8581; Two Central St., Rockport). Photography, cinematography, television production and other related courses for the aspiring and experienced photographer. All are taught by established professionals from around the country. The workshop also operates an excellent gallery on the premises and a good retail store with photographic equipment and accessories.

Pierre Monteux School for Conductors and Orchestra Players (422-3931 and 422-6251; Monteux Hall, off Rte. 1, Hancock). Named for the conductor who made his home here, this is where one goes to learn to lead in the musical sense.

Shelter Institute (442-7938; 38 Center St., Bath 04530). Energy efficiency for the new age is what they teach at this school for prospective home builders. Three-week daytime courses are offered in the summer; night classes are given during the winter.

WoodenBoat School (259-4651; P.O. Box 78, Naskeag Point Rd., Brooklin 04616). Founded by the management at WoodenBoat magazine, this is where readers and armchair seafarers come to live out their dreams. The school offers more than 75 courses on topics like navigation, boat building and sailing for around 700 students every summer.

National Audubon Ecology Camp at Hogg Island (203-869-2017; or write National Audubon Society Ecology Camps and Workshops, 613 Riverside Rd., Greenwich CT 06831). For more than 50 years campers have studied wildlife on the island, an Audubon reserve well known for its birdlife. They learn from well-known naturalists, the likes of Roger Tory Peterson and Olin Sewall Petingill. About 50 adults are chosen for each two-week session. Rustic accommodations are provided.

Penobscot School (594-1084; P.O. Box 7, Rockland 04841). Founded in 1986, this school began as one woman teaching French to area children. Today the school offers 10-12 week classes in conversational Arabic, Japanese, Spanish, French, Italian and German and occasional intensive French and Spanish courses — most taught by native speakers. During the summer they teach English as a second language and provide informal cultural seminars (a recent series was taught by visiting professors from China).

Rockport Apprenticeshop (236-6071; Box 539, Rockport 04856). These folks are dedicated to keeping the art of wooden boat building alive. Students learn wooden boat building techniques by doing two-year apprenticeships, six-week internships, six-week volunteer stints or summer workshops.

CHAPTER FIVE

Shore Food

RESTAURANTS & FOOD PURVEYORS

Tom Hindman

The proper way to demolish a lobster.

Mainers love to cook and they love to eat. They always have. Coastal Native Americans introduced settlers to lobsters, clambakes, oysters, smoked salmon, maple syrup and baked beans, fiddleheads, popcorn, potato chips, vanilla, cornflakes and what we call Indian pudding (the best on the coast can be had, and should be had, at The Seaman's Club in Portland's Old Port). If that's not enough, ice cream was invented in Maine by ice dealer David Robinson as a treat for the Marquis de Lafayette on his visit to Portland in 1825. That may explain why Mainers eat more ice cream than people from other states. Of course, ice cream also goes well with pie, another food so many people here are expert at making.

There are thousands of restaurants along the coast. Except for San Francisco there are more restaurants per capita in Portland than any other city in the country. The competition has produced enough good places to eat and the promise that the quality of food will remain high. If the homegrown cooks weren't good enough already, the coast has managed to attract highly skilled outsiders. Usually these fine cooks are drawn to the quality of life here and their happiness is well reflected in their cooking. We all benefit as a result.

Here then is a select list of restaurants, some coastal legends, a few new finds, places we found out about by badgering reluctant residents and neighbors, places we liked and places we didn't but were outvoted, plus places written up and sent in by friends, all experienced or professional eaters. It's a list long enough to get you up or down the coast and back.

We've noted the restaurants' serving times and seasons as they were when we made the final survey for this book. As with all things, they are subject to change according to the changing seasons and demands of the economy. Call first. If you can, make reservations in summer. Things can get pretty busy at the great places, especially during July and August. Many restaurants, even white tablecloth ones, don't take reservations, though. So if you're really hungry, plan to arrive early enough to stake a good place in line.

The general price range we list is meant to reflect the cost of a single meal, usually dinner unless the review talks about breakfast or lunch. What we've tried to represent as a typical meal is an appetizer, entree, dessert and coffee, although several of the places we review are not appetizer places. We do not include the price of alcohol or other drinks in the estimated cost.

Dining Price Code	Inexpensive	Up to $10
	Moderate	$10 - 20
	Expensive	$20 - 30
	Very Expensive	$30 or more

Credit Cards	AE - American Express	DC - Diner's Club
	CB - Carte Blanche	MC - MasterCard
	D - Discover Card	V - Visa

We've also included a list of food purveyors for each of the regions on the coast. Some are delicatessens that will sell almost anything to go, others are bakeries or gourmet, ethnic food and wine stores. Visitors will want to note that wine and beer are available broadly, but hard liquor is sold only at state stores (although during the recent state budget crisis there was talk of turning over the liquor franchise to private enterprise).

Tom Hindman

Fiddleheads, the young tips of ferns that are harvested in Maine during the spring, are a great regional specialty that can be found on the menu at the coast's best restaurants.

RESTAURANTS — SOUTH COAST

Cape Neddick

CAPE NEDDICK INN
363-2899.
Rte. 1, Cape Neddick.
Closed: Mon. & Tues. off-
 season.
Price: Expensive.
Cuisine: Country gourmet.
Serving: D, SB off-season.
Credit Cards: AE, MC, V.
Reservations:
 Recommended.
Handicap Access: Limited.
Special Features: Art
 gallery.

From the outside, the Cape Neddick is all country inn. Inside, the decor is clever and rather
modern with a split-level dining room, abstract
sculptures, expressionistic canvases on the walls,
Fiestaware and funky vintage crockery on the tables.
The food is a mix of old and new, too. Wontons are
stuffed with curried beef; chicken with maple-
brandy mincemeat and cornbread; chateaubriand
with herbed French toast and a sauce of Boursin
and roasted garlic. The wine list is quite international, and desserts — especially the homemade
chocolate-cognac ice cream and chocolate bourbon
cake — are not to be missed.

Tom Hindman

*Collecting maple syrup
during the winter when the
sap is running. Maine
annually produces an
excellent grade of the sweet
sauce, which is sold at many
roadside stands.*

The Kennebunks

ALISSON'S
967-4841.
5 Dock Square,
  Kennebunkport.
Open daily.
Price: Moderate.
Cuisine: American.
Serving: L, D.
Credit Cards: AE, MC, V.
Handicap Access: Limited.

Alisson's is a neighborhood breakfast establishment and later-day burger joint. Because the neighborhood happens to be Kennebunkport, that means that this place is going to be jammed in the summer. There's a butcher block bar to ease the wait. Regardless of the size of the crowd, the help is affable and on-the-ball. On the menu, it's burgers, burgers, plus soup, sandwiches, salads, bar appetizers, fried seafood and daily dinner specials. Some of the names may be too cute, but the burgers make up for it. The French fries and onion rings are good, too. Alisson's makes a noteworthy raspberry chocolate cake.

1810 EATERY
985-2858.
17 Main St. (Rte. 1),
  Kennebunk.
Closed: Sun.
Price: Moderate.
Cuisine: Mostly northern
  Italian, some southern
  Italian.
Serving: L, D.
Credit Cards: MC, V.
Reservations: No.
Handicap Access: Steps at
  entrance.

"Affordable and fair, what Italian dining should be," says the menu. That's just what you get at this modest and comfortable family restaurant with its pumpkin pine floors and stenciled fireplace. The most expensive entree, Shrimp in Garlic-Wine Sauce, runs $7.45 — and includes garlic bread and a green leaf salad with good pepper-Parmesan dressing. Northern Italian standards, such as fettucini Alfredo and vegetable lasagna, dominate the menu. There are also a few southern Italian offerings such as lasagna and eggplant Parmesan, as well as some 1810 originals: haddock with bread crumbs and white wine and chicken with rosemary. In summer, it's nice to dine *al fresco* on the small outdoor deck.

**ROSE ARBOR TEA
  ROOM**
967-8098.
Port Road (Rte. 35),
  Kennebunk.
Closed: Tues.
Price: Moderate.
Cuisine: British, Irish and
  Scottish "tea" fare,
  breakfast items.
Serving: Afternoon tea
  noon-6, B on
  weekends, dessert in the
  evenings in summer.

There's more chintz here than in your great-aunt's parlor. Stepping through the pink door of this two-story Victorian house is like strolling into another century. Three of the rooms are decorated with vintage tapestry couches, crockery and antique lace; the fourth is a high-tech fantasy with glass table, purple aluminum chairs and electric blue floors. Why? Who knows? The food is faithful to what everybody makes such a fuss about in Agatha Christie novels. The "Edwardian" tea is elaborate— paper-thin cucumber sandwiches, watercress and egg, smoked salmon, baked ham, tender currant

Credit Cards: MC, V.
Reservations: Yes.
Handicap Access: Steps at entrance.
Special Features: Antique couches, crockery and table linens; gift shop; BYOB.

scones with whipped cream, mini-brioches and sweets like rum balls and almond meringue. All is artfully arranged on a three-tiered silver tray. (The pot of tea is extra.) Try the Sandwich Sampler (just the sandwiches and scones) or what's referred to as the "Cream Tea" (scones, cream and jam); a heartier alternative is the Ploughman's Lunch (salad, cheese, sourdough rolls and oatmeal jumbles). The tearoom also serves weekend breakfasts beginning no earlier than the respectable hour of 8 a.m. And there's a dessert roster during p.m. hours in the summer.

Kittery, Kittery Point

CAP'N SIMEON'S GALLEY
439-3655.
Rte. 103, Pepperell Rd., Kittery Point.
Closed: Tues. in winter.
Price: Inexpensive to Moderate.
Cuisine: Seafood.
Serving: L, D, SB.
Credit Cards: AE, MC, V.
Special Features: Great view.

This is the perfect place to pop sweet scallops in your mouth or curl up with a nice French fry and gaze out the window at the sea. That's if you can get a window seat. The lobster — usually brought in earlier in the day to the docks below — may take more of your concentration, but it's worth it. The interior has the feel of an old boat that has been sealed up tight with yearly coats of shellac. There is nothing fancy going on in here with the food, either. These people know what they're doing and have been doing it for years. The purpose here is to see that you're properly filled full of fresh seafood and side orders and send you on your way. But not before you're ready to leave.

CHAUNCEY CREEK LOBSTER POUND
439-1030.
Chauncey Creek Rd., Kittery Point.
Open: May-Sept.
Price: Moderate.
Cusine: Lobster.
Serving: L, D.
Credit Cards: MC, V.

We can't think of any place we'd rather be up the creek. This old-fashioned lobster pond actually sits against the edge of an embankment rising from a creek. Across the way are thick woods, making this like a nice homey treehouse where you can lay waste to a lobster or two (there are no nautical distractions). They start serving at 10:30 a.m., and we've known friends to indulge in a late lobster breakfast now and then. The steaming mounds of clams and mussels are succulent and legendary. The service is to the point, probably because they don't indulge in any frills or side dish fanfare here. You want potato salad. Well, then, bring it yourself. Chauncey's is out of the way (thoroughly removed from the shoppers' bustle in nearby Kittery) but well known and well worth the side trip for the crowd that comes back year after year.

"It is apparent to serious shellfish eaters that in the great evolutionary scheme of things crustaceans developed shells to protect them from knives and forks."

Calvin Trillin, *Alice, Let's Eat*

Lobsters in the ocean are the color of seaweed and walk along the floor. "A shoe with legs," is how poet Anne Sexton described them. Lobsters are caught by lobstermen who heave a string of box-shaped wooden or vinyl-coated wire traps over the side of their boat. They bait their traps with fish heads and tails and species that don't normally sell well at the fish market. (Somehow it's not surprising to learn that lobsters are carnivores.) With luck, when the lobstermen returns and pulls up the trap, there will be a legal-sized lobster in it. (A waterlogged trap may weigh as much as 70 pounds.) A "keeper" measures at least 3.25 inches and is no more than 5 inches from its eyes to the beginning of the tail. It may or may not weigh a pound or more.

Lobsters in a pot of boiling water turn red. Before the 1800s, lobsters were in such abundance you could simply pick them off the beach, take them home and cook them. People who could afford it didn't. Lobsters were considered a low-class food. Nineteenth-century prisoners were forced to eat them three times a week, and on Boston's Beacon Hill the servants ate them, although there was a limit to the number they would eat a week.

Finally, in the mid-19th century, fishermen began lobstering by boat, and scarcity produced demand. In 1989, the Maine fleet landed a lobster catch valued at just less than 60 million dollars with an average price per pound of $2.55.

How to Eat a Lobster

Always with gusto.

Rip off both claws, grab nutcracker, hammer or rock. Crack open, remove meat, dip in butter and eat.

Next, grab tail in one hand, body in other, and bend back until it cracks and the meat inside can be removed. Once removed, tear off end flippers, grab fork or long narrow stick, insert, push out tail meat and eat.

Next, tear off small claws, suck out the meat and eat. Next, remove the body from the back, crack open sideways, remove the meat and eat.

Finally, eat the green tomalley (liver) which many consider the best part.

Ogunquit

ARROWS
361-1100.
Berwick Rd., Ogunquit
Closed: Mon. & Tues.
Memorial Day–
　December; also closed
　Jan.–March and most
　of April.
Price: Very Expensive.
Cuisine: Regional
　American with ethnic
　accents
Serving: D.
Credit Cards: MC, V.
Reservations:
　Recommended.
Handicap Access: Limited.

A wildly romantic setting and fabulous food is a rare combination, which is why Arrows is such a find. Outside the many-windowed dining room is a garden that's pure English country. Inside are fine linens and weathered oak, hurricane lamps and bright bursts of flowers. The menu, which changes daily, is limited, but first rate. Unusual wines are available by the glass and bottle. Service is all one could ask for — efficient and low-key. Here is food that's as good looking as it is inventive. Spicy lamb sausage, lobster ravioli, almond shrimp fritters for starters; duck with lemon couscous and sauteed ginger — and pepper-coated salmon with sesame mayonnaise as entrees. The homemade ice creams are creamy and rich. So is the chocolate truffle cake.

Arrows

Chefs Mark Gaier and Clark Frasier made their culinary reputations in San Francisco before opening Arrows.

HURRICANE
646-6348.
Perkins Cove, Ogunquit.
Open seven days a week.
Price: Moderate to
　Expensive.
Cuisine: Seafood and
　American with ethnic
　touches.
Serving: L, D.
Credit Cards: AE, V, MC.
Reservations:
　Recommended for
　dinner and large parties.

Chef Brooks MacDonald gets his seafood fresh off the cove's fishing boats. He grills it and often dresses it in an elegant sauce. It's that simple. The setting, like the food, is simple but dramatic. There are two fireplaces in the dining room and views of the Atlantic from every seat. Appetizers include deviled lobster cakes served with fresh tomato and cilantro salsa, and roasted little neck clams with fresh pasta and marinara sauce. There's an extra effort to make everything fresh here, even the house salad that's made from field greens, pistachios and roasted shallots. Three or four varieties of fresh grilled fish are offered daily and may include grilled sea scallops served with lemon creme fraiche and caviar; crispy whole fish served with Oriental black bean sauce; and black tie shrimp served scampi-style over fresh *tagliatelle*. There's hope for folks tired of seafood, too, including lovely grilled chicken served with a fresh strawberry-mint salsa, and chianti-braised veal, served with wild mushrooms and shallots over fresh pasta. (Friends of ours are crazy for Chef MacDonald's burgers — served only at lunch.)

JACKIE'S TOO
646-4444.
Perkins Cove, Ogunquit.
Open all year.
Price: Inexpensive to
　Moderate.
Cuisine: American.
Serving: B, L, D in
　summer; L in winter.
Credit Cards: V, MC.
Handicap Access: Yes.

Jackie's Too is known for the generosity with which they pack their lobster rolls, among the least expensive in town, and a lobster dinner that includes steamed clams, mussels, knockwurst and corn on the cob. The knockwurst is, we think, a brave break with tradition and a savory addition. We also are partial to their chicken tenderloins sauteed with jumbo shrimp in wine, butter and garlic. In the summer, the best seats are on the deck, within a stone's throw of the rocky cove. The atmosphere is casual and comfortable. In the off-season, you get a spectacular, albeit protected, view of the water.

JONATHAN'S
646-4777.
2 Bourne Ln., Ogunquit.
Open all year.
Price: Moderate.
Cuisine: New England
　and Continental.
Serving: L, D.
Credit Cards: MC, V, AE.
Reservations: Yes.
Handicap Access: Yes.

For 16 years this has been a popular stop for area residents and returning visitors. Jonathan's offers a raw bar and an extensive menu that leans toward seafood and pasta but also includes dishes like Jamaican Grilled Chicken and, of all things, Jaeger Schnitzel. Owner Jonathan West's art collection covers the dining room walls and represents 25 well-known local painters, past and present. If they don't grab you, there's a 600-gallon tropical saltwater reef aquarium in the main dining room. Or you can take in the carefully tended gardens visible through the dining room windows. Jonathan's also provides an old-fashioned bright spot in the local nightlife with their convivial piano bar and nightly sing-alongs.

OGUNQUIT LOBSTER POUND
646-2516.
Rte. 1, Ogunquit.
Closed: Mid-Oct.—early May.
Price: Moderate to Expensive.
Cuisine: Seafood.
Serving: L, D.
Credit Cards: AE, MC, V.
Handicap Access: Yes.

This airplane hangar of a restaurant is the next best thing to a bonafide lobster bake. Picnic tables painted camp green are lined up on the lawn near the giant steamer and the feel is that of a down-home barbecue. Inside isn't quite as charming, but what's more important, food or atmosphere? Regulars would say the former. Steamers, lobster stew, broiled and fried seafood, and of course lobster are all on the menu. The Pound prides itself on heavyweight contenders — 2½- and 3-pound lobsters — though there are smaller clawed wonders, as well. After a meal like that, you might not have room for dessert, but if you do, the deep dish pies are the way to go.

Tom Hindman

The fascination of some of Maine's famed blueberries.

ROBERTO'S
646-8130.
82 Shore Rd., Ogunquit.
Closed: Dec.—April.
Price: Moderate to Expensive.
Cuisine: Italian.
Serving: D.
Credit Cards: MC, V.

Roberto's is housed in a restored 1850s farmhouse. The wood floors have been left bare, and the tables are simply patterned with red and white checkered tablecloths. The local saying about this popular Ogunquit restaurant is that, "Rain or shine, there's always a line." That's because chef-owner Robert Cammarota won't take reservations. The best tactic is to get there early or wait it out at the bar. Specials change with the season: lighter in the warm days of summer and heavier in the fall. The fact all dishes are cooked to order might slow things on occasion, but think of all the hours that went into making the tomato sauce. That should help put what's important in life back into perspective.

Old Orchard Beach

JOSEPH'S BY THE SEA
934-5044.
55 West Grand Ave., Old
   Orchard Beach.
Closed: Nov.—March.
Price: Moderate.
Cuisine: French with
   regional touches.
Serving: B, D, SB.
Credit Cards: AE, V, MC.
Reservations: Suggested.

Joseph's is known as "an oasis in a honky-tonk sea." In a town of snack bars and pack-'em-in surf-and-turf joints, this is where to go for escargots served with native "dulse" seaweed or Wild Mushroom Torte and Fettucini Genovese (fresh pasta with artichokes, shitake mushrooms, spinach, raisins, pine nuts and lemon basil olive oil). Joseph's is known for its Angel Hair Pasta Maison (made with shrimp, scallops and fish sauteed in sun-dried tomatoes, garlic, herbs and cream). Steak au Poivre and Lobster Stuffed with Scallops are also big among the restaurant's aficionados. So is the Saco Bay soup — scallops, mussels and local fish in a bouillabaisse. Once a private house, its hardwood floors and handcrafted white birch archways, awnings and mantels are well looked after. Most people prefer to eat outside on the screened-in porch, which overlooks a manicured lawn with gardens, the dunes, the beach, the ocean, islands and sky. Our optometrist first told us about Joseph's. She didn't want us to let too many others in on one of the region's best-kept dining secrets. We've broken her confidence, I'm afraid. This is too good a place to hide.

VILLAGE INN
934-7370.
213 Saco Ave., Old
   Orchard Beach.
Closed: Mon.
Price: Moderate.
Cuisine: American.
Serving: L, D.
Credit Cards: AE, V,
   MC, D.
Handicap Access: Yes.

So what about the location — a busy intersection — and the distance from the sea. During summer nights at any one time 400 customers are here busy eating, while people wait up to two hours to get in. Nautical pictures have been tacked up around the enormous, light-blue dining room in case anyone really wants a view. Ample helpings and moderately priced food may also be the reason the Village Inn and its twin in Auburn are two of the state's biggest-grossing restaurants. Favorites here include the Seafood Platter, Lobster Stew, Fish Chowder and Haddock Parmesan. They also offer an extensive children's menu and some "landlubber" specials — prime rib, thick steaks and roast turkey. Some of their shoreside specials have an Italian accent — manicotti, spaghetti and meatball Parmesan, lasagna and veal Parmesan. Everything comes with a potato, vegetables and hot rolls and is brought to you by a wait staff capable of dealing with any hitch or glitch in the food chain.

Saco

CORNFORTH HOUSE
284-2006.
893 Portland Rd. (Rte. 1),
  Saco.
Closed: Mon. in season;
  Jan. & Feb.
Price: Expensive.
Cuisine: Continental.
Serving: L (Tues.—Fri.),
  D, SB.
Credit Cards: MC, V.
Reservations:
  Recommended.
Handicap Access: Yes

The Cornforth House is an elegant sidelight on busy Rte. 1 — probably the last place on earth one would expect to find a country inn. Still, once inside, the mood is romantic with gilt-framed artwork and ornate fireplaces in the several small dining rooms. The service is warm, if a bit too eager. Food ranges from classics like steak au poivre, rack of lamb, prime rib and veal marsala to more creative notions like Veal Sausage in Puff Pastry and Pecan Chicken. Desserts are fantastic creations: a leprechaun-green *creme de menthe* mousse cake and a monster ice-cream-filled profiterole with hot fudge.

Scarborough

**CARSON'S FAMILY
  RESTAURANT**
883-4400.
433 U.S. Rte. 1,
  Scarborough.
Open year round.
Price: Inexpensive.
Cuisine: Seafood, diner
  food.
Serving: B, L, D.
Credit Cards: D, MC, V.
Handicapped Access: Yes.

From the outside it looks like one of those roadside stops that could be either a great find or a terrible mistake. It's a find. Frilly white and pink curtains give a homey touch to the booths. (There's also a counter.) The waitresses call you "honey" and treat everyone with a sisterly brand of kindness. The menu is huge and put together with the traveling family in mind. There are hamburgers and cheeseburgers for the kids; meatloaf and center cut pork chops for those wanting to experience the cuisine of their childhood; salad plates for the dieter; a 12 oz. prime rib for the big eater, as well as a dazzling selection of fresh seafood. Ask for yours with a side of their great mashed potatoes. The pie and strawberry shortcake are homemade.

**SPURWINK COUNTRY
  KITCHEN**
799-1177.
150 Spurwink Rd.,
  Scarborough.
Closed: Late Oct.—
  Mother's Day.

Popular with the people of wealthy Cape Elizabeth, Wally Stone and staff serve Yankee fare that doubles as good fog food, so comforting when one of those pea soupers has you socked in. Feathery macaroni and cheese, solid baked beans and simple fish, buttery rolls that should not be allowed

Price: Inexpensive to
Moderate.
Cuisine: Family.
Serving: L, D.
Credit Cards: None; they
accept personal checks.
Handicap Access: Limited.

to be plastered with any more. The decor is Yankee shabby. The waitresses dote on you like attentive granddaughters. Sometimes Wally walks around offering complimentary slices of baked goods. Eileen makes the pie, for which local legislators should consider making her a Maine State treasure.

Wells, Wells Beach

**BILLY'S CHOWDER
HOUSE**
646-7558.
1 Mile Rd., Wells Beach.
Open daily.
Price: Moderate.
Cuisine: American
seafood.
Serving: L, D.
Credit Cards: MC, V.
Handicap Access: Yes.

Friends of ours, a fisherman and an artist, know people from the Berkshires who, when they hanker for fried clams or boiled lobsters, come here. Then they go home. All in the same day. Our friends understand this. They tell the story to make a point. The portions are huge. What you can't eat, take with you. The fried stuff is delicious and light — a true guilty pleasure that's so good you have a hard time believing it's bad for you. The service is bustling and efficient. This place has a hard New England beauty that you can't beat. Pine boards inside, wetlands and water outside.

MAINE DINER
646-4441.
Rte. 1, Wells.
Open all year.
Price: Inexpensive.
Cuisine: Seafood and
American.
Serving: B, L, D.
Credit Cards: MC, V.

This little spot on the town line between Wells and Kennebunk occupies a warm spot in many local resident's hearts. It used to close every Memorial Day and reopen after Labor Day when the tourists left. That's changed, but the lobster pie hasn't. The locals still come here, too, all of which says something about the power of good food.

The Yorks

FLO'S HOTDOGS
Unlisted phone.
Rte. 1, York.
Open all year.
Price: Inexpensive.
Cuisine: American.
Serving: L.
Credit Cards: None.

It's not the hot dog. They sell the same dog, a Shultz, at Rick's (see below). It's the sauce, the abuse, the atmosphere and probably something deeper than all that. Just past Pie in the Sky on Rte.1, this one-story shack with no real sign is the destination of experienced travelers, rich and poor, who come here from all over the country. There's no real parking lot. You just kind of pull over. Inside, not only is there no view, there are no windows, just a few old yellow wooden swivel stools and an order counter. "Here the customer is never right," says Gail, Flo's daughter-in-law. Ah, delicious.

ONE FISH, TWO FISH
363-8196.
Rte.1, York.
Open all year.
Price: Expensive.
Cuisine: Seafood.
Serving: L, D daily in
    summer; L daily in
    winter, D Fri., Sat. and
    Sun.
Credit Cards: V, MC, AE.
Reservations:
    Recommended.
Handicap Access: Yes.
Special features: White
    wine list.

In spite of its Rte. 1 location, this relatively new restaurant already has made ardent fans among people who live nearby. Chef Ron Siegel calls what he creates "contemporary seafood." He can call it what he likes, because it's good. Appetizers include roasted garlic and eggplant soup with red pepper *aioli*, and oysters with house smoked salmon and a lime-vodka *creme fraiche*. Entrees are imaginative: lobster ravioli with black pepper roasted asparagus, basil, Pernod and Parmesan; Portugese clams and pork, brine-cured and grilled with tomatoes, pasta and kale; and swordfish with white bean ragout, sun-dried tomato butter and tapenade-polenta croutons. The menu is not only contemporary, it changes frequently. Siegel, who obviously believes the rule "white with fish," offers 30 chardonnays on his wine list. His wife Cynthia bakes dessert.

**RICK'S ALL SEASONS
    RESTAURANT**
363-5584.
240 York St., York Village.
Open every day.
Price: Inexpensive.
Cuisine: Rick's American.
Serving: B, L, (D on Wed.
    and Thurs. only).
Credit Cards: None.
Handicap access: Limited
Special Features: Breakfast
    from 4 a.m. to close.

Rick's is a back-down-around-the-side-of-the-building kind of place where everybody seems to be in a good mood. The decor is dark, wooden and cavernous with red and white checkered tablecloths. There is no view, and nobody seems to mind. Rick's caters to all ages in need of breakfast and beyond. The staff works well with bulkie rolls, homemade chowder, chili and cheesecake. They also make a decent morning muffin. Service is fast and the attitude is offhand. Rick's also makes a dessert called Cheryl Plouff's Carrot Cake that kind of goes "plouff" when you bite into it.

YORK HARBOR INN
363-5119.
Rte. 1A, York Harbor.
Open all year.
Price: Moderate to
    Expensive.
Cuisine: American.

We're not crazy about this place, but everybody else is. In the summer there's a long line that possibly feeds on itself. The inn is certainly old and quaint — everything an inn is supposed to be. But the small dining rooms with their low ceilings make us slightly claustrophobic. It simply could have been because the service was snail's pace the day we ate there, and that got to us. Looking out on to an obstructed view of the harbor,

Serving: L, D, SB.
Credit Cards: AE, MC, V.
Reservations:
  Recommended.
Handicap access: Yes.

eating broiled scrod, knowing this was the place to be, somehow wasn't enough. Reportedly the soup of the day, presumably a regular feature, was developed by the resident chefs "exclusively" for the inn. It's hard to imagine the chefs doing otherwise. In addition to the long lines, they are distinguished by their seafood chowder, which won first prize from the Yorks Chamber of Commerce in 1986.

RESTAURANTS — CASCO BAY

Brunswick

ROSITA'S
729-7118.
212 Main St., Brunswick.
Open daily.
Price: Inexpensive.
Cuisine: Mexican.
Serving: L, D, SB.
Credit Cards: None.
Special feature: Huevos
  rancheros on Sunday.

E very college town needs a Mexican restaurant and Rosita's is the South of the Border outpost nearest to Bowdoin College. The term "casual" is an understatement here. Beer comes out of a cooler and one orders food cafeteria-style. But the folks behind the counter are eager to please and the place has a friendly feel. All the usual suspects are on the menu: *burritos, tostados, nachos, tacos, enchiladas, chili, fajitas* and *tamales*. Besides the standard beef, pinto bean and chicken trio, there are *chorizo,* the spicy Spanish sausage, and black beans, too. Salsas come in hot and mild strengths and the overall firepower of most fixings is quite tolerable. Sunday breakfasts are unusual featuring bacon and egg tacos and huevos rancheros.

Casco Islands

CHEBEAGUE INN
846-5155.
John Small Rd.,
  Chebeague Island.
Closed: Mid-Sept.—
  mid-May.
Price: Moderate to
  Expensive.
Cuisine: Continental.
Serving: L, D.
Reservations:
  Recommended, even for
  lunch.
Credit Cards: AE, MC, V.

T he Chebeague Inn has an old-fashioned feel. Maybe it's the cane-backed rocking chairs on the porch, a perfect spot to while away a lazy (and hot) afternoon. Or because it's so remote (by ferry it is an hour or so from Portland and 13 minutes from Cousins Island). Or maybe it's the food. Old-timey fare like real Maine chowder with potatoes and bacon, baked ham sandwiches on thick warm-from-the-oven bread, tuna with celery and mayo and homemade lemonade and iced tea. Desserts run along the same lines — a mile-high devil's food wedge being the attention grabber. The dinner menu,

Handicap Access: Limited.
Special Features:
  Verandah with Casco
  Bay view.

which is quite extensive, is a mix of country cooking and continental fare.

JONES' LANDING
766-5542.
Next to the ferry landing
  on Welch St., Peaks
  Island.
Open daily.
Price: Moderate.
Cuisine: Burgers, fried
  seafood, barfood.
Serving: L, D; L only
  Thurs.—Sat. in winter.
Credit Cards: MC, V (with
  $10 minimum).
Handicap Access: Limited.

The outdoor deck with its sweeping view of Casco Bay and Portland's skyline is the place to be when the mercury hits 90. Though indoors doesn't have half the charm, the family-style booths and smoky bar are welcome refuge when a storm comes up. Most people don't come here for the food or the service. The food is perfectly acceptable diner-style fare: tuna melts, strip steaks, pizza, burgers, seafood and specials like New England boiled dinner and baked stuffed clams. The service is casual to occasional. Off-season, Jones is very much a local hangout. But in summer, half of Portland can be found hoisting a glass on the deck. Small wonder, since it's only a 20-minute ferry ride from town.

Freeport, South Freeport

HARRASEEKET INN
865-9377.
162 Main St. (Rte. 1),
  Freeport.
Open daily .
Price: Expensive.
Cuisine: Regional
  American.
Serving: B, L, D.
Credit Cards: AE, MC, V.
Reservations:
  Recommended
Handicap Access: Yes.
Special Features: Tableside
  cooking.

Sam Hayward, late of Twenty-Two Lincoln (a former favorite spot north of Freeport), has set up camp here and, oh, what a camp it is. Hayward has brought with him the best of his innovations and an extensive knowledge of wines and cheeses. The result is a dining room more sophisticated than most in Maine. Decor is understated — white linens, fresh flowers and flickering candles. Menus change weekly and there are nightly additions as well. Service is attentive, yet not as overbearing as it can be in places of this sort. Start with salmon Napolean napped with light tarragon cream or potato soup with saffron. Salads, included with entrees, are a lively mix of greens and edible flowers. Main courses run from rabbit with cider cream and wild mushrooms to lamb brochette perfumed with cumin. There are also classic dishes like rack of lamb and chateaubriand carved with great fanfare at your table. Wines by the glass are as interesting as half and full bottles, a rare treat, and dessert is a must — a Rolls Royce of a sundae with dense homemade chocolate ice cream and caramel and fudge sauce, apple pie with a scoop of rich vanilla, fresh fruit sorbet. For those who prefer dessert a la Francaise, cheese and fruit is also on the roster.

HARRASEEKET LUNCH & LOBSTER
865-4888.
End of Main St., South Freeport.
Open: May to mid-Oct.
Price: Inexpensive to Moderate.
Cuisine: Seafood.
Serving: L, D.
Credit Cards: None.
Handicap Access: Partial.

Twenty minutes from downtown Portland, this is a favorite city getaway for lobster on the deck and a protected view of boats, pine-topped islands and Wolf's Neck. During the height of the season the line is long and the help gets a little overwhelmed. For those who can make do with just lobster, clams and corn, there's another window around the side of the shack where there is rarely anyone waiting. All the seafood tastes heavenly, the fries have that nice, dry clean taste and the corn is worth ordering two ears at a time. The pies are okay; the homemade ice cream is better.

Georgetown

FIVE ISLANDS SEAFOOD
371-2145.
Off Rte. 27 at Five Islands, Georgetown.
Closed: Mid-Oct.—April.
Price: Inexpensive to Moderate.
Cuisine: Lobster in the rough.
Serving: L, D.
Special Features: Outdoor pier dining; BYOB.

This working pier happens to be an ideal spot to crack open a lobster and suck down some steamers. Picnic tables on the dock are about it for amenities. But the panorama — sailboats on the Sheepscot River and pine-blanketed islands — more than makes up for it. Order corn, steamers and lobsters at the pound. Then step next door for coleslaw, french fries, chili, burgers, etc. Five Islands also makes one of the best lobster rolls on the Maine coast, so if you're feeling lazy, go for it. Dessert runs from double-dip ice cream cones to homemade pies.

THE OSPREY
371-2530.
Robinhood Marine Center (off Rte. 127), Georgetown.
Closed: Tues. in spring and fall; Mon.—Wed., Jan.—early March.
Price: Expensive.
Cuisine: Eclectic; classics to regional American.
Serving: L and SB in summer season only; D.
Credit Cards: MC, V.
Reservations: Appreciated.
Special Features: Cooking classes; wine-tasting dinners.

An extensive, creative menu and a dramatic water view have garnered the Osprey a wide following. The porch is the place to be in summer, and if luck's with you, you'll get a glimpse of the feathered creatures the restaurant's named for. Almost everything — breads, sorbets, ice creams — is made on the premises, and much of it is quite good. A few dishes don't work, but with such a large menu that's not unexpected. Mushrooms in puff pastry, brie in filo and the coastal sampler are among the better starters. Wiener Schnitzel, Pork Roquefort, stuffed filet mignon and linguini with lobster, shrimp and scallops grab kudos on the main course roster. The largesse extends to the dessert menu: peanut butter-fudge ice cream, profiteroles, cheesecake, devil's food cake and an intense chocolate torte with the fitting name: "Obsession."

The Harpswells

DOLPHIN MARINA BASIN
833-6000.
Basin Point., off Rte. 123, South Harpswell.
Open all year.
Price: Inexpensive to Moderate
Cuisine: Seafood.
Serving: B, L, D.
Credit Cards: MC, V.
Handicap Access: Yes.

This is where the fishermen come for food. They're the ones sitting at the counter with meaty burgers piled with ketchup. You can get burgers in the city. Try the chunky lobster stew. Watch lobsterboats or sailboats tie up. Wash it all down with coffee and a slice of one of their fresh fruit pies in season.

ESTES LOBSTER HOUSE
833-6340.
Rte. 123, South Harpswell.
Open Memorial Day to Labor Day.
Price: Inexpensive.
Cuisine: Lobster.
Serving: L, D.
Credit Cards: None.

It's about at this point on the coast that travelers have to start making choices about which isthmus or peninsula they explore. The advantage to overcoming any indecision you may have is that once you've acted, you feel like you've taken possession of the place — and its food. Temporary ownership has a terrific taste here. This is the sort of out-of-the- way place where you can watch fishermen work around their boats. It gives you a larger appreciation of that delicious haddock sandwich you're holding. If you want something naturally sweet, try a mess of clams.

RICHARD'S
729-9673.
Rte. 123, North Harpswell.
Closed: Sun. & Mon.
Price: Moderate.
Cuisine: German, American.
Serving: L, D; D Thurs. to Sat. in winter.
Credit Cards: MC, V.
Reservations: Recommended.
Handicap Access: Limited

German beers and victuals are the thing here. The beer roster is prodigious, with numerous offbeat selections. And beer is just what one needs to wash down hearty fare like wiener schnitzel, smoked pork chops, sauerbraten, wursts, potato salad, and sauteed cabbage. There's also an American menu for the unadventurous. It includes chicken, haddock and steaks. Though the dining room is sedate with dark wood, hanging plants and shades of green and white, the mood is lively and the wait staff particularly good-natured. Tortes and streudels for dessert.

Portland

ALBERTA'S
774-0016.
21 Pleasant St.,
  Portland.
Open all year.
Price: Moderate.
Cuisine: American
  regional.
Serving: L, D.
Credit Cards: MC, V.

Regulars talk about Alberta's ups and downs, but most consider it to be the best all-around in town. The menu is always a fresh mix of Tex-Mex, blue fish, *etouffee* or whatever is big in cities to the south. The service is always consistently fine and friendly. We saw then-Vice President Bush here one January. He did not seem adverse to drinking beer out of a bottle next to a guy with a pony tail. At least not here. Then we once ate dinner here with a lady from Palm Springs who hated it. Go figure. This place invented Death by Chocolate. We love the poppy seed cake.

Michael Loomis

Even President Bush knew about Alberta's.

BACK BAY GRILL
772-8833.
65 Portland St., Portland.
Closed: Sun., Memorial
  Day & July 1.
Price: Expensive.
Cuisine: Regional
American grill.
Serving: D.
Credit Cards: AE, MC, V.
Reservations:
Recommended.
Handicap Access: Limited.

This trendy grill in an untrendy part of town has a lot of style. Slick, simple lines, handsome paintings on the walls — and, don't laugh at us, wonderfully comfortable chairs. They also have what many believe is the best food in Portland. The menu changes weekly, as do wines by the glass (there's an interesting selection); the beer list is not bad, either. The wait staff is extremely knowledge-able about everything. No hemming and hawing when you want to know exactly what kind of vin-egar is in the salad dressing. Look for starters like charred eggplant with roasted red peppers and *aioli* or littleneck clams with bacon butter. Though grill-ing is the thing here (quite often there are grilled vegetables and at least one grilled dessert), the changing menu is by no means one-dimensional. It can range from linguini with whole clams or Idaho trout to lobster with Thai curry cream. There are always lamb, pork and beef dishes, too. *Crème Brulee* is a signature finish that's been on the menu since the restau-rant opened, but newer innovations like Plum Napolean, Sauternes Cake and Chocolate Dim Sum shouldn't be ignored.

CAFE ALWAYS
774-9399.
47 Middle St., Portland.
Closed: Sun. & Mon.
Price: Expensive.
Cuisine: Regional
American.
Serving: D.
Credit Cards: AE, MC, V.
Reservations:
Recommended.

C afe Always may not appear to be as hard-edged these days as when it first opened. The black-and-yellow high-tech look has given way to rosy impressionistic florals. But the cooking and service are as sharp as ever — and right up there with the best in town. Tapping on Mexican, Indian, Italian and Far Eastern influences, the repertoire changes daily. Breast of pheasant with carmelized apples, Japanese scallion rolled beef and ravioli filled with salmon mousse are the sort of fare one can expect. There's always a vegetarian item on the roster, too. And though by-the-glass wine selections are limited, half and full bottles are plentiful. Hip crockery is one reason to order dessert. But even if the poppyseed cake and peanut butter-and-chocolate ice cream *bombe* were served on Styrofoam they'd be worth it.

STREET & COMPANY
775-0887.
33 Wharf St., Portland.
Open daily.
Price: Moderate.
Cuisine: Seafood, pasta.
Serving: D.
Credit Cards: AE, MC, V.
Special Features: Patio
dining.

G arlic perfumes the air at this casual subterranean retreat off a funky cobblestone alley. Dried flowers and rough wood make for a countrified atmosphere and family-sized cans of olive oil and tomatoes give the place an ethnic feel. Pasta and grilled seafood pretty much make up the menu. Salmon, swordfish, scallops and shrimp are constants. There's also a soup of the day and changing specials like tuna Nicoise and sole meuniere. Pastas come with a variety of creative seafood sauces. Homebaked pies are the only desserts — fresh peach, apple crumb and strawberry-rhubarb — and are enough to make one forget all about mousse cake and sorbet.

South Portland

UNCLE BILLY'S
SOUTHSIDE B-B-Q &
TAKEOUT
767-7119.
60 Ocean St., South
Portland.
Open daily.
Price: Moderate.
Cuisine: Southern
barbecue.
Serving: L (except
Sunday), D.
Credit Cards: MC, V.

A pig fancier would go hog wild at Uncle Billy's. Lots of pig loot and lore here. This is barbecue Texas-style. Ribs, brisket, links, chicken, smoked fish. Smoked fish? We're in Maine, and it's mandatory you have something for the seafood-loving crowd. Fiery barbecued beans, peppery corn bread and snappy coleslaw are the finger- and fork-licking sides. The barbecue sauce comes in two strengths — hot and mild. There are also items like *jambalaya* (Louisiana is right next to Texas) and spicy spaghetti. The best dessert is the Death-by-Chocolate

Special Features: On premises smoker; takeout.

Sundae — chocolate ice cream loaded with chocolate shavings and doused with thick fudge sauce.

Michael Loomis

Uncle Billy's smokes and then barbecues their ribs and chicken. We're partial to their beans and cornbread, too.

Yarmouth

THE CANNERY
846-1226.
Lower Falls Landing,
   Royal River, Yarmouth.
Open daily.
Price: Moderate.
Cuisine: American,
   Continental.
Serving: L, D, SB.
Credit Cards: MC, V.
Reservations: For groups
   of 5 or more.
Handicap Access: Yes.
Special Features: Deck;
   river view.

But for the name, you would never figure this for a former shrimp factory. These days the Cannery has a dramatic, West Coast look with lots of glass and wood, cathedral ceilings and potted plants. The outdoor deck overlooking the Royal River is a nice spot for a summer lunch and the indoor "porch" dining for a romantic dinner in winter. Lunch is a mix of offbeat salads and sandwiches like roast chicken with tarragon, lobster and crab roll, and crab cakes. The dinner menu is heavy on the seafood — steamed lobster, broiled scallops, fried clams, grilled salmon and seafood pasta. Desserts run from cheesecake and pies to the luscious Lemon Charlotte Cake. This isn't a favorite place of ours, but you can't beat the setting.

MUDDY RUDDER

846-3082.
Rte. 1, Yarmouth.
Open daily.
Price: Moderate to
   Expensive.
Cuisine: American, New
   England.
Serving: L, D, Sat. and
   Sun. B.
Credit Cards: AE, D, DC,
   MC, V.
Reservations:
   Recommended.
Handicap Access: Yes.

With its extensive all-day menu, the Muddy Rudder is a good option when the troops can't agree. Choices run from burgers and sandwiches to lobster and steaks and the price is right too. Service is of the "My name is . . ." variety, but that's okay in a casual setting like this. Potted plants and trees give the dining rooms an outdoors feel, and most tables have a view of the Cousins River. Among the best picks are lobster pie with its delicate crust and a light creamy filling, and grilled or blackened fish. Brownie pie with vanilla ice cream, apple cobbler, cheesecake and apple spice cake all make satisfying endings.

RESTAURANTS — MIDCOAST

Bath

KRISTINA'S

442-8577.
160 Center St., Bath.
Closed: Sun. evenings and
   Mon. and Tues.
   evenings in winter;
   Jan.—mid-Feb.
Price: Moderate to
   Expensive.
Cuisine: American eclectic.
Serving: B, L, D.
Credit Cards: MC, V, D.
Special Features: Bakery
   takeout.

A bakery case crammed with gingerbread, Danish, cookies and cakes is the first thing you see when you walk into Kristina's. It might be tempting to stop right there, but then you'd miss the good cooking within. Kristina's brunches are full of possibilities — a crabmeat omelet, *huevos rancheros*, eggs florentine, homebaked raisin-bread toast, fresh fruit, spiced yogurt. Lunch is a meal of soups, salads, sandwiches and burgers. Dinner runs from such standards as lamb chops and grilled salmon to the exotic Indian tofu. There's also a light menu that includes *quiches* and *burritos*. Kristina's upstairs dining room is casual and loungelike; downstairs is bright, homey and cheerful with butcher block tables and potted plants.

TRUFFLES CAFE

442-8474.
21 Elm St., Bath.
Closed: Tues.
Price: Moderate.
Cuisine: Eclectic soups and
   sandwiches.
Serving: B, L.
Reservations:
   Recommended.

Truffles offers welcome relief from the lunchtime blahs. Yes, the menu is mostly soups, salads and sandwiches, but everything is done with a deft touch, and even the simplest dish is full of surprises. Take the corn chowder. Not only is it dairy-free, but it comes with diced red pepper and scallions for flavor and crunch. Chicken salad goes beyond the mayonnaise-encrusted cliché with a Southwestern spiced Russian dressing. The grilled cheese gets a new spin when it's an oozing mass of spinach and brie. Breakfasts cover the usual egg dishes plus a couple of specials like waffles with blueberry butter and smoked salmon and scrambled eggs. The ultra-rich coffee-coated truffles are the only dessert you will need, even when you have several other homemade choices available.

Belfast

DARRES
338-1884.
57 Main St., Belfast.
Open daily in summer;
closed Sun. in winter.
Price: Inexpensive.
Cuisine: American.
Serving: B, L.

Here, local pols plot their next moves in wooden booths over steaming bowls of fish chowder and homemade yeast rolls while alternative types take advantage of the luncheon bar with miso soup and macrobiotic muffins. Dark and busy on the inside, Darres has a hometown hotbed feel. Shoppers take a break over turkey melts while mothers pacify small children with good old peanut butter and jelly (on whole wheat). Try the fresh haddock sandwich with a side of slaw. Slurp down a real milkshake. Waitresses call out orders over the din, their voices cut through the thick smell of onion rings and burgers. You can have your java hot and black or opt for Japanese tea. The blackboard usually boasts a full slate of seasonal pies, cheesecake and fruit-sweetened delights for those watching their sugar intake.

**90 MAIN
RESTAURANT**
338-1106.
90 Main St., Belfast 04915.
Open all year.
Price: Moderate.
Cuisine: Eclectic.
Serving: L, D.
Credit Cards: V, MC.

This place is a mix of Down East, New Age and New York — a common cultural crossroads in Belfast these days. Clean and woody upstairs and down, you can have your ham and havarti on a buttery roll; baked goat cheese on fresh greens with raspberry vinaigrette; steamed mussels in wine, garlic and herbs served with butter broth and crusty bread; seaweed salad, or regular stuff like a cheeseburger; turkey-bacon melt or reuben. We didn't care for the twig tea. It tasted twiggy. On the other hand, now we can say we had it. The pie's okay, we tried the apple and blueberry. Flan, unfortunately nearly everywhere, is impossible to make well.

**PENOBSCOT
   MEADOWS INN**
338-5320.
Rte. 1, Belfast.
Closed: Tues.; Nov.—Mar.

A fine collection of Big Band tunes is one reason to stop at Penobscot Meadows, but it's not the only one. There's dining on the cozy porch under flickering hurricane lamps and decorative quilts. There's also a fine wine list — and the food. The

Price: Expensive.
Cuisine: Country gourmet;
   regional American.
Serving: D.
Credit Cards: D, MC, V.
Reservations: Required.
Special Features: Deck
   dining with a view of
   Penobscot Bay.

wines hail from Chile, Spain, California and France and are available by the glass and in full and half bottles. The menu borrows from country gourmet, regional-American and whatever else grabs the chef's fancy. Even the familiar takes on a new edge in such capable hands. Sate of shrimp, pork and chicken; spinach-stuffed mushrooms; shrimp crepes and escargots are among starters. Main courses run from an interesting mixed grill and Szechuan veal to champagne lobster. Breads and salads are carefully conceived as well. Desserts are wonderful — creamy homemade ice creams, lemon mousse in an edible chocolate cup, triple chocolate terrine, and a truly stellar peach ice cream and chocolate cake roll.

Boothbay Area

**LOBSTERMAN'S
WHARF**
633-3443.
Rte. 96, East Boothbay.
Closed: Mid-Oct.–early
   May.
Price: Moderate.
Cuisine: American.
Serving: L, D.
Credit Cards: MC, V.
Feature: Kid-proof dining;
   deck with river view.

Wedged between two old shipyards, this family restaurant is festive and fun. Best of all, there's plenty to keep the kids occupied. The long, paneled dining room has the look of an ocean liner, and just in case you don't get it, lobster traps, buoys, and paddles hang from walls and ceilings. In fair weather, dine on the deck overlooking the Damariscotta River. Otherwise, grab a table in the large dining room. Unlike places that are all gimmick and no substance, the Wharf has good food and an enthusiastic staff. Tasty biscuits and corn muffins. Savory starters like deep-fried artichokes. Bright salads. And interesting entrees. A mixed grill with kielbasa, sirloin and chicken is a winner as is the baked flounder stuffed with chunks of crab. There are occasional disappointments, but these can be avoided by sticking to basics. For dessert, brownie sundaes.

Camden

**CAPPY'S CHOWDER
   HOUSE**
236-2254.
Main St., Camden.
Open all year.
Price: Moderate.
Cuisine: American.
Serving: B, L, D; call for
   winter hours.

Right downtown, the compact size belies the huge staff required to make this place run. They claim sooner or later everyone shows up here, and they run it like they're ready for your arrival, morning, noon and night. Great chowder, good burgers, a good short stack of ribs and bouyant pancakes (at breakfast). They also are quite competent with locally caught fish. Many a time we have

Credit Cards: MC, V.
Handicap Access: Limited.
Special Features: Bakery.

stood packed in the doorway or at the bar waiting for a table or preferably a booth. Even once you've been seated in the varnished and bric-a-bracked joint, you feel like you're a character in a triple-decker sandwich.

CASSOULET
236-6304.
31 Elm St. Camden.
Closed: Sun. & Mon. in
    season; Sun.—Tues. off-
    season.
Price: Expensive.
Cuisine: French,
    Mediterranean.
Serving: D.
Credit Cards: MC, V.
Reservations:
    Recommended.
Special Features: Outdoor
    dining in summer.

The name may be French, but the cuisine at this storefront bistro is really more Mediterranean. As is custom on the other side of the Atlantic, a meal can go on for hours — not because the service is slow, but because time is necessary to savor the flavors. Make no mistake, these flavors are worth lingering over: rabbit paté with dried fruit; shrimp over linguini with garlic, shallots and feta; *moussaka* (Greek lamb and eggplant casserole); and *cioppino* (Italian fish stew). Hot french breads and salads with homegrown greens are also well-conceived, rather than an afterthought. Desserts are a match for the rest of the menu: chocolate mousse, cranberry-pear cobbler and a truly outstanding chocolate-apricot torte.

**PETER OTT'S STEAK
    HOUSE**
236-4032.
16 Bayview St., Camden.
Closed: Mon. in winter.
Price: Moderate.
Cuisine: American.
Serving: D.
Credit Cards: MC, V.

There's something reassuring about the dark wood and friendly greeting at this Camden institution; somehow you know you'll end up with a decent steak and salad and walk out humming. And you do. Red meat's the thing here. Several cuts are available daily, and occasionally there are specials like black angus ribeye with a burgundy/green peppercorn sauce. Broiled fish and specials like Haddock Caribbean style, as well as pastas of the day, round out the menu. The chef prides herself on ridiculously fattening desserts such as the concoction called Chocolate Decadence, but you can always jig it off at the Irish pub downstairs.

THE WATERFRONT
236-3747.
62 Bayview St., Camden.
Open daily.
Price: Moderate.
Cuisine: American;
    seafood.

Camden's harbor may be the most beautiful in the midcoast region, and the Waterfront is the place to watch it from. In summer, the restaurant opens its roomy terrace to salty breezes — the better to enjoy your lobster and clams by. Seafood, in some cases with a certain stylish twist, is the kitchen's hallmark. Fresh fish, crab cakes, crab pie,

Serving: L, D.
Credit Cards: MC, V.
Handicap Access: Yes.
Special Features: View of
Camden Harbor.

linguine with sun-dried tomatoes and fresh scallops share the menu with steaks and specials like breast of chicken with olive oil and blueberry vinegar. At lunch, sandwiches and salads are teamed with chowders and soups. This is a charming spot to while away a couple of hours. Crack open a chablis, dig into a halibut steak, and enjoy the water lapping at the docks.

Newcastle

THE NEWCASTLE INN
563-5685.
River Rd., Newcastle.
Closed: Mon., June—Nov.;
Sun.-Thurs. rest of year.
Price: Expensive to Very
Expensive.
Cuisine: Country gourmet.
Serving: D.
Credit Cards: MC, V.
Reservations: Required.

There's only one seating at the Newcastle Inn each evening. Such regimentation might be off-putting if the food were not so good and the experience enjoyable. The small dining room is lighted by candles and has white linens, fresh flowers and classical strains. The five-course meal —there's a single set menu each night — is $33. This includes hors d'oeuvres on the sun porch, a starter, soup, homebaked cream biscuits, salad, a main course and dessert. The menu changes nightly and is on the order of an onion tart, *risotto primavera*, corn custard, beef tenderloin, chicken with champagne sauce, duck with lingonberry turnovers, and salmon with orange glaze. Dessert might be an airy souffle or some other creation like luscious lemon-layered ice cream cake.

Rockland

THE BROWN BAG
596-6372.
606 Main St., Rockland.
Open: Year round.
Price. Inexpensive.
Cuisine: Country eclectic.
Serving: B, L.
Credit Cards: None;
personal checks
accepted.
Handicap access: Yes,
through the back.

In 1987 four sisters founded this breakfast and luncheon spot. They do well — especially at the most important meal of the day, breakfast. Fresh roasted Green Mountain coffee, an edible still life of warm croissants, sticky buns and giant blueberry muffins and cooling loaves of fresh shredded wheat (yes, fresh!). The oatmeal is also homemade and the cinnamon swirl French toast is laced with real Maine maple syrup. Congenial customers line up to place their orders for *huevos rancheros,* brown bag pockets (their version is scrambled eggs with three cheeses in a whole wheat pita). The toad 'n holes are hands-down winners with kids. Lunch is hearty sandwiches and sister Claire's famous soups and chowders. Grab a juice or seltzer from the cooler and decide whether the mood warrants falafel with

Two Rockland locals who know good pie when they've had it.

Michael Loomis

lemon tahini sauce or a roast beef/boursin sub (the beef is marinated and roasted on the premises). The owners devote a whole blackboard to their changing dessert menu; their seasonal pies, cheesecakes, puddings and cookies are all made from scratch.

CAPTAIN'S TABLE
596-6870.
Rte. 1, Rockland.
Open year round.
Price: Inexpensive.
Cuisine: American.
Serving: B, L ,D.
Credit Cards: V, MC, AE, D.
Handicap Access: Yes.

Driving north into "downtown" Rockland on Rte. 1, don't miss the scruffy-looking residential hotel on your left called the Wayfarer. The hotel's restaurant — the Captain's Table — is where the fishermen eat. From brobdingnagian stacks of flapjacks to eggs with ham and fish cakes (potato, onion and flaked fish formed into patties and grilled —delicious), this is the way to keep body and soul together through a morning of sightseeing, sailing or any more strenuous activity. There are also low-priced lunch and dinner specials, but come in the morning. The Ritz it ain't, but you've been living in the city too long if you can't enjoy this real slice of Maine life.

The Nickerson Tavern in Searsport.

Michael Loomis

Searsport

NICKERSON TAVERN
548-2220.
Rte.1, Searsport.
Closed: Mon. in summer;
    call for fall and winter
    hours.
Price: Moderate.
Cuisine: American.
Serving: D.
Credit Cards: AE, MC, V.
Reservations:
    Recommended.
Handicap access: Yes.

The Nickerson has become a favorite in the Midcoast area. Owners Tom and Linda Weiner parlay their respective skills in the kitchen and dining room to produce a wonderfully polished evening. Begin with the *escargot*, redolent with garlic and baked in pastry caps, or the Carolina crabcakes, pure crabmeat lightly seasoned, then panfried and served with roasted pepper puree. The house salad with chilled fresh greens and pepper Parmesan dressing is excellent. So is the raspberry and hazelnut encrusted chicken and the locally caught scallops baked with artichokes and mushrooms in a light garlic and cheese sauce. A daily fish of the day special might be pan-blackened catfish or grilled red snapper or a poached salmon with dill *bearnaise*. The dessert cart circulates constantly and is filled with creme-filled pastry shells, lemon curd tarts, and *cappuccino* cheesecakes, but you have to ask for the ice cream of the day. Ginger is a sure-fire winner.

Thomaston

**HARBOR VIEW
TAVERN**
354-8173.
Off Main St. on public
    landing, Thomaston.
Open year round.
Price: Moderate.
Cuisine: Seafood,
    continental.
Serving: L, D.
Credit Cards: MC, V.
Handicap Access: Yes.

The funky interior of the Harbor View belies the serious cooking that goes on here. Old photos, gilded mirrors, mobiles and musical instruments cover every inch of wall space. The building itself is nothing more than a slightly off-kilter vintage boathouse, and during the summer it is filled to overflowing with visiting yachtsmen and local merchants. The kitchen's specialty is New England seafood with a French flair — Lobster Provençal with garlic butter and herbs; steamed lobster stuffed with scallops and finished with a wine and cheese sauce; stuffed shrimp; plus steaks and pasta. For lunch, look for filling items like the steak-and-cheese sandwich and fried seafood. Desserts run from carrot cake to richer confections like Chocolate Chip Pie and brownie a la mode.

Vinalhaven

THE HAVEN
863-4969.
Main St.,
  Vinalhaven.
Open all year.
Price: Moderate.
Cuisine: Seafood; exotic
  regional.
Serving: B, D; call for
  schedule.
Credit Cards: None;
  checks accepted.
Reservations: Yes.

Favored by residents, summer people and visitors, the Haven has been a popular gathering place for more than a dozen years. The menu changes often to incorporate the day's catch, ripening wild berries or chanterelles harvested from the surrounding spruce woods. Two dining rooms are open in the summer. The back room offers a more traditional seafood-restaurant atmosphere. The front room, once a storefront, is a favorite place to dine surrounded by the works of local artists, many of whom are well-known outside of this close-knit community.

Waldoboro

MOODY'S DINER
832-7468.
Rte. 1, Waldoboro.
Closed: Fri. & Sat. between
  midnight and 5 a.m.
Price: Inexpensive.
Cuisine: Diner food.
Serving: B, L, D.
Handicap Access: Yes

What distinguishes a really great restaurant is when the locals don't leave after it's been discovered by tourists. Everyone shares counter seats and booths at Moody's: Waldoborans, summer people, tourists, fishing boat captains and yacht owners. The corned beef hash is legendary. The cheeseburgers and meatloaf are, too, as is their walnut pie and any of their cream pies. You like the food? Leave with stomach full and one of their cookbooks, on sale next to the cash register.

The Pie State

"The feast was a noble feast, as has already been said. There was an elegant ingenuity displayed in the form of pies, which delighted my heart. Once acknowledge that an American pie is far to be preferred to its humble ancestor, the English tart, and it is joyful to be reassured at a Bowden [sic] reunion that invention has not yet failed."
— Sarah Orne Jewett, *The Country of the Pointed Firs and Other Stories.*

The Maine coast is nothing if not for pie. And it wouldn't take much retooling to change Maine's nickname from the Pine State to the Pie State.

Maybe Maine's having a drowned coast, which resulted from those two tectonic plates crashing together before being smothered by the glaciers, explains why so many people here understand the importance of a good crust and pie a la mode.

Apples ripen earlier here than in other New England states, and Maine Macs and Cortlands are often the nation's first taste of autumn.

Roy Zalesky

Maine even has several filling seasons (see "Berry and Apple Picking" in *Recreation*, Chapter Six).

There are two kinds of Maine pies. Fruit and Cream.

The saying should be, "As American as blueberry pie." The Europeans brought the apples. The blueberries were already here. Cream pies probably were invented in Maine. Somebody looked out the window on a cold wintery day at the snow blanketing a blueberry barren and her thoughts turned to filling.

In 1825, David Robinson, a local ice dealer, supposedly invented ice cream and by extension, pie a la mode. *Yorkie's,* the best pie place in the history of civilization, flourished in Camden until the last decade. Sigh. Pie gone by.

Here are several pie places, some legendary, some secret and wrangled from friends and some our own favorites.

South Coast
Hattie's Deli (282-3435) in Biddeford Pool. Blueberry.

Casco Bay
Spurwink Country Kitchen (799-1177, Cape Elizabeth). Pastry chef Eileen Esposito is a genius.

McMag's (871-9019, Portland). Their apple is not too sweet and not too tart, and oh, the crust.

Midcoast
Kristina's Bakery and Restaurant (442-8577; 160 Center St., Bath). Try the orange-walnut.

Dip Net Coffee Shop (372-6275; Port Clyde). This could very well be the true "Son of Yorkie's" (see above).

Weaver's Bakery (338-3540; 19 Main St., Belfast). Any flavor.

Moodys Diner (832-7468; Rte. 1, Waldoboro). Famous for strawberry-rhubarb since 1927.

Mrs. Marples (Friendship Rd., Waldoboro). Self-service pie sold on the honor system. Select your pie and leave her money.

Dick, who runs a restaurant of the same name in Ellsworth, makes a fine pie.

Roy Zalesky

Down East/Acadia
Dick's (667-7220; 42 Main St., Ellsworth). Pie and counter conversation.

East of Schoodic
Arlene's Harbor Side (963-2311; Corea). If you're lucky you can have some. But to be sure, call and order a day in advance.

Helen's (255-8423.; Rte. 1, Machias). Her famed strawberry.

Westport

THE SQUIRE TARBOX INN
882-7693.
Rte. 144, Westport Island.
Closed: Nov.—mid-May; open seven days in season.
Price: Expensive.
Cuisine: American.
Serving: D.
Credit Cards: AE, D, MC, V.
Reservations: Required.
Special Features: Goat cheese made on premises; dairy open year round.

Dinner is served every night during the busy months in the 1763 portion of this pretty farmhouse. It's a hearty and lavish meal — five courses of good country cooking. The menu changes daily, but you can count on that there will be plenty of their homemade goat cheese on it — whether it's their spreadable and tasty farmstead *chevre* (fashioned after French-style goat cheese) or *caerphilly*, an aged, waxed cheese with a smooth texture and mellow flavor — smoked or plain. You never leave hungry, either, because they fill you up with great vegetables and a selection of dinner meats that can include roast fish, poultry, chops or their goat salami (it's pretty tasty, too). They often offer Sin Pie for dessert, rich with, you guessed it, chocolate.

Wiscasset

LE GARAGE
882-5409.
Water St., Wiscasset.
Closed: Mon.; Dec. and
Jan.
Price: Expensive.
Cuisine: New England.
Serving: L, D.
Credit Cards: MC, V.
Reservations:
Recommended.
Special Features: River
view.

Candelabra, cathedral ceilings and two half-sunk schooners set the scene at this former auto garage right on the river. The effect is dramatic — especially on one of those gray, misty days the coast is so famous for. As atmospheric as Le Garage is, the food is surprisingly down to earth. Starters like *ratatouille,* savory charbroiled items like chicken, steak, pork chops, fresh seafood, unusual pastas, light salads and desserts. Yes, we think there is an overabundance of cream sauce on the menu, but this is easy enough to avoid if you are so inclined. We suggest you save the calories and cholesterol for dessert — homespun favorites like Grapenut pudding, ice cream cake, apple crisp and gingerbread.

RESTAURANTS — DOWN EAST/ACADIA

Blue Hill

THE BLUE HILL INN
374-2844.
Union St., Blue Hill.
Open: Weekends and
holidays in winter;
every evening beginning
Memorial Day.
Price: Expensive.
Cuisine: Continental.
Serving: D.
Credit Cards: MC, V.
Reservations: Required.
Special Features: No
smoking; six-course
prix-fixe dinner.

With its many chimneys and six-over-six windows, The Blue Hill Inn has been a beacon in the night for travelers since 1840. The last five years it has attracted visitors for chef Art Wallace's elegant six-course dinner, as well. One cool fall evening before dinner, we sat in the common room enjoying warm brie, a glass of Medoc and a crackling fire. When time for dinner came, we moved to the romantic dining room, candlelit by sconces and an enormous chandelier. The first course, butternut squash and apple soup, was rich and flavorful, warmed by nutmeg and thickened with *créme fraiche.* The second was a rainbow trout wrapped around a delectably smooth salmon *mousseline,* surrounded by a light mushroom sauce. After that they offered us a "breather" with grapefruit ice, a tart lead-in to the two main courses: noisettes of lamb, medium rare, juicy and with sauteed red pepper and shallots; and lemon-and-bourbon-marinated quail with sides of scallions and summer squash. We especially liked

The Blue Hill Inn, where most of the year chef Art Wallace serves a stomach-expanding six-course prix-fixe feast.

Blue Hill Inn

the quail. It had no trace of gaminess and was crisp on the outside. We finished with a dark chocolate *gateau* and good strong coffee for the road. Ah, the lucky travelers who had the foresight to stay the night here, too.

FIREPOND
374-2135.
Main St., Blue Hill.
Closed: Labor Day—
    Memorial Day.
Price: Expensive.
Cuisine: Classic gourmet;
    regional American.
Serving: D.
Credit Cards: D, DC,
    MC, V.
Reservations:
    Recommended.
Special Features: Screened
    porch overlooking
    creek.

Lady Chatterley would have been fond of Firepond. A rushing stream below and rough-hewn wood beams give it the feel of a romantic lair. But with lighted candles and pale linens this is more elegant than anything Lawrence might have dreamed up. The food encourages amorous visions, as well. Homemade little breads and rolls, offbeat salads like warm spinach with tomato and buffalo mozzarella. Starters include smoked trout, patés, and baked brie with almonds; main courses, pork tenderloin marsala, steak au poivre and lobster with fresh pasta and a three-cheese sauce. For dessert look for fresh fruit tarts, homemade ice cream or flourless chocolate cake. Oh, there might be an occasional misstep — but every great romance has its low point, too.

**LEFT BANK BAKERY &
    CAFE**
374-2201.
Rte. 172, Blue Hill.
Open daily.
Price: Moderate.

The Left Bank has a counterculture feel not unlike those coffeehouses Bob Dylan and Joan Baez used to hang out in. A fieldstone chimney, pine paneling and windows facing the garden (much of the food is homegrown) make for a rustic dining room. The help, although perfectly polite and efficient, has that I-was-at-Woodstock look. Not

Cuisine: Eclectic
  homegrown; some
  vegetarian.
Serving: B, L, D.
Reservations:
  Recommended.
Special Features: Bakery
  takeout; live music after
  8 p.m.

Castine

THE CASTINE INN
326-4365.
Main St., Castine.
Open daily mid-May—
  Nov.
Price: Expensive.
Cuisine: New England
  regional.
Serving: D.
Credit Cards: V, MC.
Reservations: Yes.
Special Features: Porch
  dining in good weather.

surprising then that the pickings are wholesome and homespun. Breakfast is a real eye-opener with more than a dozen options — challah-bread French toast; exotically stuffed omelets; pancakes; granola; oatmeal; homemade whole wheat bagels; muffins; cinnamon puffs and smoked salmon. Lunch includes homemade pizzas; main course streudels and pies; sandwiches and pastas. Dinner may be a Thai noodle dish called *Pad Thai,* a curried orange chicken, fish stew or a French country pizza. There's a children's menu as well.

O pen only for dinner, the restaurant at the Castine Inn is one of the best in Maine. The fare is New England regional — simple cooking with classic underpinnings, a tendency toward seafood and a good view of the harbor. Chicken and leek pot pie is a specialty here, as are crabmeat cakes with mustard sauce. The menu varies with the seasons, depending upon the harvest of local farmers and fishermen, and always offers half a dozen appetizers (the salmon ravioli with a tomato saffron sauce is excellent). Entrees include a delicious roast duck with peach chutney. The dessert list is solid, too: *créme brulee;* almond cake with a cherry sauce; blueberry cobbler; or rhubarb crisp. Service is friendly and efficient. Smoking is permitted only in the pub, where appetizers such as Mussel Bisque or oysters on the half shell are served. Weather permitting, seating is available on the porch overlooking the handsome gardens.

Kathy Gould

The Castine Inn, where you can dine on the porch overlooking manicured gardens.

DENNETT'S WHARF
326-9045.
1 Sea St., Castine.
Open: Late spring—
    mid-Oct.
Price: Moderate.
Cuisine: American.
Serving: L, D.
Handicap Access: Yes
Special Features: View of
    working harbor and
    beyond.

This place boasts the longest raw bar in New England. That may be one reason it's a favorite stop for cruising sailors, Maine Maritime cadets, tourists and year-round residents. Dollar bills have been stuck to the high, barnlike ceilings, and the waiter says it costs a buck to find out how. The food is as good as the company and about as refined: seafood lasagna, grilled marinated swordfish steak. This is the sort of place you hope will take you in as soon as you walk in the door. It gets particularly wild during sailboat racing season. There's an impressive view of working boats, yachts, the imposing shadow of the Maine Maritime's training ship *State of Maine* and a thick forest across the harbor. Great homemade desserts and decent coffee.

Deer Isle

**EATON'S LOBSTER
    POOL**
348-2383.
Blastow's Cove, Little Deer
Isle.
Open: Mother's Day
    through Oct.
Price: Moderate.
Cuisine: Lobster.
Serving: L, D.

Eaton's sits on one of those incredibly perfect Maine coves with small islands silhouetted against the horizon at dusk. Indoors or out, bibbed families lay waste to some of Maine's finest: steamed clams, lobster, chowder, French fries, coleslaw, blueberry pie and coolers of beer (it's BYOB). When we were kids, Eaton's was exactly the same way.

East Orland

DUFFY'S
469-3777.
Rte. 1, East Orland.
Open all year.
Price: Inexpensive.
Cuisine: American.
Serving: B, L, D.
Handicap Access: Yes.

Homestyle food, muffins the size of softballs and a clientele that looks like Norman Rockwell models. The silverware doesn't match and the chairs wobble. No extra charge for that. The motto on the menu says succinctly: "We here at Duffy's are a native orientated restaurant. We aren't fussy and we're certainly not fancy. If you are, Ellsworth is 12 miles east and Bucksport is 7 miles west." Recently Duffy's opened a lobster pound and clambake next door.

Ellsworth

DICK'S
667-7220.
42 Main St., Ellsworth.

Vintage luncheonettes are going the way of the dinosaur, which is why Dick's is such a find. This Ellsworth institution is the quintessential cor-

Closed: Sat., Sun. & holidays.
Price: Moderate.
Cuisine: American.
Serving: B, L.
Handicap Access: Limited.
Special Features: Pie to go.

ner hangout. A place that still serves all those lunch-counter favorites: grilled cheese, fried eggs, pepper steak, franks and beans. Dick's looks the part, too, with Formica counters, vinyl-covered stools and a tired-looking screen door. Besides the typical breakfast and lunch choices (burgers, fried fish, etc.) there are usually a couple of specials. They're known for their pies — hearty main course versions like turkey and beef and those for dessert like pumpkin, banana cream, apple and blueberry. All have the same perfect crust. Yes, there really is a "Dick." He and his wife run the place and are always ready to offer a friendly word.

THE WOK
667-3555.
173 Main St., Ellsworth.
Open: Year round.
Price: Inexpensive.
Cuisine: Thai.
Serving: L, D.
Credit Cards: V, MC.
Handicap Access: Yes.
Special Features: Spicy take out.

We'd been hearing about this restaurant for a couple of years but never seemed to be there when a table was available. Suspended paper umbrellas hover above red-clothed tables, local artwork eclipses the walls, and six small booths fill the available floor space of Ellsworth's only Thai restaurant. Sneakered clientele sit back to back with those more coiffed, and conversation runs from cruise lines to the latest channeling techniques. The service and food are four-star. We had *Tom Kha Gai* — a delicious chicken soup with galanga and coconut milk and the Spicy Fish, perfectly deep-fried fish topped with a tangy, moderately spiced tamarind sauce. The *Masaman Curry* —chicken, pineapple, sweet potatoes and bamboo shoots — is so good, you'll be tempted not to share. This is a good alternative for those who've been fished out on the way up or down the coast.

Gouldsboro

CHARLIE'S LOBSTER HUT
No telephone.
Rte. 186, Prospect Harbor Rd., Gouldsboro.
Open Memorial Day to mid-Oct.
Price: Inexpensive.
Cuisine: Lobster.
Serving: Takeout.

Charlie would be out lobstering again if he had $100,000 for a boat, but he doesn't. So instead he sells lobsters, crabmeat, clams and chips out of the cabin he was born in out here by the side of the road. You can get the lobsters live, or cooked in the big blackened half-barrel filled with water that contains his "secret solution." Although you might not think so, people from all over the world have stopped by. This is lobster to the right of rough. People say it tastes better here. Charlie says, "I know how I want it, so it suits me, and that's how I do it for everyone else."

Hancock

LE DOMAINE
422-3395.
Rte 1., Hancock.
Closed: Nov.—May.
Price: Expensive.
Cuisine: French.
Serving: D.
Credit Cards: AE, MC, V.
Reservations: Required.

Here is excellent French country cooking and an encyclopedic wine list (all French with many obscure regional labels) right in the heart of Down East. Everything that comes out of the kitchen is wonderful — dense rich chicken liver *paté* (now available by mail order as well), garlicky escargots, rabbit with prunes, stuffed savoy cabbage. Vegetables (baby string beans and carrots) are from the garden as are the salad greens. Desserts are not to be missed: Chestnut Coupe — a vanilla ice cream and chestnut parfait, bread pudding, mousses and tarts. Even the dining room has a *Provençal* feel. A walk-in fireplace at one end dominates and doubles as a rotisserie. Copper pots, wine maps and red-and-white linens give the place the feel of a bistro, while dark wood and classical music add an elegant touch. Service is professional and knowledgeable without being the least bit pretentious — all in all a rare find anywhere.

**TIDAL FALLS LOBSTER
  POUND**
422-6818.
Half a mile off Rte. 1,
  Hancock.
Closed: Late Sept–
  late June.
Price: Moderate.
Cuisine: Lobster.
Serving: L, D.
Special Features: Dining
  on the banks of Sullivan
  Harbor.

Tidal Falls has all the makings of a great lobster shack — a fine location and equally fine food. Everything is country casual — picnic tables under a row of weeping willows, or, on blustery days, a pine hut with plants and skylights. Even though this is an order-your-food-and-wait-till-your-number-is-called place, the menu is more ambitious than most. Besides lobster au natural, look for steamed mussels with garlic butter, bakery French and garlic breads, lobster stew, crab rolls and Dove bars for dessert.

Le Domaine

The crisp, casual atmosphere belies the serious — and excellent — French country cooking going on at Le Domaine.

Mount Desert Island

**FISHERMAN'S
LANDING**
288-4632.
35 West St., Bar Harbor.
Closed: Oct.–May.
Price: Moderate.
Cuisine: Maine specialties.
Serving: L, D.
Handicap Access: Yes.

S teamers, lobster and crab are the fixings at this seafood shack overlooking Frenchman's Bay in downtown Bar Harbor. On fair days the picnic tables on the outdoor deck are the ones to grab, but when the weather turns foul, retreat to the indoor dining room. Unlike other lobster shacks, which are strictly BYOB, Fisherman's Landing serves liquor. Except for the bar, everything's self service, and the college students behind the counter are a conscientious friendly bunch. Shellfish in various incarnations, onion rings, potato salad, fries and slaw are all good bets.

JORDAN POND HOUSE
276-3316.
Park Loop Rd., Mount
　Desert Island.
Closed: Late Oct.–
　late May.
Price: Moderate.
Cuisine: American.
Serving: L, D, afternoon
　tea.
Credit Cards: MC, V.
Reservations:
　Recommended.
Handicap Access: Yes.
Special Features: Outdoor
　dining.

Y es, this is a touristy spot smack in the middle of Acadia National Park, but every once in a while tourists know the score, and this is one of those times. With an outdoor patio and a many-windowed dining room, the restaurant makes the most of its location on Jordan Pond. Tea, a repast of meltingly good popovers and raspberry preserves, is served at long tables on the lawn; lunch and dinner can be had on the patio or indoors. So what if the service can be a bit relaxed? Why would you want to rush off anyway? Look for lobster roll, curried chicken salad, sandwiches and quiches at lunch; steaks, chicken and lots of seafood at dinner. Be sure to try the iced tea or lemonade — both home-made. For dessert the Chocolate *Paté* is a standout.

PORCUPINE GRILL
288-3884.
123 Cottage St.,
　Bar Harbor.
Closed: Sun.–Thurs.;
　Oct.–June.
Price: Expensive.
Cuisine: Regional
　American.
Serving: D.
Credit Cards: MC, V.
Reservations:
　Recommended.

T he Porcupine Grill is a stylish stop in what can really be a tacky town. Antique oak, chic window swags, and oversized black-and-white photos of the Porcupine Islands give the place a big city look. Start with one of the classy cocktails — fresh fruit daiquiris, sparkling cider, peppered vodka. The wine and beer lists are interesting, too. Food is clever and modern: homemade breads like poppyseed dill and cranberry walnut; olive oil grilled vegetables; offbeat salads like a Caesar with garlic fried clams; pork chops with cornbread stuffing and homemade applesauce; steak with caramelized onions; poached salmon. Desserts can be hit or miss, though, so stick to sure bets like the chocolate fudge pie, cheesecake or truffle tarts.

Winter Harbor

CHASE'S
963-7171.
Rte. 186, Winter Harbor.
Open daily.
Price: Moderate.
Cuisine: American; New
  England diner.
Serving: B, L, D.
Credit Cards: MC, V.

Chase's is Maine's answer to the diner: chowder, burgers, sandwiches and broiled and fried seafood served in a no-nonsense, no-frills setting. The lights are bright and the chairs worn, but the food is right on the mark and the help on their toes. When was the last time you saw waiters carry three plates on an arm? Among the better picks: broiled fresh haddock, fried clams, chowder and specials like a fried flounder basket. For dessert, try the carrot cake or chocolate raspberry torte. Afterwards, take a spin out to Schoodic Point and work it all off by climbing along the rocks.

**FISHERMAN'S INN
  RESTAURANT**
963-5585.
Newman St., Winter
  Harbor.
Open June through
  early Oct.
Price: Inexpensive to
  Moderate.
Cuisine: Seafood.
Serving: L, D.
Credit Cards: MC, V.

Lobster served seven ways — from boiled and served whole to lobster pie and lobster rolls — and other local seafood, as well as staples like chopped sirloin with mushrooms and a salad bar with limited but crisp vegetables, lettuce, coleslaw and potato salad. There are no frills in this modest dining room lined with spartan wooden booths and linoleum-topped tables. And the service could have been friendlier. But that was a little easier to overlook at the meal's sweet finale —hot, gingery Indian pudding and a nicely eggy custard pie.

RESTAURANTS — EAST OF SCHOODIC

Eastport

FLAG OFFICER'S MESS
853-6043.
73 Water St., Eastport.
Closed: Mon.; Jan.–March.
Price: Moderate.
Cuisine: Seafood.
Serving: L, D.
Credit Cards: AE, V, MC.
Reservations: Yes.
Handicap Access: Yes
  (downstairs).
Special Features: Harbor
  view.

The dining room upstairs is actually a small hall with a high ceiling and windows almost as big as the view of the fishing fleet in Eastport's harbor. All that makes it a great place to sit and watch the fog roll in. The salmon doesn't get any fresher than what they serve here: it's brought in from salmon farms out in nearby Cobscook Bay. Both it and the scallops are fresh and sweet and would be divine without so much butter. The salad bar is limited, but fresh. The bar downstairs is a popular night spot.

ROLANDO'S
853-2334.
118 Water St., Eastport.
Closed: Mon.; Tues. in
  winter.
Price: Expensive.
Cuisine: Italian.
Serving: D.
Credit Cards: MC, V.
Reservations:
  Recommended.

Hearty Italian cooking is what's on the burner at Rolando's. Not that you'd guess it. This 19th-century captain's home is pure New England with its cozy rooms and antiques. The menu runs from pizzas, calzones and gyros to fancier preparations like stuffed shrimp, several versions of fettuccine Alfredo, char-broiled steaks and chicken. There are also such southern Italian standbys as spaghetti, lasagna and ravioli, which with the meaty marinara, meatballs or sausage are the picks of the house. Desserts include the sinful Chocolate Purgatory Pie, cream cheese pie and cannolis.

WACO DINER
853-4046.
Bank Sq., Eastport.
Closed: Sun. L and D.
Price: Inexpensive.
Cuisine: American diner.
Serving: B, L, D.

It's tempting to mispronounce the name of this place, but just try it and a dozen people will correct you. Wack-o is the right way to say it, and the name is suitable for this quirky little spot. Lunch counter standards — clam chowder, corned beef hash, grilled frankfurters, fish and chips and all sorts of pies — make up the bulk of the menu, but there are some surprises: scallop stew, tuna noodle casserole, fried clam rolls, homemade English muffin toast and Grapenut pudding. Best of all, the place looks as if it's been around for eons with worn vinyl stools, old-timey booths and counter all crammed in a space the size of a postage stamp. Service may be a little surly, but that only adds to the charm.

Machias

HELEN'S RESTAURANT
255-8423.
Rte. 1, Machias.
Open all year.
Price: Moderate.
Cuisine: American.
Serving: B, L, D.
Handicap Access: Yes.

As the tour buses in the parking lot suggest, Helen's, famous coast to coast, is very good at hooking hungry travelers and putting up with any odd request you throw at them. For them it's faster to do it than think about it. All fried foods are cooked in cholesterol-free oil, which means you can then go ahead and get your dose from one of their fine cream pies. We had a rib-sticking pork sandwich with homemade mashed potatoes and gravy because Helen's makes you feel that way. That feeling stuck all the way to Eastport. There's good parking.

MICMAC FARM
255-3008.
Off Rte. 92, which is off
Rte. 1, Machiasport.
Closed: Mon.
Price: Expensive.
Cuisine: Country gourmet.
Serving: D.
Reservations: Required.

This 18th-century farmhouse may be out of the way (that is to say, at the end of a rutted dirt road), but it's worth seeking out for the sheer romance of the place. Flickering candles give a refined glow to the rustic rooms with wide floorboards and low beams. There are usually five dinner choices; the night we were there they included Filet Mignon with Bordelaise Sauce; Shrimp-and-Crab Stuffed Sole; Chicken Piccata; and Beef Stronganoff. Desserts are inspired creations on the order of their light-as-air Bavarian Cream and Meringue Glacé. Machiasport is dry, so if you want wine or beer with dinner, you'll have to bring your own.

SANDWICH SHOP
255-8032.
Rte. 1, Machias.
Open every day.
Price: Inexpensive.
Cuisine: American.
Serving: B, L, D.
Handicap Access: Yes.
Special Features: Home-
    baked breads.

Recently expanded, but the servers here are not quite as skilled as the waitresses at Helen's; they also don't yet have that road-weary look. This is a small, step-up-and-order operation that focuses on quality. All the sandwiches are made on homemade bread and are the type that remind you of the simple comforts of home. They make a nice PB&J. We'd also recommend their chicken burgers and crab meat roll. We finished with a piece of Blueberry Spice Cake and coffee. The case is full of other wholesome baked goods, including great hamburger buns.

Maine Food Festivals

As we said before, Mainers love to eat. They also love to celebrate food. Here is a list of some of the annual food-centered celebrations on the coast:

Annual Damariscotta River Oyster Festival (563-8340). Mid-July. Ancient inhabitants used to feast on oysters here, and people are expected to enjoy the local harvest at this annual festival well into the next century.
Annual Winter Harbor Lobster Festival (963-7638; 800-231-3008 out-of-state). Mid-August. Almost as famous as Rockland's Lobster Festival (see below). A main attraction are the lobster boat races.
Bay Festival, Belfast (338-2896). Last week in July. This used to be called the Broiler Festival on account of its being a big chicken town. There used to be so much chicken here, you would think twice before visiting. These days, most chickens have moved out of town, but they still celebrate their broilers.

Maine Lobster Festival, Rockland (596-0376). First weekend in August. A parade, pageant and the world's largest lobster cooker. This festival has been famous for more than 45 years.

Wild Blueberry Festival, Machias (255-4402). Mid-August. Two days celebrating one of the state's biggest crops. This is the home of the wild blueberry.

Yarmouth Clam Festival (846-3984). Third week in July. Every year for almost 30 years, the folks in Yarmouth pay tribute to the clam. They eat lots of fried ones, then they go take a ride on the roller coaster at the midway.

Diana Lynn Doherty

People enjoying themselves at one of the many strawberry festivals on the coast.

FOOD PURVEYORS

BAKERIES

South Coast

Whistling Wings Farm (282-1146; 427 West St., Biddeford). Berries from this farm and kitchen end up on tables all over the world. The jams, jellies and syrups contain no preservatives or juice concentrates, and in summer the bakery offers berry sweets for immediate consumption.

Porpoise Pastries (967-5846; Main St., Cape Porpoise). They're open from spring to mid-October and are worth the ride for their blueberry cream cheese Danish, homemade English muffins, bagels, pastries and cakes.

Chase Hill Bakery (967-2283; Chase Hill Rd., Kennebunk). An unassuming gray clapboard house with old-fashioned bakery cases and a table or two. They sell comforting chicken pot pies, breads, cakes and pastries.

The Cookie Loft (967-2812; 46 Dock Sq., Kennebunkport). Grab a cookie or cake to go. They'll even decorate when you have a birthday on the road. Or stop for cappuccino on the back deck by the river.

Bread & Roses (646-4227; 28A Main St., Ogunquit). Fresh pastries and bread baked on the spot.

Danny's Deli & Bake Shop (934-9332; 4 Temple Ave., Old Orchard Beach). This is where the New England Baptists come in the summer for fresh baked goods and sandwiches to go.

Casco Bay

The Port Bakehouse (773-2217; 205 Commercial St., Portland). You'll find their wholesome rolls and buttery cakes and tortes in stores and restaurants around Portland or you can go straight to the source. They make a different bread every day of the week. Everybody likes the prairie bread because it's packed with nuts and grains and pumpkin seeds.

Midcoast

Kristina's (442-8577; 160 Center St., Bath). Pastries and tortes to fuel your way up the coast. They also make great French toast for a sit-down breakfast.

The Cookie Gallery (236-6011; 3 Sharp's Wharf, Camden). Cookies, coffee and homemade ice cream cookie sandwiches.

The Donut Hole (963-7074; Main St., Winter Harbor). Homemade donuts, pies, and pastries. Also a good spot to grab a grilled cheese, take in the view of Henry's Cove and maybe run into Tom Selleck.

Down East/Acadia

Cottage Street Bakery and Deli (288-3010; 59 Cottage St., Bar Harbor). You can have a sit-down meal here or you can grab a sweet to go. We weren't nuts about their muffins, but everything else was pretty good.

Left Bank Bakery & Cafe (374-2201; Blue Hill). Handmade, homemade bagels, peasant bread and European pastries are baked fresh here every day.

East of Schoodic

Arlene's Harbor Side (963-2311; Corea Harbor, Corea). Arlene makes great pies and a superb cheese roll. During the summer she serves breakfast and lunch on the patio of her tiny harborside home.

The Sugar Scoop (546-7048; Main St., Milbridge). Pies, cookies, squares and a heavenly bakery smell.

BREWERIES AND WINERIES

Casco Bay

Geary Brewing Company (878-2337; 38 Evergreen Dr., Portland). They brew a fine ale here, and if you can't make it to the brewery you can find it at almost any grocery store or gourmet shop in the area.

Gritty Mcduff's (772-2739; 396 Fore St., Portland). They brew their own downstairs.

Down East / Acadia

Bartlett Maine Estate Winery (546-2408; Old Rte. 1, Gouldsboro). A tasting here is pretty relaxed. Honey wine, apple wine and wines of pear, blueberry, raspberry. Robert and Kathe Bartlett have been making their fruit wines since 1983. We especially like their dry pear and apple combination. Weekends in May/June to October: Tuesday to Saturday 10 to 5, Sunday noon to 5; November to December: Tuesday to Saturday 10 to 5, Sunday noon to 4. Closed holidays.

Down East Country Wines (667-6965; Rte. 3, Bar Harbor). More than 40,000 bottles of fruit wines are produced in this old blacksmith's barn. Semi-sweet or medium dry wild blueberry, spiced apple and blue blush, a blend of apples and blueberries. Tours are available.

CANDY AND ICE CREAM

South Coast

Sweet Temptations (283-4755; 364A Elm St., Rte. 1, Biddeford). They make their fresh fruit yogurt to order.

Harbor Candy Shop (646-8078; 26 Main St., Ogunquit). European-style chocolates are made and sold here in a very elegant atmosphere.

The Goldenrod (363-2621; York Beach). A vacation at the beach wouldn't be the same without saltwater taffy. They make it right here and call it "kisses." Watch it being made or grab an ice cream soda in their old-fashioned soda fountain.

Casco Bay

Browns Apiaries (829-5994; 239 Greely Rd., Cumberland). They raise bees here and sell the sweet by-products. Honey, strained and with the comb, in half-pound to one gallon sizes, candles, honey candy and bee keeping supplies. They're open year round, five days a week, but it's best to call ahead.

Ben & Jerry's Ice Cream (865-3407; 83 Main St., Freeport). This grew from a one-room shack on the curb outside L. L. Bean to a much larger one room shack, big enough to accommodate long lines in all kinds of weather. Sometimes you need ice cream after a long day shopping.

Wilbur's Chocolate Shoppe (865-6129; 13 Bow St., Freeport). All-natural chocolate — creams, berry flavors or rich and dark. They have a hotline for chocoholic emergencies: 729- 4462.

Midcoast

Round Top Ice Cream (563-5993; Bus. Rte. 1, Damariscotta). For years they made ice cream at this dairy. Thirty flavors. Now they make music and theater here as well.

The Downeast Ice Cream Factory (633-5178; Rte. 96, East Boothbay). They make the ice cream, you make the sundaes. They also make homemade candies.

Miss Plum's (596-6946; Rte. 1, Rockport). A reporter friend of ours thinks this is the best ice cream on the coast. They also sell sorbet, frozen yogurt and baked desserts.

East of Schoodic

K-K-K-Katies (454-8446; Rte. 1, Mill Cove, Robbinston). They hand dip all of their homemade chocolates and use recipes from well-loved Passamaquoddy Bay candymakers of old. Check out their Maine potato candy. It's better than it sounds.

COFFEE STORES

Casco Bay

Green Mountain Coffee Roasters (773-4475; 15 Temple St., Portland). They were Portland's first roast-and-serve place and are credited with making yuppies and normal people alike dedicated to their brews.

Portland Coffee Roasting Co. (761-9525; 111 Commercial St., Portland). They roast their own here, and we particularly like their French roast, rich and buttery. Get your coffee here by the cup or the pound before you head down the street to the ferry.

DELIS AND TAKE-OUT

South Coast

Gitano's (967-3564; Dock Sq., Kennebunkport). They have pizza and other Italian specialties to go. Good bets are the pesto and chocolate-hazelnut torte.

Old Salt's Pantry (967-4966; Dock Sq., Kennebunkport). Don't be fooled by its size. This tiny deli offers a huge menu of take-out from sandwiches, subs and burgers to gourmet tidbits, wine and beer.

Einstein's (646-5252; 2 Shore Rd., Ogunquit). Eat-in or take out in this deli on the main drag. A favorite breakfast spot for residents.

Anthony's Food Shop (363-2322; 679 Rte. 1, York). Beer, apples, pizza, but best is a selection of great Green Mountain coffees like Columbian Supremo with real cream. There are small sizes for short hops and large sizes for long hauls. If you didn't get a decent cup of coffee for breakfast, stop here and rectify the situation.

Casco Bay

Portland Wine & Cheese (772-4647; Middle and Exchange sts., Portland). Great deli sandwiches in the basement of an Old Port office building. Eat it there or get it to go. They also have a nice selection of wines.

Midcoast

Camden Deli (236-8343; 37 Main St., Camden). New York-style sandwiches, wine and beer, and great desserts.

FAST FOOD
South Coast

Bob's Clam Hut (439-4233; Rte. 1, Kittery). Fried clams, sweet and steaming, are served here year round. The ultimate in finger-fast food.
Fancy That (646-4118; 7 Main St., Ogunquit). Good, fast sandwiches. Friends of ours are regulars here.

Casco Bay

Mark's (corner of Exchange and Middle sts., Portland). Mark is out there through all kinds of weather selling his dogs and smoked sausages from a little red cart. There's a park next door for you to sit in, if it's warm enough.
The Good Egg Cafe (773-0801; 705 Congress St., Portland). Where all the good people go including the police chief. Great eggs, great muffins. A coffee and muffin to go is only a buck.
McMag's (871-9019; 230 Commercial St., Portland). Fast food on the working waterfront. Great fresh fish sandwiches, steamed mussels and clams to go.
Porthole (774-3448; 20 Custom House Wharf, Portland). The place for a quick breakfast or lunch before heading out to the Casco Islands for the day (the ferry used to leave from here, but now you have to walk a few blocks down the street).
Raff's and Emily K's (773-7763; 285 Forest Ave., Portland). Wholesome fast food: organic beef burgers; baked and grilled chicken; rotisserie chicken; and an organic salad bar in two adjoining restaurants.

Midcoast

Brud's Hot Dogs (East Side, Boothbay Harbor). Hot dogs, fast and inexpensive. Since 1948. Sold out of a cart on the east side of town.

Lady Millville Store (236-6570; 113 Washington St., Rte. 105, Camden). Fresh dough pizza, subs, burgers, hot dogs, even fast food seafood and chicken.

El Taco Tico (594-7568; Main St., Rockland). Fast and cheap, their Mexican food is addictive.

Wasses (594-7472; 2 North Main St., Rockland). *The Washington Post* likes their hot dogs. Their "waffles" are pretty good, too — vanilla ice milk, Spanish peanuts and thick fudge in a crispy waffle cone.

Michael Loomis

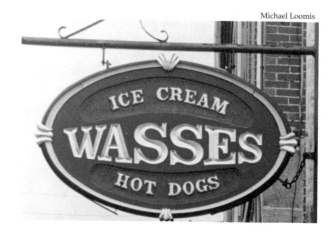

Wasses, famous for its chili dogs and homemade ice cream sandwiches.

Cod End (372-6782; near town landing; Tenants Harbor). From Memorial Day through mid-October they serve up fresh, fast seafood, including good lobster rolls and chowder. Take it with you or eat it on their picnic tables.

Down East/Acadia

Bubba's (288-5871; 30 Cottage St., Bar Harbor). Soups, sandwiches and a full bar, for those who choose to linger. You wouldn't guess by the name that this would be a small art deco palace, would you?

Epi Sub & Pizza (288-3507; 8 Cottage St., Bar Harbor). Homemade calzone, pizza, pasta and other quick stuff like crabmeat rolls, quiche and salads.

The Deacon Seat (244-9229; Clark Point Rd., Southwest Harbor). They serve breakfast and lunch here from 5 a.m. to 4:30 p.m. every day except Sunday. Eat it as fast as you want.

East of Schoodic

The Crossroads (726-5053; Rte. 1, Pembroke). Located at the site of an old iron works, this little carry-out attached to a roadside motel serves the best lobster roll around.

GOURMET FOOD STORES

South Coast

Chickadee Acres Sugar Bush (361-1922; Josiah Norton Rd., Cape Neddick). Fresh maple syrup. By appointment only.

The Tipsy Mouse (967-3853; Chase Hill Rd., Kennebunk). Lilliputian, but crammed with wheels of Camembert and brie and a nice selection of wines.

An inviting window display at a Maine island general store.

State Development Office

Casco Bay

Micucci's (775-1854; 45 India St., Portland). A tiny Italian grocer at the foot of Munjoy Hill, they have all the fixings for an authentic Italian feast, including fresh mozzarella on Wednesdays.

Micucci's

Micucci's in Portland is the place to get the fixings for an authentic Italian picnic.

Midcoast

Weatherbird Trading Company (563-8993; Main and Church sts., Damariscotta). Locally made *patés*, imported beers and French scents in a 1754 saltbox cape.

Wicked Wild Maine Preserves (882-7772; Rte. 27, North Edgecomb). Jams and jellies for toast or cooking; some are made with no sugar at all. Especially interesting are their hot sauces and their run-for-water mustard. Call ahead.

Ducktrap River Fish Farm (763-3960, 800-828-3825 out-of-state; Pitcher Pond Rd., Lincolnville). Naturally smoked Atlantic salmon and rainbow trout raised here and at fish farms nearby. Open year round, Monday through Friday. We like their smoked bluefish and scallops best.

State of Maine Cheese Company (596-6601; 75 Front St., Rockland). Peter Kress, cheesemaker, is responsible for these distinct cheeses: Penobscot cheddar, Katahdin cheddar, Cumberland smoked, Aroostook Jack and more, all made from all natural Maine milk.

Kohn's Smokehouse Inc. (372-8412; Rte. 131, St. George). They make and sell fine smoked meats and seafood. Bacon, sausage, bratwurst, salami, even poultry. In the winter they're open Monday through Saturday; in the summer seven days a week.

Great Eastern Mussel Farms (372-6317; Long Cove Rd., Tenants Harbor). They've taken the lowly mussel and cultivated it. Call ahead and ask for a tour of their plant.

Morse's Sauerkraut (832-5569; Rte. 220, Waldoboro), and **Morse's Sauerkraut II** (563-8833; "Sauerkraut Alley" off Main St., Damariscotta). Every once in a while they run a simple ad in the paper that says, "Kraut's ready." Maybe eating sauerkraut wouldn't be considered a chore if it were all as good as the fresh stuff made here. It's so popular, they've expanded to a second carry-out location in Damariscotta. Both places garnish their kraut with knockwurst, bratwurst, kielbasa and the humble dog. Sandwiches available.

Mystique (832-5136; Friendship St., Waldoboro). Open daily 4 p.m. to 7 p.m. They sell French-style goat cheeses, smoked *chevon*, which is goat meat, goat salami, herbs and scented geraniums. This is all raised locally and the goats providing the milk and meat are registered.

Foggy Ridge Gamebird Farm (273-2357; West Branch Rd., Warren). They raise, dress and smoke game birds. They also sell live ones. Pheasants, partridges and quails. Call for an appointment.

Down East/Acadia

Lunt & Lunt (334-2922; Frenchboro Island). The tin shed behind their dock is where Frenchboro Island Seafood packs mason jars of lobster delicacies for Bloomingdale's in New York City. The labels say, "We catch our seafood in the waters around our home and cook it ourselves — only 24 jars at a time — in kitchens, not factories." They do all this on an island that is mostly owned by the Rockefeller family.

East of Schoodic

Jim's Smoked Salmon (853-4831; Washington St., Eastport). Jim smokes Atlantic salmon raised on farms in Cobscook Bay. He will also wrap your salmon gift in a beautifully crafted wood box that he builds himself.

J. W. Raye & Co. (853-4451; Rte. 190, Eastport). They've been making mustard here since 1903, first for the sardine canning industry that used to flourish here, now for the mass market. Visit their gift shop or get a tour and learn how they make the stuff at the Mustard Museum.

Maine Wild Blueberry Company (255-8364; Elm St., Machias). These people have the biggest wild blueberry business in the world. You can buy frozen, canned and dried blueberries right from the factory. They call the dried ones "wild chews." They taste like raisins but like blueberries.

The joys of a farmer's market in Maine.

Tom Hindman

HEALTH FOOD AND FARM MARKETS

South Coast

Haycroft (439-6522; Picott Rd., Kittery). Fresh and freezer lamb by reservation. They raise New Zealand Romneys and Black and White Finn sheep. They also have strawberries in season.

A. Z.'s Fresh Foods Markets (934-2097; 11 Heath St., Old Orchard Beach). A good place to get healthy at lunch.

Casco Bay

Basics Natural Food Store (767-2803; 537 Shore Rd., Cape Elizabeth). Whole and health foods, organic meats and poultry, including a knockout organic bacon. There's a small coffee shop to the rear.

Whole Grocer (774-7711; 118 Congress St., Portland). They call the people who shop here "granolas." Okay, it's fine to have a little fun with folks, but those whole-grain lovers really know how to live. This place has an absolutely beautiful fresh fruit and vegetable department.

Wolfe's Neck Farm (865-4469; Wolf Neck Rd., off Flying Point Rd., Freeport). Lean, delicious organic beef and lamb raised on a beautiful saltwater farm run by the state university system. They ship to New England and elsewhere, but it's better yet to take the trip down the long dirt road and get a slab to thaw out for a seaside barbecue. This farm has been operating for more than one hundred years and selling natural beef since 1959.

Midcoast

Belfast Co-op Store (338-2532; 67 Main St., Belfast). Whole foods, local produce, fresh bread and other baked goods. Bona fide good things brought to you in a macrobiotic town.

Fiddler's Green Farm (338-3568; Lincolnville Ave., Rte. 52, Belfast). Baking mixes and hot cereals, 100 percent organic; buckwheat and whole wheat pancakes; oats 'n' barley pancake and baking mix; buttermilk spice cake and cookie mix; and Penobscot porridge. They also sell organic vegetables. Open May to October.

The Last Stop Poultry Farm (273-4029; Rte. 1, Boothbay). Fresh native broilers and roasting chickens. Fresh native turkeys. Homemade chicken and turkey pot pies.

School House Farm (273-2440; Rte. 1, Boothbay). Late June through Thanksgiving. Seven days a week. They raise and sell 24 varieties of apples, six of plums and four of pears. They also have fresh vegetables in season.

Maine Maid Products (563-8904; Lessner Rd., Bristol). They sell regular, low-sugar and no-sugar jams, as well as a line of gourmet liquors. Pickles, relishes and sauces. It's best to call ahead.

The Green Grocer (563-3229; Rte. 1, Lincolnville). Choice fruit, native produce in season, honey, State of Maine cheese, homemade jellies, maple syrup and baked goods. They also have an ice cream parlor. Open from the end of June to early October.

Apple Hill Farm Orchard (563-5415; Rte. 215, Newcastle). While you're out leaf peeping, this is a good place to stop for a crispy Mac, Cortland, Red Delicious, Northern Spy or some cider, apple butter or dried apple rings. They're open mid-September through Christmas, all day on the weekends, but call ahead during the week.

Fresh Off The Farm (236-3260; Rte. 1, Rockport). Native produce and berries in season; apples and cider in season; natural foods, vitamins, herbs, jams, jellies, maple syrup and candy, pickles, relishes, blueberry syrup, chutney, mustards, dried beans and local honey year round. Lots of things to take home to your friends.

Down East/Acadia

Hay's Farm Stand (Rte. 172, Surry Hill, Blue Hill). From July to October, Monday through Saturday, they sell certified organic vegetables, strawberries, raspberries, tomatoes, corn, potatoes and lamb. They also sell farm sausage, jams and their homemade Old Goat Soap.

Darthia Farm (963-7771; West Bay Rd., Rte 186, Gouldsboro). They offer a selection of organic fruits, vegetables and herbs, as well as homemade jams, vinegars, pesto, yogurt, herb cheeses and fresh butter.

Entropia Farms (288-4930; Rte. 3, Bar Harbor). Open year round. They sell six varieties of garlic, as well as chemical-free beef, vegetables, forest products, eggs and pond grown trout.

H.O.M.E. (469-7961; Rte. 1, Orland). It stands for Homeworkers Organized for More Employment and, in addition to crafts, they sell fresh vegetables in season and storage crops like potatoes and squash. They also have a good selection of locally grown spices, flour in bulk, grains and dried fruit.

East of Schoodic

Cross Farm Road (497-2640; Off Rte. 187, Jonesport). Organic isn't a fad here. They've been farming that way for more than 20 years and are certified. More than 200 types of vegetables, 50 kinds of potatoes and unusual salad greens, squashes and onions.

Little Valley Ranch (255-8230; Rte. 1A, Whitneyville). Native beef by the side, quarter or whole if you have room. They also raise farm fresh brown or colored araucana eggs. Blueberries and raspberries in season. Call ahead.

CHAPTER SIX

By The Sea, By The Sea
RECREATION

*Windjamming on the
schooner* Mary Day, *based
in Camden Harbor.*

Tom Hindman

Many of the recreational opportunities along the coast and on its islands center around, you guessed it, water. Your time spent here will likely include swimming in water; sailing, canoeing or kayaking on it; windjamming through it; camping by it, or biking, hiking, climbing, horseback riding or cross-country skiing to get a view of it.

Of course, there are many other things to do. The coast also has its share of skating rinks, bowling alleys and water slides, and in this chapter we will explore many different possibilities for you and your family.

Fun on the coast used to be a one-season affair. Nineteenth-century tourists came here to enjoy cool breezes when cities to the south — Boston, New York and Philadelphia — sweltered in the summer sun. French Canadians early on discovered Old Orchard Beach, the closest sand beach of note to Montreal and Quebec. Today the Maine coast holds plenty of chances to enjoy yourself the year round. Although most people choose to hike and camp here in the summer, many know to take advantage of the off seasons and avoid the crowds. Leaf peeping has become a popular pastime for autumn visitors. Several resorts and parks have extensive cross-country ski trails. There's even downhill skiing at the Snow Bowl in Camden. Spring is mountain bikes and kayaks and the chance to have Acadia National Park all to yourself.

Whatever season you visit, remember the weather. The outlook often changes quickly, and the combination of ocean wind and water can make 40 degrees Fahrenheit seem much colder. Bring along a good selection of warm clothes and rain gear (See "Climate and What to Wear" in *Information,* Chapter Eight).

Acadia National Park

Acadia National Park on Mount Desert Island is the most visited place in Maine. It has more than 100 miles of trails through forests and past lakes; eight climbing peaks, most suitable for family hikes; great biking on old carriage roads; camping facilities; wonderful views; good rock climbing, canoeing and cross-country skiing; lovely beaches and the only fjord on the eastern seaboard.

You can wander through the Wild Gardens of Acadia and see over 200 species of plants, trees and shrubs indigenous to the island; climb to the summit of Cadillac Mountain, the highest point on the eastern seaboard, and enjoy the grand views, including Frenchman Bay; swim at freshwater Echo Lake or saltwater Sand Beach; see the high tide surge at Thunder Hole, a tidal cavern carved by wave action with water spouts as high as 40 feet, and sea kayak along the New England coast.

Part of Acadia National Park is on the Isle au Haut, a lightly populated island that is eight miles out to sea from Stonington, where there is good biking, hiking, swimming and fishing.

A third part of Acadia is Schoodic Point, at the tip of the Schoodic Peninsula in Winter Harbor, where there are great views of the rocky coastline from hiking trails that ascend to overlooks, and a scenic 13-mile biking loop.

AUTO RACING

The chance to see auto racing is rare on the coast. *Beech Ridge Motor Speedway* (883-6030; 70 Holmes Rd., Scarborough) features stock car racing on a 1/3 mile track. Starting time is 1:33 p.m. (to let you know they run the show like a well- oiled machine) beginning the last Sunday in April and running until mid-May, then again from the Sunday after Labor Day until the third week in September. Starting time between May and September is 7:03 p.m. every Saturday evening.

BALLOONING

Most balloon flights originating near the coast are overland. Balloonists talk about one pilot who often dares saltwater flights. He and his passengers have been rescued three times.

Even if the winds are blowing inland, you are almost assured a good view from the White Mountains to the shore. Spring flights are tricky — and often canceled — due to the changeable Maine weather. September and October tend to be the busiest months because of foliage flights, so be sure to make your reservations early. Experienced balloonists say winter flights are the most spectacular, when the air takes on a crystalline clarity. Dress warmly, though; it will be much colder at an 800-foot altitude than it is on the ground.

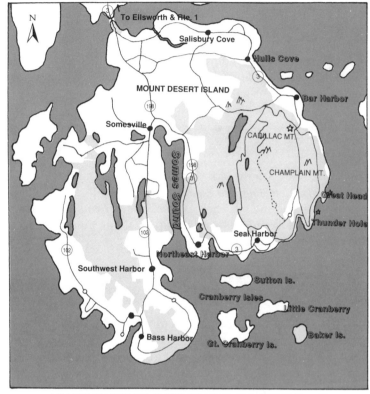

ACADIA NATIONAL PARK ON MOUNT DESERT ISLAND

ACADIA ON ISLE AU HAUT

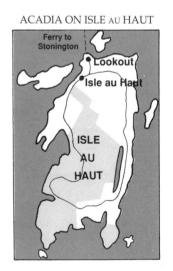

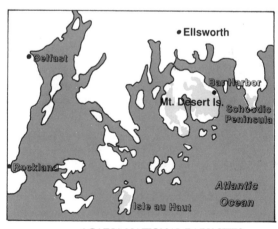

ACADIA NATIONAL PARK SITES

ACADIA NATIONAL PARK

The Casco Bay region is a hotbed for balloonophiles: for what it's worth, **Balloon Sports** (761-8373; 145 Glenwood Ave., Portland) boasts having "Coastal Maine's oldest balloon pilot." Pilot Bob Schuerer of **Freeport Balloon** (865-1712; Beech Hill Rd., Freeport) offers intimate champagne flights (just two passengers and the pilot). **Hot Fun — Manned Balloon Flights** (761-1735; Portland) offers flights year round as well as balloon gift certificates.

BASEBALL

T he Boston Red Sox are the closest professional home team. Locally there is the **Northern New England Semipro League** with teams in South Portland, Portland, Bath and inland. There is also an **American Legion** league. Both play a full summer schedule. For information about times and locations of games, consult the nearest daily or weekly newspaper.

BEACHES

M aine's beaches are the crown jewels of the coast. Almost all are flanked by the rugged terrain that gives the coast its distinct beauty and character — jagged outcroppings of metamorphic rock, sheer cliffs and exhilarating Atlantic surf. More than 40 percent of the visitors to the coast make the South Coast their destination. That's where most of the sand beaches are, and **Old Orchard Beach** and the long, broad stretches of sand at **York** and **Ogunquit** are the most famous southern Maine beaches. These beaches have lovely sandy bottoms perfect for swimming. Mainers will tell you the water's a little cool.

We have our favorites. The swimming is great at **Ferry Beach,** in Scarborough, where water over a long, shallow sandbar warms up early in the summer and is kept protected by Prouts Neck. **Higgins Beach** in West Scarborough is a beautiful, broad stretch of sand bound by a modest, old-fashioned summer village (there is no boardwalk in sight and dogs run free after 4 p.m.). Then there's **Jasper Beach** near Bucks Harbor, where the surface is littered with almost perfectly round, palm-sized pieces of granite and crystalline quartz. Further Down East, the beaches become colorful. At **Perry,** the beach is deep red; at **Bailey's Mistake** it's black, and at **Jonesport,** it's brilliant white. These beaches are separated by only 40 miles.

Mainers work hard to keep their beaches and shore beautiful. According to *Down East* magazine, in 1990 more than 300 volunteers picked their way along 190 miles of shoreline and came away with 18,000 cigarette filters, 12,000 pieces of glass, 9,000 pieces of Styrofoam, 8,000 lengths of plastic rope, a tent, a toilet, a door, plastic eggs, flowered slippers, a Barbie doll, five grocery carts, a rug, a beer keg, a sled, a motorcycle, eight surfboards, a bag of onions, a bathrobe, twenty cough-syrup bottles and a dead horse. Mercifully, they cleaned all that up, so they and visitors alike can truly enjoy the beach. Below, we've listed the major beaches, but we can't tell you how to get to all of Maine's beaches. All along the coast you will find dozens of lovely little sand beaches tucked here and there, many of them with public access. Just keep your eyes open.

Protecting Maine's beaches.

State Development Office

South Coast

Crescent Beach and Seapoint beaches; Seapoint Rd., Kittery. Crescent Beach, a 625-yard sand beach and its 550-yard sister beach Seapoint across a small peninsula are nice, but have limited parking.

Drakes Island and Laudholm beaches; Rte. 1 to Drakes Island Rd., Wells. This is really one beach with two names, in addition to being a well-kept secret among South Coast beachgoers. It's comparatively quiet here in the height of the summer, even when nearby Moody is jammed. It is 940 yds. with accompanying saltwater farm and nature center; limited parking.

Ferry and Western beaches; Rte. 207 to Ferry Rd., Scarborough. Actually three beaches, including two that wrap around a rocky point and lead up to tony Prouts Neck. The tide rips right at the point, and at high tide you can almost reach out and touch the lobster boats in the harbor. You can let your dog run free after 4 p.m. Total of more than 1,700 yds.; limited parking.

Ferry Beach State Park; Rte. 9, Saco. A fine sand beach that stretches more than 4,500 yds. It is part of a 117-acre state park with all the facilities, including picnic tables, toilets and bathhouse. Fee is charged at gate. Parking.

Fortunes Rocks Beach; Rte. 208, Biddeford. Long sand beach that's great for swimming. 3,740 yds.; parking limited.

Gooch's Beach; Rte. 9 to Sea Rd., then left onto Beach Ave. past Kennebunk Beach, Kennebunk. The beach of choice for Kennebunkport residents and summer people including surfers, this is a crescent-shaped sand and shingle beach with a rocky point; 1,300 yds.; parking is limited to those with permits, so take the trolley. It's well worth the ride.

Goose Rocks Beach; Rte. 9 to Dyke Rd., then left onto King's Hwy., Kennebunkport. Lovely beach that attracts both swimmers and birdwatchers (there's a salt marsh at the southeast end); 3,600 yds.; parking limited.

Hills Beach; off Rtes. 9 and 208, Biddeford. An excellent, if short, swimming beach, on a 530-yd. sand spit protecting Maine's largest tidal basin. People like to birdwatch here (see below). Facilities nearby; parking limited.

Kennebunk Beach; Rte. 9 to Sea Rd., then left onto Beach Ave., Kennebunk. Sand and shingle beach popular among families and surfers. It's hard to park here, and illegal if you don't have a sticker; take the trolley instead; 820 yds.

Long Beach; Rte. 1A, York, and **Short Sands;** Rte. 1A, York Beach. Long Beach, at 2180 yds., and Short Sands, 410 yds., are two of the South Coast's most popular beaches. The surfers like the waves. Parents like Short Sands, because it is near the heart of York Beach, so tired young beach bums can easily refuel with a snack. There are lifeguards and restrooms at both. Parking is limited, so arrive early.

Moody Beach; Rte. 1 to Bourne Rd., then right onto Ocean Ave., Wells. A couple of years ago in a heated courtroom battle, residents tried to cut off public access to the beach. In a blow to the coastal aristocracy, they failed. It is 2,750 yds.; facilities nearby; fee for parking.

Ogunquit Beach; Rte. 1 to Beach St., Ogunquit. People love the sand here. It's refined, white and abundant (1,620 yds.). One local newspaper describes this as "very popular with the gay community"; another publication says that it is "near summer art colony." We call it fun. Facilities; fee for parking.

Old Orchard and Surfside beaches; Rte. 9, Old Orchard Beach. Some call this the Canadian Riviera, and more often than not the language spoken here is French. Lovely fine white sand beaches with a total length 3,320 yds. Bathhouse. Fee for parking.

Parsons and Crescent Surf beaches; Rte. 9 to Parson's Beach Rd., Kennebunk. You get to these two pretty beaches along a private way owned by the Parson family. Total is 1,700 yds.; no facilities; limited parking.

Pine Point and Grand beaches; Rte. 9, Scarborough. Two fine white sand beaches and sand spit totalling 2,500 yds. Facilities nearby; fee for parking.

Scarborough Beach State Park; Rte. 207, Scarborough. This is a barrier beach and dunes that protect a freshwater marsh. It's so popular among swimmers and surfers that it often fills to overflowing by noon on a hot day; 2,060 yds.; picnic tables, grills, bathhouse, fishing; fee for parking.

Wells Beach; Rte. 1 to Mile Rd., then left onto Atlantic Ave., Wells. Motels and condos line the beach; 4,000 yds.; facilities; fee for parking.

Casco Bay

Crescent Beach State Park; Rte. 77, Cape Elizabeth. The *Maine Times* calls this "one of Maine's best family beaches." Sand and stone beach; 1,560 yds.; picnic tables, snack bar, fishing.

Winslow Memorial Park; Rte. 1 onto South Freeport Rd. (at the Big Indian) and follow to Staples Rd., South Freeport. Nestled in the middle of a pretty, immaculate town-run park and camping area, this is another great beach for the family. The small, man-made beach is sheltered although untended by a lifeguard. Picnic tables, playground, rest rooms; entrance fee charged.

Midcoast

Pemaquid Beach Park; off Rte. 130, New Harbor. About a half-mile long and backed by dunes. There's a bathhouse, picnic tables, rest rooms. Entrance fee.

Reid State Park; Rte. 127 to Seguinland Rd., Georgetown. A half-mile open barrier spit, this is another great beach. There's a salt marsh, sand dunes, rocky ledges, tidal pools, a bathhouse, picnic tables, fireplaces and a snack bar. Decent parking. Entrance fee.

Crescent Beach; Crescent Beach Rd., Owl's Head. Popular swimming beach near summer colony. Length, 1,100 yards. Nearby facilities; limited parking.

Popham Beach State Park; Rte. 209, Phippsburg. Not only fine sand, but a fine beach. In fact, one of the finest. More than two miles long; there are picnic tables, rocky outcrops and tide pools and plenty of parking, which fills up quickly on a hot day. Entrance fee.

Sandy Point Beach; Stockton Springs. About a mile long; there's not much here except beach. No facilities and little parking.

Down East/Acadia

Sand Beach; off Park Loop Rd., near Cadillac Cliffs, Acadia National Park. Possibly more people have driven by this famed pocket beach than any beach in the country. It's on the Loop Road. There are no facilities. There are so few parking spaces and so many people who want to stop, they sometimes have to close it off during the height of the summer. It's a beauty. The sand is actually shell fragments. Entrance fee to national park.

Lamoine Beach; Lamoine State Park, Rte. 184, Lamoine. Best swimming beach in the area with great views of Mount Desert Island across the bay. Picnicking; camping; no bathhouse; parking; entrance fee.

East of Schoodic

Jasper Beach; off Starboard Rd., Bucks Harbor. This beach is made up entirely of polished pebbles. It's beautiful, even if it makes for difficult swimming.

Sand Beach in Acadia National Park is one of the few sand beaches east of Portland.

Courtesy, State of Maine

Roque Bluffs Beach; Roque Bluffs Rd. off Rte. 1, Roque Bluffs. There's also **Simpson Pond** next door for freshwater swimming, a playground, picnic tables, grills, a bathhouse, bathrooms, and parking. Sand and shingle beach; 910 yds.

BERRY & APPLE PICKING

Wild blueberries, wild red and black raspberries and berries of the cultivated kind, including strawberries, somehow taste better in Maine. Maybe it's because spring here is usually a long, cold and damp affair. Maybe it's because you get to pick them yourself, sneaking a taste now and then to determine whether the big ones or smaller ones are sweeter this year. Whatever the reason, berry season in Maine is heavenly, beginning with strawberries in late June to early July, blueberries in late July right through August Down East.

Good wild berrypicking spots, like fishing holes, are well-guarded secrets passed down from parent to child. Better-known berry spots are the tops of *Blue Hill* and *Schoodic Mountain.* Knowing those two will put you ahead of millions of visitors, but get there early. If you want to do better than that, we recommend you find a local family willing to adopt a berrypicker.

Here are some places that, for a fee, will let you pick cultivated berries to your heart's content. We've also listed a few apple orchards for fall visitors in search of a crisp Mac or Cortland. Call ahead for picking prospects.

South Coast

Spiller Farms (985-2575; Rte. 9A, Wells Branch). Strawberries and raspberries. June 20 to end of season. Apples. Daily 10–6.

Whistling Wings Farm (282-1146; 427 West St., Biddeford). Raspberries. July to Labor Day. Daily 8–5.

Jordan's Farm (799-1466; Wells Rd., Cape Elizabeth). Strawberries. End of June through August 1. Mon.–Sat., 7–7.

Maxwell's Farm (799-3383; off Rte. 77 near Two Lights, Cape Elizabeth). Strawberries and raspberries. Mid-June–mid-July. Mon.–Sat., 7 a.m.–8 p.m. Closed Sun. Call ahead.

Double T Orchard (829-3316; 17 Orchard Rd., Cumberland). Apples every day during apple season, 8–4.

Juniper Edge Strawberries (725-6414; Harpswell Rd., Rte. 123, Brunswick). Strawberries. June 15 to end of season. Tue.–Sun., 8–6.

Lipovsky Gardens (725-7897; Church Rd., Brunswick). Blueberries. Call ahead for an appointment.

The Ledges (666-8827; Rte. 138, Bowdoinham). Apples, plums and raspberries. June–Oct. Daily 8–6.

Hilltop Raspberry Farm (737-4988; Post Rd., Bowdoinham). Raspberries. July 15–Oct. Daily, 9–6.

Prouts Vegetable (666-5604; Brown Point Rd., Bowdoinham). Strawberries. Late June–mid-July. 7 a.m.–dusk. Closed Sundays.

Midcoast

Spear Farm & Greenhouse (273-3818; Rte. 1, Warren). Strawberries. Open daily through season; call for hours.

School House Farm (273-2440; Rte. 1, Warren). Daily, 9–6.

Watson's Chase (236-3188; 289 Beech St., Rockport). Blueberries. Last week of July through third week in Aug. Mon.–Sat., 8–5; Sun., noon–5.

Down East/Acadia

Bagaduce Farm Orchard (326-9013; Rte. 166, Castine). Daily, 10–5.

Silveridge Farm (469-7836; McDonald St., Bucksport). Strawberries and raspberries. By appointment. Late June to end of season; daily, 8–8.

C and G Growers (326-9311; Rte. 175, South Penobscot). Strawberries. Starting in late June; daily, 9–5.

Bay View Farm (359-2719; Ridge Rd., Sedgwick). Blueberries. Last week of July to first week of Sept.; daily, 9–5, weather permitting.

Christies Hill (359-2701; Sedgwick). Blackberries. Last week of July through first week of Sept. Call for hours.

Richard's Orchard (667-7287; Oak Point Rd., Trenton). Call for information.

Ben's Berry Patch (244-3944; Love Pond Rd., Southwest Harbor). Blueberries. Aug. 1–Sept.10. Daily.

East of Schoodic

Welch Farm (225-8451; Roque Bluffs Rd., Roque Bluffs). Blueberries. Call for season information.

Crows Brook Farm (726-3971; 66 Little Falls Rd., Pembroke). Strawberries. Daily in season, 9–7.

John Metzger

Biking on Old Orchard Beach.

BICYCLING

First, here's what The Law says:
    You need to have brakes so you can stop within a reasonable distance. (Seems fair.)

You need a head lamp if you're riding at night; night being that time when cars by law should have their headlights on.

The head lamp has to produce a white light someone in front of you can see from at least 200 ft.

You need a rear red reflector visible from at least 200 ft. and reflector strips on your bike pedals and handlebars.

Helmets are not the law for cyclists in Maine, but we suggest them. Coastal paved roads, dirt roads and trails open to cyclists are often narrow and winding as they follow the terrain. Traffic at the height of summer can make those byways even more dangerous. Wearing a helmet will help protect you from injury should you hit a bad piece of road or path. It also could save your life should you encounter a car wanting more than its share of the road. We'd also like you to consider that biking — and any other outdoor activity in Maine — requires paying careful attention to weather conditions. Be sure to dress properly. Even if it promised to be a warm day, take along a windbreaker that will help you ward off a sudden damp fog.

Now, here's a roundup of biking on the coast: There are three highways closed to cyclists: the Maine Turnpike, the interstate highway system and Rte. 1 between Brunswick and Bath.

Otherwise, go crazy. Great areas to pedal through include: *Cape Elizabeth*, which has bike lanes on Rts. 77 and 207 leading through coastal marsh areas and past several great beaches; the stretch of *U.S. Rte. 1* littered with old sea captains' homes between *Belfast and Bucksport*; the perimeter of *Megunticook Lake* and on to Lincolnville; the carriage paths and *Park Loop Rd.* in Acadia National Park; the *Park Loop Rd.* on Schoodic Peninsula; the lovely, flat, uncrowded terrain *East of Schoodic*; *Islesboro*; *Monhegan*, and any other island with paved roads. During the summer of 1990, state ferries carried 5,000 cyclists to Maine's islands. That's about the same number of cars traveling along Acadia's Loop on a busy day or two. Bike and rider fares range from $4 to $47.

Several chambers of commerce offer bike tour maps of their areas. The Rockport–Camden–Lincolnville Chamber of Commerce does. (See "Tourist Information" in *Information*, Chapter Eight.) If you want to make your own way, the state publishes excellent, inexpensive highway maps. Write for information from the Maine Department of Transportation, State House Station 16, Augusta, 04333–0016. Roland Roy is the state's bicycle coordinator.

DeLorme Mapping Company offers a $3.95 pamphlet titled *Bicycling*. It can be found at bookstores and large supermarkets in the magazine/map/recreation areas. Another excellent guide for cyclers is *25 Bicycle Tours in Maine* by Howard Stone (Back Country Publications, P.O. Box 175, Woodstock, VT 05091). Both books offer excellent maps and directions for touring cyclists, including sights to look for on the way.

If you want to see more of Maine than just the coast, there is the annual *"Trek Across Maine,"* a mid-June fundraiser for the Maine Lung Association. The three-day, 180-mile ride begins in the mountains at Bethel and ends on the coast in Rockland. For more information, contact the Maine Lung Association (622-6394).

If speed is the thing, there's the *Tour D'Acadia*, a 24-mile annual "citizens" bike race in late September. Most of the riding takes place on the Park Loop Rd. For more information, contact the Mount Desert Island YMCA (288-3511; P.O. Box 51, Bar Harbor 04609). There's also the *Yarmouth Clam Festival* bike race held every year during the third week in July (846-3984).

There are bike clubs along the coast. They seem to keep springing up as bicycling becomes more and more popular. Here are a few along the coast: The **Casco Bay Bicycle Club** offers two to 20 mi. bike trips that are open to non-members. For information, write to them at: 84 New Gloucester Rd., Cumberland 04121; or call 774-1118 for a recorded listing of upcoming trips.

The **Elan Velo Bike Club** in Saco sponsors Criterion, a two-day bike race in mid-July. For information check with Saco Cycles (283-2453; 294 Main St., Saco).

For offroad cycling, check in with the **Southern Maine Offroad Bicycle Association**. It is headquartered at Allspeed Bicycles, 1041 Washington Ave., Portland.

BICYCLE DEALERS

You're on the road bright and early on your first day, and bam, you hit a bump, wipe out and break a spoke. That's not to say the roads and trails in Maine are any rougher than those you're used to at home. We just say it to remind you that accidents do happen, and let you know that help is not far away.

Here's a list of bike shops on the coast. Several rent bikes; all repair them. Some are great places to go to replace the water bottle you left behind, as well as pick up information on roads and trails favored by local cyclists, tours and clubs.

South Coast

Bicycle Bob's (439-3605; 167 State Rd., Kittery).
Cape-Able Bike Shop (967-4382; Arundel Rd., Kennebunkport).
Movin' On (646-2810; 11 S. Main St., Ogunquit).
Quinn's Bike Shop (284-4632; 140 Elm St., Biddeford).
Saco Cycle (283-2453; 294 Main St., Saco).
Viking Motel (934-5443; 84 West Grand Ave., Old Orchard Beach). Rentals.
Wheels & Waves (646-5774; Rte. 1, Wells).

Casco Bay

Allspeed Bicycles (878-8741; 1041 Washington Ave., Portland).
Back Bay Bicycle (773-6906; Forest Ave., Portland).
CycleMania (774-2933; 59 Federal St., Portland).
Joe Jones Ski and Sports (761-1961; 198 Main Mall Rd., South Portland).
L. L. Bean (865-4761; Main St., Freeport).

Midcoast

Bath Cycle and Ski (442-7002; Rte 1, Woolwich).
Birgfeld Bicycle Shop (548-2916; Rte. 1, Searsport).
Maine Sport (800-244-8799; Rte. 1, Rockport).

Down East / Acadia

Acadia Bike & Canoe (800-660-8615; 48 Cottage St., Bar Harbor).
Bar Harbor Bicycle Shop (288-3886; 141 Cottage St., Bar Harbor).
Gulliver's Bicycle Shop (667-3223; 163 Main St., Ellsworth).
Southwest Cycle (244-5856; Main St., Southwest Harbor).

BIRDWATCHING

"The black-billed cuckoo taps out his hollow message in code. . . ."

— *E. B. White*

Birders on Mount Desert Island, where hundreds of different birds can be seen.

Roy Zalesky

FOR BIRDERS

Bird life in the woods, bogs, ponds, open lands, rocks and beaches of the Maine coast is amazingly rich. Though there are few year-rounders, innumerable birds drop by. Maine is the last stop for many migrants, both from the north in winter and from the south in summer.

Accordingly, human migrants from the north will be attracted in late summer to the abundant shorebird life of marshes and mudflats like *Scarborough Marsh and Biddeford Pool,* where they may hear the *coocoo* of the least bittern or catch sight of a little blue or a black crowned night heron, a snowy egret, glossy ibis or even a marbled godwit.

Southern birders, on the other hand, will head well-bundled in winter for a shore lookout like **Quoddy Head** to see flying murres, kittiwakes and other alcids, a swimming harlequin duck or a king eider. Or they may hope to see a northern three-toed woodpecker in the spruce forests along the rocky northeastern shore, the year-round habitat of gray jays, northern ravens and boreal chickadees.

Any birder north of Portland will look for bald eagles nesting. All will want to visit the extraordinary flocks of ocean birds that breed in early summer among the more than 2,000 sheltering islands and the plankton-rich waters fed by the icy Labrador current. The puffin is the most famous; other notable breeds include black headed gulls, razorbills, black guillemots and Leach's petrels, hard to spot because they fly at night.

Arctic terns arrive in mid-May like a snowstorm over the sea. In late summer they're off east again over the Atlantic, starting their incredible annual trip through Europe and Africa to the Antarctic. All these nesting creatures pose the birder's familiar dilemma: how to observe the birds without disturbing their habitat.

The ferry from **Bar Harbor to Yarmouth** is an excellent place from which to observe, and so are many shorter ferry rides (See "Ferries" in *Transportation*, Chapter Two, and "Whale Watching," below). Take a boat ride around **Matinicus Rock** (offshore from Matinicus Island), the southernmost known breeding place for puffins on the East Coast. **Seal Island** near Machias has pathways and blinds set up for birders and is worth a special trip in June. You can land for a few hours but not stay overnight.

Wonderful places to see the fall migration of shore birds are the quiet beaches near the Canadian border. One birder we've heard of spotted 100 species in one day in **Dennysville** on the Dennys River. The **Lubec and Eastport** flats host an enormous number and variety of traveling sanderlings, sandpipers, knots, willets and other beach feeders.

FOR NON-BIRDERS

If you've never watched birds, Maine raises your awareness of them. As your car crosses an inlet or shallow river your eye is suddenly caught by a four-foot-tall great blue heron — still as a post, ankle deep in running water, coiled to spear his lunch on a six-inch yellow beak. On a Maine beach you see a familiar flock of sandpipers do their tiny quickstep all together, slow down to stoop and feed together along the curl of a retreating wave, soar away together with a flash of white along each wing. It's hard to imagine these tiny creatures may have spent the winter in Palm Beach and have Arctic plans for the summer.

Keep watching. You might see among them one with longer legs or, higher up the beach, a plumper bird with a reddish back looking under seaweedy pebbles. A fellow beachgoer with binoculars will tell you the plump one is a ruddy turnstone and the tall one a yellowlegs. If you ask to borrow the binoculars to see the color of the long-jointed legs, you've taken the first step to a new interest.

Irresistible in harbor waters in winter are the diving buffleheads, chunky little black and white birds that tip up like toys, all in one motion. In tidal inlets and freshwater ponds you see not only birds shaped like farm ducks but also swimming birds of less familiar shape, maybe one with a tuft of feathers on the top or back of the head, a grebe or merganser.

Finally, there are the sea birds on the rocky shores. Even if you haven't learned to distinguish the soaring seagulls from the smaller terns that hover and dive along the surf, you may want to take the boat to **Matinicus** in June or

July. Then you can tell friends back home you've seen the unmistakable puffin, standing tall like a penguin on its large orange feet, its back black, its round stomach white, its broad beak blue, yellow and red.

FOR ALL BIRDERS

If you want to know the latest action on the wing call the *Maine Audubon* bird alert hotline at 207-781-2332. The hotline operates from 5 p.m.–8 a.m. daily. All of the beaches listed above come with birds. Following are a few places well worth looking into. Some are full-fledged nature preserves or refuges. Others are just great spots for locating birds. When possible, we have provided addresses and phone numbers.

South Coast

Biddeford Pool (Rte. 208, Biddeford). A one-mile wide tidal basin and broad mud flats at low tide. There is excellent birdwatching here, because many species of shore birds stop here en route to northern and southern climes.

Rachel Carson National Wildlife Refuge (Rte. 9, Wells). This famous refuge encompasses 1,600 acres of salt marsh, white pine forest and many, many birds. It is managed by the U. S. Fish and Wildlife Service, which offers limited access to birders and naturalists interested in viewing extensive bird life. Maps and guides to the preserve are available.

Scarborough Marsh Nature Center (883-5100; Pine Point Rd., Scarborough). The Maine Audubon Society operates an education center on this 3,000-acre saltwater marsh. They offer guided tours, including Full Moon Canoe tours during the summer when participants can experience the marsh at night. There's also a self-guided tour (you follow directions in a pamphlet available at the center). You can rent a canoe for your trip through the marsh on your quest for birds.

Seapoint Beach (Seapoint Rd., Kittery). Good birdwatching on a tiny peninsula that sticks out into the Atlantic Ocean, just southwest of Brave Boat Harbor.

Webhannet River Marsh (off Rte. 1, Wells). Good birders vantage for spotting shore birds and migrating waterfowl.

Casco Bay

Maine Audubon Society (781-2330; 118 U.S. Rte. 1, Falmouth). The Gilsland Farm Sanctuary is home to the society, as well as whoever stops by. More than 60 acres of salt marsh, fields and forest also serve as a workshop and touring ground for naturalists. There is a great bookstore for naturalists here.

Midcoast

Hog Island Audubon Camp (Muscongus Bay). Osprey drop in here, so do eagles. Audubon annually sponsors two six-day field ornithology sessions. The Todd Wildlife Sanctuary on the island hosts a variety of nesting birds.

Workshops include a one-day trip to Matinicus Rock. For more information, see "Schools" in *Culture,* Chapter Four.

Salt Bay (Rtes. 215 and 1 through Damariscotta Mills, Newcastle and
Damariscotta). If you don't want to leave your car, Salt Bay is a good spot.
Rte. 215 borders the bay along its southwest edge; Rte. 1 leads along the bay
to the east. Birds like to rest and feed in the large shallow bay and its
mudflats laid bare at low tide.

Swan Island (289-1150; Merrymeeting Bay near Richmond). The state operates
this 2,000-acre preserve and allows a few visitors to camp at shelters in the
path of a wide variety of migrating and nesting birds, including the Canada
or wild goose. Tours are available, provided you obtain the necessary (and
inexpensive) permit. Call or write Swan Island Reservation Clerk, Maine
Department of Inland Fisheries and Wildlife, 8 Federal St., Augusta 04330.

Down East/Acadia

Matinicus Rock (Criehaven Township). A mass of granite that rises 60 ft. above
sea level is home to the southernmost colony of puffins. It's also favored by
many other birds, including the rare razorbill auk.

Stanwood Museum and Birdsacre Sanctuary (667-8460; Rte. 3, Ellsworth). A
100-acre sanctuary and museum that is the former home of Cordelia

Tom Hindman

*Keeping track of the birds
near the lighthouse on Petit
Manan, one of the best places
in the country to view the
European whimbrel.*

Stanwood, a famed ornithologist and nature writer. In the museum there are stuffed birds, eggs and photos any birder will love.

East of Schoodic

Petit Manan National Wildlife Refuge (Milbridge). An 1,841-acre preserve that includes Bois Bubert, Petit Manan and Nash islands is said to be one of the best spots in the state to view the whimbrel, a small European curlew. There are nature trails on the mainland. The islands (with the exception of the northern end of Bois Bubert) are open to the public and can be reached by private boat.

BOATING

Wooden Boats

Pleasure boats and working boats come and go in all shapes and sizes in Maine, but there's something particular about a wooden boat. Museums are devoted to the wooden boat, and a magazine industry flourishes here thanks to wooden boats. There are also schools to help keep the craft of wooden boat building alive. Best of all you can still look out at the harbor — or practically anyplace else on the coast — and see them in abundance.

In spite of all the extra work wooden boats demand of their owners, many Mainers would not go down to the sea in anything else. They are a living part of the sea. A boat, said someone probably before the invention of fiberglass, is a hole in the water you keep throwing money into. Nowhere else do people throw money into their wooden boats so willingly as in Maine.

The wooden boat has as important a place in Maine's history as the glacier. The Passamaquoddy Indians cruised the coast in birch bark canoes. The graceful lines of those canoes still live in the famed Old Town canoes made in Bangor. The first wooden ship built in America was constructed in Maine by the colonists of Popham Colony in 1607. It was a 30-ton pinnace called the *Virginia*, and it carried cargo between England and Virginia for 20 years.

At first, Maine boat builders relied on the forests at their back door. As lumber along the South Coast became scarce, more boat builders moved Down East to take advantage of cheaper building materials. The industry grew. Soon it seemed like the whole coast was one big shipyard, building good, cheap cargo ships.

The earliest Maine ships were built in the tradition of their British forebears, but by the time of the Revolutionary War, Maine shipwrights had developed their own designs and style of shipbuilding. Speed became important to the merchant marine, and shipbuilders responded with the sleek, fast clipper ship; 83 clippers were built and launched in the state during the mid-1800s. The last of the famous wooden cargo ships built in Maine was a three-masted square rigger ship called the Down-Easter that was almost as fast as the clipper, but had a deeper, more spacious hull and enabled merchants to haul more with every trip.

Schooners were also built in Maine. Merchants prized them because they were even larger than the clippers and Down-Easters, and they were more economical to operate. Today they operate out of Rockland and Camden serving the tourist trade (See "Windjammers," below).

The end of the wooden boat as a merchant trading vessel came with the invention of the steamers. Steamships didn't rely on changeable winds and currents. They ran on time, and even the fastest clipper couldn't compete. Ironically, renowned Bath shipbuilder Arthur Sewall built the first steel sailing vessel, *Dirigo I,* in 1894. It weighed more than 2,800 tons.

Maine wooden boat builders took a new tack, building smaller boats for fishermen and pleasure sailors. The style of boat often depends on where it comes from: Peapods come from Penobscot Bay; Quoddy boats from Passamaquoddy Bay; the pretty, gaff-rigged Friendship Sloops from the town of Friendship on Muscongus Bay. There were also punts built to navigate a harbor or any small, calm waterway; dories to ferry people and small loads to and from shore; and pulling boats that were manned by oarsmen who literally hauled large ships that had been becalmed on windless water. Today those same pulling boats are used by Outward Bound students, their courses set on personal development.

For an invigorating taste of Maine's wooden boat heritage hard at work, watch the Friendship Sloop Races held every year in late July in Boothbay Harbor. Sponsored by the Friendship Sloop Society, the sloop races are really a week of wooden boat activities including three days of racing and events at the Maine Maritime Museum in Bath. Another wooden boat event is Windjammer Days held midweek during late June or early July. The festival offers enthusiasts the chance to check out windjammers moored in the harbor during the festival. The annual event also includes concerts, a parade and a chance to tour visiting military vessels. For information about the Friendship Sloop Races or Windjammer Days, contact the Boothbay Harbor Chamber of Commerce (P.O. Box 356, Boothbay 04009; 633-2353).

B oating on Maine's shore was once exclusively the activity of members of the Abenaki tribe cruising the coast in well-made birch bark canoes. Today few people venture on saltwater in modern fiberglass and aluminum canoes, let alone birch bark. Most recreational boating is now done in sailboats, motor boats and kayaks. Some will argue that ferries — a way of life for many Mainers — are also a form of recreational boating. They certainly are a good

Diana Lynn Doherty

During the summer on Mount Desert Island narrated nature cruises introduce visitors to the wonders of Maine's birdlife, geography and seals.

way to gain access to some of the best sights on the coast (See "Ferries" in *Information,* Chapter Eight). Windjammers and sightseeing cruises to view puffins and whales are two types of boating we list later in this chapter.

Whatever boat you choose, watch the weather. Spring often brings weather systems moving through the Gulf of Maine at a fast clip. Summer fogs can last for days. Fall and winter nor'easters can combine driving winds and rain with a high tide to make life on the water miserable if you are unprepared.

CANOEING AND SEA KAYAKING

Canoeing is rare off the Maine coast these days. Most boaters prefer something larger or smaller and more self contained. Where canoeists reign is on the small inland waterways, fresh and saltwater ponds and salt marshes.

A kayaker negotiating whitewater in Maine.

Roy Zalesky

Extended solo sea kayak trips are not stuff for amateurs. It's not so much the kayak as the elements that can cause problems. Weather changes quickly, currents and tides can be dangerous and tricky. Knowing how to handle your kayak properly will give you an edge out on the water. You can learn the basics in a couple of hours on a few weekends. You begin with wide, stable kayaks, then you learn how to flip. After a while, it won't feel too tippy.

The varied coastline of *Deer Isle* is a wonderful place to canoe and kayak. *Camden Harbor* is also a favorite stopping place for kayakers on the way east or west. There you see them bouncing in the waves next to windjammers. The inlets and harbors of *Mount Desert Island* are popular, too. So are the islands of *Casco Bay.* A great reference for kayakers is *Sea Kayaking Along the New England Coast* (AMC Books, $14.95). It contains an excellent round-up of information on everything about coastal kayaking conditions throughout New England, including the Maine Island Trail (see sidebar in this chapter).

The following places offer gear, lessons, rentals and half-day to five-day trips.

South Coast

Kittery Rent-All & Sales (439-4528; Rte. 1, Kittery). Canoe rentals.

Scarborough Marsh Nature Center (883-5100; Pine Point Rd off Rte. 1, Scarborough). Hourly canoe rentals and self-guided canoe tours of the marsh.

Also guided tours, including "full-moon" tours during the summer. The center is open from 9:30 a.m.–5:30 p.m.; last canoe rental at 4. Open from mid-June until Labor Day.

Casco Bay

H2Outfitters (833-5257; P.O. Box 72, Orrs Island 04066). Canoe and kayak instruction for groups or individuals, as well as three-hour guided tours of waters near Bailey and Orrs islands. Classes offered year round.

L. L. Bean Outdoor Discovery Program (865-4761, ext. 7800; Main St., Freeport). Throughout the summer, the L.L. Bean store staff gives canoe and kayak lessons on a nice, easy stretch of the Royal River in Yarmouth. The academic wing of the outdoor store also hosts an annual Sea Kayak Symposium in early August and the Annual North American Canoe Symposium in early June.

New Routes in Harpswell (729-7900; Harpswell). Private and group lessons. One day trips or longer. Rentals.

Saco River Outfitters (773-0910; 127 Marginal Way, Portland). Canoe and kayak rentals, instruction and gear, as well as guided trips on Casco Bay. Every week during the summer, they sponsor kayak midweek get-togethers at East End Beach in Portland.

Tommy's Hardware (772-5357; 273 Congress St., Portland). Open and closed boats for rent; lessons and guided tours. This is also a great place to learn where Casco Bay kayakers like to go — the store sponsors weekly get-togethers at the East End Beach in Portland.

Midcoast

Dragonworks, Inc. (668-8481; Merrymeeting Bay). Equipment, tours and instruction for sea kayakers.

Explorers at Sea (367-2356; Maine St., Stonington). Sea kayak rentals, gear and guide service.

Indian Island Kayak Co. (236-4088; 16 Mountain St., Camden). Guided tours, instruction and sales.

Island Hopping (603-466-2721; or write Summer Workshop, P.O. Box 298, Gorham, NH 03581). The Appalachian Mountain Club offers experienced canoeists the chance to spend three days exploring the water routes the Abenaki Indians used as they traveled among the islands of Penobscot Bay.

Maine Sport (in-state 800-244-8799; out-of-state 800-722-0826; Rte. 1, Rockport 04856). Guided tours and rentals.

Sea Touring Kayak Center (236-9569; P.O. Box 691, 123 Elm St., Camden 04843). Sea kayak rental, instruction and guided tours.

Tidal Transit Co. (633-7140; Boothbay Harbor). Hourly lessons and custom trips for sea kayakers.

Down East/Acadia

Acadia Bike & Canoe (288-9605, 228-5483 or 800-526-861548; 48 Cottage St., Bar Harbor). Canoe and kayak rentals. The store also offers sea kayaking tours and instruction for coastal waters.

Caribou Kayaks (244-5703; P.O. Box 362, Bass Harbor 04653). Handcrafted kayaks that many Maine kayakers will swear by.

Mansell Boat Rental (244-5652; Shore Rd., Southwest Harbor). Canoe rentals.

National Park Canoe Rentals (244-5854; Long Pond, Acadia National Park). There are 32 canoes available, but reservations are suggested as all canoes are often rented by 9 a.m. Open daily 8:30–5. Paddles, life jackets and instruction provided.

Reversing Falls

Maine with its dramatic tides has several good reversing falls, favorite proving grounds for kayakers and canoeists. What makes reversing falls interesting is the water speed and direction change as the tide changes. The rapids run inland as high tide approaches, and they run out to sea as the tide ebbs. Here are some favored by small boaters in Maine:

Blue Hill Falls (under Rte. 175 bridge, Blue Hill Falls). The best time to negotiate these rapids, which are only about 100 yds. long, is about 3 hours before high tide. The coast near here also offers some good exploring for people in small boats. Parking is limited, and access to the falls is hampered by traffic. Be careful walking to and from the water.

Damariscotta Reversing Falls (Damariscotta/Newcastle; Rte. 1 bridge or Rtes. 129 and 130 bridges). Two locations to practice your whitewater canoe and kayak skills.

Bagaduce Falls (Brooksville). It's easy to park and find these reversing falls between Snow Cove and the Bagaduce estuary.

Goose Falls (Brooksville). Reversing falls at outlet of Goose Pond.

Sullivan Falls (Sullivan). Great scenery at these reversing falls between Taunton Bay and Sullivan Harbor.

Maine Island Trails

The Maine Island Trail Association was founded in 1987. The waterway is a kind of Appalachian Trail for boaters. It begins with islands in Casco Bay and follows the coast Down East past Machias. The trail includes 70 islands where travelers can put ashore and camp for the night. Thirty are privately owned islands; the rest are owned by the state and governed by the Bureau of Public Lands.

"What makes the Maine Island Trail a pleasure is its 'connect the dots' character, the 'dots' being islands. Without access to islands along the way, there would be no trail," wrote kayaker Michael Burke in a recent *Yankee* magazine.

Members have access to prudent use of the islands on the trail — or what the association calls "permissive trespass." Members receive a copy of *The Maine Island Trail Book*, a guidebook packed with charts and information. There are about 2,000 members of MITA, 200 of whom regularly make litter-picking forays to islands they have "adopted."

For information about the organization, write to the Maine Island Trail Association, 60 Ocean St., Rockland, ME 04841.

CRUISING

For the sailboat or motorboat cruiser, the coast could be considered a paradise. There are hundreds of deepwater anchorages, beautiful fishing villages like Jonesport and quaint albeit sophisticated towns such as Camden (a true pleasure sailor's town). Islands make for great side trips. The smallest are great places to anchor and enjoy a swim on a warm summer day and lobster on the rocks; the largest offer almost all the amenities of the mainland.

An excellent guide for pleasure boaters in Maine is *A Cruising Guide to the Maine Coast* by Hank and Jan Taft (International Marine Publishing; Camden, ME; $32.50). It's packed with charts, tips and history for those viewing the coast from the water. If you don't have your own boat, here is a list of dealers who sell and rent sailboats and motorboats.

CHARTERS AND RENTALS

There are not a lot of people willing to rent you their boats. More are willing to take you. Boat people are like that.

South Coast
Threshold (283-4007; Saco). Crewed half-day, full-day and overnight sails on a
35-foot wooden ketch.

Casco Bay
Palawan (773-2163; Custom House Wharf, Portland). Half-day, full-day and
evening trips aboard a vintage 58-foot ocean racing sloop.

Midcoast
Sun Yacht Charters (236-9611; Elm St., Camden). Bareboat charters from 19 ft.
day sailors up, with a three-day minimum. Season runs from mid-June
through September.
P.G. Willey & Company (236-3256; Camden). Day sailers for full- and half-
day rentals.
Gladiator (354-8036; Friendship). Sail on Captain Bill Zuber's Friendship sloop
from the place these famed boats were built.
Surprise (372-6366; The East Wind Inn at Tenants Harbor). Sail Muscongus
Bay, three trips daily aboard this vintage Friendship sloop.

Learning to sail in Maine.

Tom Hindman

Down East/Acadia

Chance Along Sailing Center (338-1833; Belfast). Sailboats from the tiny (Sunfish) to the small yacht (23 foot). Half-day, full-day and week rentals.

Gull Haven/Manset Boat (244-9223; Clark Point Rd., Southwest Harbor).

Hinckley Yacht Charters (244-5008; Bass Harbor). Bareboat sailboat charters to qualified sailors. Forty boats available from 30 to 44 feet. Reservations suggested.

Indian Point Yachts, Inc. (288-5258; Indian Point Rd., Mount Desert). Bareboat or crew sailboat charters for one week or more. Up to 50 boats of all sizes available. Reservations required.

Libbys Sailboat Rentals & Charters (288-3604; 5 Stephens Ln., Bar Harbor).

Mansell Boat Rental (244-5625; Main St., Southwest Harbor). Day sailors and canoes for the day.

Western Bay Charters (667-3411; 98 Maine St., Ellsworth). Bareboat sailboat charters to qualified sailors for one day or more. Seven boats avail∂¹ from 25 to 32 feet. Reservations suggested.

SAILING LESSONS

Chance Along Community Sailing Center (338-1833; 140 High St. Belfast). Lessons to get around the harbor or down the coast. Rentals from Sunfish to 23 ft. boats; 1/2 or full day and weekly rates.

Maine Sailing School (967-5043; Ocean Ave., Kennebunkport). Adults, kids, short time, long time, big boats, little boats, even speedboats, just like George Bush's.

Narrad Sailing School (549-7855; Christmas Cove, South Bristol).

Sawyer's Sailing School (783-6882; Mere Point, Brunswick). Three-day instructional cruises aboard a 28-foot sloop.

Spring Point Sailing School (767-9500; Southern Maine Technical College, South Portland). Classes for beginning and advanced sailors, including private lessons by appointment.

WoodenBoat School (359-4651; Brooklin). Weeklong instructional programs, part of the boat-building school and run by *WoodenBoat* magazine.

BOWLING

There are two types of bowling. Tenpin is known to most of the world as "bowling." In New England — and Maine — candlepin is often the game of choice.

Candlepin bowling is a great way to spend a rainy — or any other — day. Unlike the tenpin's duck pin shape, the sticks in candlepin are cylindrical and tapered at both ends. Candlepin balls are the size of coconuts and, because there is no need, there is no place to insert your fingers. The balls travel much faster. There is none of the lumbering, none of that crowding the pins back off the alley. When one of the small balls hits the pins, they fly out of the way like just-split wood, but you know the ball has pretty much given it all it's got. Even with three chances every frame, candlepin scores are lower. That's part of the challenge.

South Coast

Big 20 Bowling Center (883-2131; Rte. 1, Scarborough). 20 candlepin lanes.

Roll-A-Way Lanes (282-1713; 480 Elm St., Biddeford). 24 candlepin lanes.

Vacationland Bowling Center (284-7386; Rte. 1, Saco). 20 candlepin lanes.

Casco Bay

Pride's Corner Bowling (797-2699; Elmwood Ave., Westbrook). 14 tenpin; 12 candlepin lanes.

Yankee Lanes of Brunswick (725-2963; Bath Rd., Brunswick). 32 tenpin lanes.

Midco~

~wling Center (594-5661; Park St., Rockland). Candlepin.

\rk Bowling (594-7525; Rte. 1, Rockport). 12 candlepin lanes.

Acadia

\wling Center (469-7902; Rte. 46, Bucksport). 12 candlepin lanes.

\ling Lanes (667-9228; Triangle, Ellsworth). 12 candlepin lanes.

CAMPING

There are hundreds of private and public campgrounds along the coast. Many offer priceless views of the water at camper's prices. Some are no bigger than a modest parking lot. Others are mammoth. Because the summer camping season is short in Maine, we recommend calling well ahead for reservations — especially if you are planning to visit Acadia over the July 4 weekend. Once Labor Day weekend ends and school begins, most coastal campgrounds become lovely, quiet and wonderfully available.

Below we've listed some of the best municipal, state and federal campgrounds on or near the coast. For a complete list of private campgrounds, contact the *Maine Campground Owners Association* (782-5874; 655 Main St., Lewiston 04240). The *Maine Publicity Bureau* also publishes a camping guide. Call or write for one (582-9300, 800-533-9595 out-of-state; P.O. Box 2300, Hallowell 04347).

Casco Bay

Recompence Shores Camp Sites (633-2700; Burnett Rd., Freeport). This small oceanside campground is run by the state university system. Tent and RV campsites, showers, electrical hookups and one of the best views in the area. Next door is a state-run organic beef farm. Ask when you check in and you can get a couple of thick steaks to grill during your stay.

Winslow Memorial Park (865-4198; Staples Point Rd., Freeport). Small, municipally run park with camp and picnic sites and a lovely man-made beach.

Midcoast

Camden Hills State Park (236-3109; two mi. off U.S. Rte. 1). Often this lovely campground is full. It's near one of the most popular seacoast towns in Maine, as well as within striking distance for hikers headed up Mount Battie. You should have a reservation to make sure you have a spot during July and

State Development Office

Camping in beautiful Camden Hills State Park.

August. But you're almost certain to get one the rest of the season if you arrive before 1 p.m. Showers. Nominal fee. Open May 15–October 15.

Mullen Head Park (867-4433; South Shore Rd., North Haven). You need permission from the town office to camp here in this well-run, shoreside park. If you don't get it, console yourself with a good swim or picnic. You can get here by state-run ferry out of Rockland.

Warren Island State Park (Isleboro). Access to this spruce-covered island and its ten primitive campsites is limited to private or commercial boat. But the trip is worth it, if only to sleep overnight on a pretty little island in Penobscot Bay. Hiking, swimming, fishing; freshwater; open May 30 through September 15. You can get to Isleboro on a ferry from Lincolnville.

Down East/Acadia

Acadia National Park (reservations through Ticketron: 804-499-0853 or write Ticketron, P.O. Box 62429, Virginia Beach, VA 23462). There are two campsites in the national park. The larger of the two, Blackwoods, is located off Rte. 3, five mi. south of Bar Harbor; Seawall is on Rte. 102A, four mi. south of Southwest Harbor. Both have attractive, wooded sites and most amenities during the season (electrical hookups excluded; showers and a camp store are within 1/2 mi.). Only Blackwoods is open mid-October to mid-May, and facilities then are limited to picnic tables, fire rings, pit toilets and a hand pump for drinking water. Reservations, made at least 56 days in advance, are a must between Memorial and Labor days. Campsites are easier to come by during the off season.

Lamoine State Park (667-4778; off Rte. 3 on Rte. 184, Lamoine). This is one of the best-kept secrets for campers visiting Acadia during the high season. While sites in the national park are crammed, there are usually available waterside spots in this pretty little campground with 61 sites, as well as great views of Cadillac Mountain and Mount Desert Island. There's a lovely pebble beach nearby, too.

East of Schoodic

Cobscook Bay State Park (726-4412; six mi. south of U.S. Rte. 1 at Dennysville). This is a jewel of a campground with 106 camping sites. Most are for tents and many with water views. There are even showers (unusual in a Maine state campground). The 864-acre park has picnic benches, hiking and cross-country ski trails (see below.) Mid-May–mid-October.

McLellan Park (Wyman Rd., Milbridge). Washington County operates this family recreational area. You can camp here. There are also picnicking facilities and hiking trails.

CLAMMING

How to clam. Get a bucket, a pitchfork or a clamming rake, which looks like a gardener's claw with a long handle — that kind of thing — then go down to the beach, preferably at low tide, when your clam is at its most vulnerable. Stomp on the beach. If you see a stream of water squirt up, start digging. Warning: before you begin, look around for signs warning not to dig because of red tide. Clams and mussels drink in this rust-colored algae and collect it in a concentrated form. Cooking the clam or mussel won't help. If you eat some you can develop paralysis.

CROQUET

C roquet. The game that makes mergers and acquisitions look like sandbox. If you don't believe it, go watch the annual *Claremont Croquet Classic,* played early August on the lawns of the Claremont Hotel (244-5036; Southwest Harbor). You're invited.

FISHING

P eople have fished in Maine's waters since before history. Tribes of the Algonquin nation used to erect weirs — traps of net and wood that fish swim into, but can't get out of — in the bays and inlets of the coast. The Portugese are thought to have fished here long before the coast of Maine was first "discovered" by the British and French. The cold waters off the coast were famous for their abundant supply of bluefish, striped bass, mackerel and tuna. Today, the waters are not as populated as they once were. Commercial fisheries during this and the last century have depleted much of the natural supply of saltwater fish.

While large schools of fish are now rare on the coast, there are many opportunities both in salt and freshwater fishing. President Bush's fishing tackle master Bob Boilard, one of the most knowledgeable sports fisherman in the Saco Bay area, suggests bottom fishing for cod, pollock and mackerel. Well-known spots for saltwater fishing are Saco Bay off York, Ogunquit, Kennebunkport and Saco; Casco Bay from Portland to South Freeport; Boothbay Harbor; the waters off Rockland; and Passamaquoddy Bay near Eastport. (Bush often fishes in a small boat off Parsons Beach in Kennebunk.)

Beach and shore fishing is also popular in the fall when sunbathers have left. Good beach or shore fishing spots are *Popham Beach* near where the Kennebec River empties into the Gulf of Maine near Bath; the *Presumpscot, Saco and Mousam rivers* in the South Coast; and the southern beaches including *Crescent, Laudholm, Moody and Ogunquit.*

If you're a competitive fishermen or you like to be there when the pros weigh their fish, there are two saltwater tournaments held on the coast. *Tuna Tournament & Small Fish Rodeo* usually takes place from late July to early August. Fair game include codfish, bluefish, mackerel and cusk. For more information contact Brown's Wharf (633-5440) or the Boothbay Harbor Tuna

Club (633-4414; P.O. Box 28, Boothbay Harbor 04538). The *New England Bluefish Open* is held every year in mid-August in the waters near Bath. For more information, contact Eastern Sport Fishing Promotions (923-3301; RFD 6, Box 112, Augusta 04330).

Fly fishing in inland waters Down East.

State Development Office

When your taste runs more to trout and bass, try the rivers near the coast. Late spring and early summer are traditionally good seasons for freshwater fishermen. Then hungry fish come to the surface to feed on insects and their larvae. Atlantic salmon fishing is big in the rivers of Washington County, including the Dennys River. The season usually runs from mid-August through September.

Freshwater fishing licenses may be bought at the *Kittery Trading Post* in Kittery, *L. L. Bean* and *Peregrine Outfitters* in Freeport, as well as many other Maine sporting goods stores (no licenses are required for saltwater sport fishing). The rate for a one-day license is about the price of a movie. The longer you plan to fish, the cheaper it gets. Junior licenses are available for those ages 12 to 16. For more information call or write the *Department of Inland Fisheries and Wildlife* (in-state 800-322-1333; 289-3371; State House Station 41, Augusta 04333). They also can give you dates for the freshwater fishing season and send maps showing waters open and restricted to fishing.

If you want to learn how to fish, you can learn from the pros at "fly fishing school." *L.L. Bean's Outdoor Discovery Program* every year offers intense fly fishing instruction in addition to frequent free programs about fishing. For more information about those classes call the outdoor school (800-341-4341, ext. 7800).

DEEP SEA FISHING BOATS

Following is a partial listing of boats that offer full- and half-day deep sea fishing excursions. Some provide rods, reels and bait, but it's good to check when you make reservations.

South Coast
Judy Marie II (361-1969; Town Dock, York Harbor). Capt. Ken Young, Jr. Full- and half-day trips. Mid-May–mid-October.

Enterprise (363-7407; York). Capt. Kirk Snader. Sport fishing charters. Six passengers. Full- or half-day trips.

Bunny Clark (646-2214; Perkins Cove, Ogunquit). Mid-March–mid-November. Full- and half-day trips as well as 12-hour "fishing marathons."

Ugly Anne (646-7202; Perkins Cove, Ogunquit). April–November. Half-day trips only July–Labor Day. Full-day trips April–July and Sept.–Nov.

Midcoast

Henrietta (594-5411; Public Landing, Rockland). Capt. John Earl. All-day fishing trips.

Down East/Acadia

Dolphin (288-3322; Harbor Place, Bar Harbor). 4-hour trips.

GOLF

T he first golf courses built in Maine were built along the coast at the turn of the century, just as the game was beginning to take hold in this country. The 18-hole course at *Kebo Valley Club* in Bar Harbor, built in 1892, has the distinction of being the oldest operating golf grounds in America. Mark Twain, who once said that "Golf is a good walk spoiled," learned how to play golf at a course in York County. President Bush is still learning the intricacies of the game at a course in York County.

Many of the courses listed here are set right on the shore. If you don't make par, at least you've earned a great view. Call for current rates and hours.

South Coast

Dutch Elm Golf Course (282-9850; Brimstone Rd., Arundel). 18 holes, 6,230 yds., par 72. Cart and club rental, pro shop, clubhouse, lessons.

Webhannet Golf Club (967-2061; Kennebunk Beach). 18 holes, 6,136 yds., par 71. Cart rental, pro shop, lessons. Call 24 hours in advance.

Cape Arundel Golf Club (967-3494; Old River Rd., Kennebunkport). 18 holes, 6,000 yds., par 69. Cart and club rental, pro shop, clubhouse, lessons.

Old Orchard Beach Country Club (934-4513; Ross Rd., Old Orchard Beach). 9 holes, 3,006 yds., par 36, cart & club rental, pro shop, clubhouse.

Biddeford-Saco Country Club (282-5883; Old Orchard Rd., Saco). 18 holes, 6,200 yds., par 71, cart and club rental, pro shop, clubhouse, lessons.

Pleasant Hill Country Club (883-9340; 38 Chamberlain Rd., Scarborough). 9 holes, 2,400 yds., par 34. Cart and club rental, pro shop, clubhouse, snack bar.

Willowdale Golf Club (883-9351; Willowdale Rd., Scarborough). 18 holes, 5980 yds., par 70. Cart and club rental, pro shop, snack bar.

Casco Bay

Brunswick Golf Club (725-8224; River Rd., Brunswick). 18 holes, 6,600 yds., par 72. Cart and club rental, pro shop, clubhouse, lessons. On weekends, private until 10 a.m.

Val Halla Golf Course (829-2225; Greely Rd., Cumberland). 18 holes, 6,353 yds., par 71. Cart and club rental, pro shop, clubhouse, lessons.

Freeport Country Club (865-4922; Old County Rd., Freeport). 9 holes, 2,960 yds., par 36. Cart and club rental, pro shop, clubhouse.

Riverside Municipal Courses (797-3524 or 797-5588; 1158 Riverside Dr., Portland). Two courses: 18 holes, 6,520 yds., par 72; and 9 holes, 3,152 yds., par 36. Cart and club rental, pro shop, clubhouse, lessons.

Sable Oaks Golf Club-Marriott (775-6257; 505 Country Club Dr., South Portland). 18 holes, 6,359 yds., par 70. Cart rental mandatory, club rental, clubhouse, pro shop, snack bar, lessons.

South Portland Municipal (775-0005; Wescott Rd., South Portland). 9 holes, 2,071 yds., par 33. Cart and club rental, pro shop, snack bar.

Midcoast

Bath Golf Club (442-8411; Whiskeag Rd., Bath). 9 holes, 3,212 yds., par 35. Cart and club rental, pro shop, clubhouse, lessons, practice range.

Boothbay Region Country Club (633-9885; Country Club Rd., Boothbay). 9 holes, 5,620 yds., par 70. Cart and club rental, pro shop, clubhouse.

Bucksport Golf Club (469-7612; Duckcover Rd., Bucksport). 9 holes, 3,413 yds., par 36. Cart and club rental, pro shop, clubhouse, lessons.

Goose River Golf Course (236-8488; Simonton Rd., Camden). 9 holes, 2,910 yds., par 35. Cart and club rental, pro shop, clubhouse.

North Haven Golf Club (867-2061; Iron Point Rd., North Haven). 9 holes, 2,060 yds., par 35. Cart and club rental, lessons.

Northport Golf Club (338-2270; Northport). 9 holes, 3,044 yds., par 36. Cart and club rental, pro shop, clubhouse, lessons.

Rockland Golf Club (594-9322; Old County Rd., Rockland). 18 holes, 6,300 yds., par 70. Cart and club rental, pro shop, clubhouse, lessons — $18 weekdays, $20 weekends and holidays.

Samoset Resort (594-1431; Warrenton St., Rockport). 18 holes, 6,384 yds., par 70. Cart and club rental, pro shop, clubhouse, lessons.

Down East/Acadia

Kebo Valley Club (288-3000; Eagle Lake Rd., Bar Harbor). 18 holes, 6,200 yds., par 70. Cart and club rental, pro shop, clubhouse, lessons.

Castine Golf Club (326-8844; Battle Ave., Castine). 9 holes, 2,977 yds., par 35. Pull cart rental, pro shop, lessons.

Island Country Club (348-2379; Rte. 15A, Deer Isle). 9 holes, 3,865 yards, par 31. Cart and club rental, pro shop, clubhouse, lessons.

White Birches Golf Course (667-3621; Thorsen Rd., Ellsworth). 9 holes, 2,800 yds., par 34. Cart and club rental, pro shop, snack bar.

Northeast Harbor Golf Club (276-5335; Sargent Drive, Northeast Harbor). 15 holes, 4,557 yds., par 57. Cart and club rental, pro shop, lessons.

Causeway Club (244-3780; Fernald Point Rd., Southwest Harbor). 18 holes, 4,718 yds., par 65. Cart and club rental, pro shop, lessons.

Bar Harbor Golf Course (667-7505; Rtes. 3 & 204, Trenton). 18 holes, 6,621 yds., par 71. Cart and club rental, pro shop, clubhouse, lessons.

Grindstone Neck Golf Course (963-7760; Grindstone Ave., Winter Harbor). 9 holes, 3200 yds., par 36. Cart and club rental, pro shop, lessons.

East of Schoodic

Great Cove Golf Course (434-2981; off Rte. 1, Roque Bluffs). 9 holes, 1,694 yds., par 30. Cart and club rental, snack bar, clubhouse.

HANG GLIDING

Island Soaring (667-SOAR; Hancock County-Bar Harbor Airport, Trenton). Soar over Mount Desert Island. Avoid the crowds and the entrance fee to the Loop.

HARNESS RACING

Standardbreds pulling a two-wheeled sulky and driver compete against each other for your betting pleasure. There's only one harness racing track on the coast of Maine — *Scarborough Downs* (883-4331; exit 6 off the Maine Turnpike, Scarborough, just southwest of Portland). It also happens to be the largest of its kind in New England. Races run Tues.–Sat., 7:30 p.m.; Sun., 1 p.m. The season varies; call for schedule.

HEALTH CLUBS

Here is a list of health clubs along the coast. Health clubs come and go. Call first to find out about guest and visitor policies, and check the phone book for new clubs that may have opened.

South Coast

Ironhouse Gym (883-3858; 415 Rte 1., Scarborough). Weights, lifecycles, stair masters and fitness machines.

New England Health & Racquet Club (284-5953; 329 North St., Saco). Pool, sauna, whirlpool, racquetball, aerobics, weights, lifecycles, stair masters and fitness machines.

Women's Fitness Studio (883-8324; 70 Rte. 1, Scarborough). Aerobics, weights, stairmasters, lifecycles, treadmills and rowing machines.

YMCA (283-0100; Alfred Business Park Rd., Biddeford). Aerobics, fitness machines, Bio climbers, Nautilus, rowing machines, lifecycles, pool and sauna.

Casco Bay

Merrymeeting Health and Fitness Center (729-8433; 120 Harpswell Rd., Brunswick). Tennis and racquetball.

Merrymeeting Health and Fitness Center (729-0129; 120 Main St., Topsham). Pool, tennis, aerobics, weights, racquetball, sauna, whirlpool, fitness machines and lifecycles.

The Racquet and Fitness Center (775-6128; Congress Ave., Portland). Racquetball, tennis, aerobics, weights, fitness machines, lifecycles and sauna.

Union Station Fitness (879-9114; 274 St. John St., Portland). Aerobics, weights, treadmill, stair master, lifecycles, rowing machines, Versa climber and Nautilus.

Woman's World Health Spa (773-7173; Corner Brook, South Portland). Aerobics, weights, sauna, stairclimber and lifecycles.

YWCA (874-1130; 87 Spring St., Portland). Pool, aerobics, sauna and weights.

YMCA (874-1111; 70 Forest Ave., Portland). Pools, sauna, squash, racquetball, aerobics and fitness machines.

Midcoast

Bay Area Fitness (338-2639; Searsport Ave., Belfast). Lifecycle, weights, fitness machines, stairmasters, rowing machines and nordic track.

Mid-Coast Fitness Center (442-8498; 55 Congress Ave., Bath). Nautilus, stairmasters, sauna, lifecycle, fitness machine and weights.

Oceanside Spa (338-1692; 15 Main, Belfast). Fitness machines, weights and lifecycles.

Samoset Resort (594-2511; Waldo Ave., Rockport). Pools, hot tubs, sauna, weights, lifecycles, fitness machines and aerobics.

Trade Winds Health Club (596-6889; 303 Main St., Rockland). Pool, sauna, whirlpool, steam, Nautilus, weights, fitness machines, lifecycle, stairmasters and treadmill.

YMCA (443-4112; 26 Summer St., Bath). Aerobics, pool, whirlpool, sauna, racquetball and weights.

YMCA (633-2855; Townsend Ave., Boothbay Harbor). Pool, aerobics, weights, racquetball, sauna and cardiovascular equipment.

YMCA (236-3375; 50 Chestnut St., Camden). Aerobics, racquetball, weights, pool, sauna and fitness machines.

Down East/Acadia

Maine Racquet & Fitness Club (667-3341; Rte. 1, Trenton). Pool, tennis, aerobics, racquetball, weights, sauna, whirlpool, lifecycles, rowing machines, Nautilus and stairmasters.

YMCA (288-3511; 23 Mt. Desert St., Bar Harbor). Aerobics, weights, fitness machines, Nautilus, pool, rowing machines, nordic track and toning classes.

HIKING & WALKING

Hiking and walking can be the best way to see the coast, burn off lunch or blow off the cobwebs after sitting in the car all morning. A hike on the coast can entail anything from walking a scenic island perimeter road to climbing **Cadillac Mountain** in Acadia, which at 1,530 ft. is the tallest peak on the Atlantic coast. Another favorite hiking spot is **Camden Hills State Park.** Walkers have several options there from the tame to rigorous short climbs. A map and guide to the various hikes are available at the park entrance.

State Development Office

The pleasures of family hiking include the good view at the top.

DeLorme Mapping Company offers an inexpensive booklet titled *Hiking: Volume 1 Coastal & Eastern Region.* It has several routes mapped with experience levels clearly marked and is available at many supermarkets and bookstores. Here are some of the more popular coastal hikes and walks.

South Coast

Marginal Way, Ogunquit. Begin near Rte. 1 in Ogunquit and follow the paved footpath over cliff and ledges all the way to Perkins Cove. It's about a mile and is perfect for a morning constitutional or an evening sunset stroll.

Rachel Carson National Wildlife Refuge, Wells. Follow the signs off Rte. 9 to parking area and trail head. This is another short and pretty walk. It borders the 16,000-acre Wells National Estuarine Sanctuary.

Casco Bay

Back Cove, Portland. This 3.5-mile walk around Back Cove in Portland is a popular one on a warm spring or summer evening. What's that smell? Baked beans? That's the B & M Baked Bean factory across the way putting the final touches on a new batch of the sweet beans.

Wolf Neck State Park, Freeport. Just a few miles from the commercial craziness of downtown Freeport, this is truly a cool haven in the spring and summer. The 200-acre state park is on a small peninsula jutting into Casco Bay. The park has four miles of well-marked trails that lead along Casco Bay past Googins Island (where a pair of osprey nest) through a stand of white pine and along the Harraseeket River.

Midcoast

Bald Rock Mountain, Lincolnville. From the summit, you can see Mount Desert and the Penobscot Bay islands. From Ski Lodge Rd., this is an easy ascent on a well-traveled path to the top. It is a one-half mile walk with an elevation gain of 1000 feet.

Monhegan Island. Take the Burnt Head trail along the 150-foot cliffs and through Cathedral Woods — one of the few existing stands of virgin pine in Maine. This is a good day trip. The island has about 17 miles of hiking trails and is ruled by walkers (no vehicles are allowed). Ferries leave for Monhegan from Boothbay Harbor, New Harbor and Port Clyde.

Mount Battie, Camden. There aren't many prettier walks than this one. From various lookouts you can see Mount Desert Island, Blue Hill Bay, Camden village, harbor, coast and Megunticook from the mountain's exposed summit. There's also a stone tower at the top. This walk is even prettier in the fall when the leaves change. A park nature trail joins with a short, steep trail that climbs parallel to the auto toll road. One-mile climb with a 600-foot elevation gain.

Mount Megunticook, Camden. The highest of the Camden Hills, the ridge is ascended by park trails from several directions. The views are more limited on this walk, but there are several good vistas from exposed ledges en route. The Megunticook Trail offers most direct ascent. It begins near the park entrance and passes a grotto and stream, then rises steeply to Ocean Lookout and panoramic views. Base to Lookout is a one-mile climb with an elevation gain of 1,100 feet.

Mount Megunticook/Mount Battie, Camden. More ambitious walkers can plan to do both hills in one day. The trip begins at the parking lot, continues over Mount Megunticook, across to Mount Battie and back to the parking area. The total walk is about 4.5 miles, and the top of Mount Battie is a great place for a picnic.

Ragged Mountain, Camden. An easy trail that weaves in and out of the trail and ski lift at Snow Bowl. The elevation gain is about 400 feet, and the trail is about one mile from base to summit.

Down East/Acadia

Blue Hill, Blue Hill. A one-mile climb up a Jeep trail. The path leads through open areas and woods. Look for blueberries. (500 feet.)

Mount Champlain, Isle au Haut. A mile-long easy trip to the top offering alternate routes for the way down. (400 feet.) There are several other good walking trails on the island. To get to Isle au Haut, you can catch the ferry at Stonington.

Hiking in Acadia National Park

There are eight climbing peaks in Acadia National Park on Mount Desert Island. All of them are relatively easy. The tallest and most often climbed is Cadillac, probably because most people choose to climb Cadillac in their cars. On foot, it's less crowded, and many of the best sites come before or after you make it to the top. Below we list favorite hikes in the park. You can get trail information at the park entrance.

Cadillac Mountain, Mount Desert Island. This is a gradual climb that belies the fact that it is the highest peak on the coast. From the park loop road it is about 3.5 miles with a 1,200 foot elevation gain. Make it a round trip, and you have an excellent day's hike.

Dorr Mountain, Mount Desert Island. Stone steps lead directly up this mountain passing through woods. There are some great views of Frenchman Bay and Cadillac Mountain from its ledges. Base to summit, this is a 1.5 mile walk with a 1,200 foot elevation gain.

Gorham Mountain, Mount Desert Island. This is a great hike for amateur geologists. Combined with a side trip to Cadillac Cliffs, you will walk among overhangs, arches and caves. From the summit, you can see many of the park highlights, including the Beehive, Sand Beach, Great Head, Otter Cliffs and The Bowl. If you want to continue on, a trail leads along the ridge to Champlain Mountain. This is a one-mile hike to the summit with a 500 foot elevation gain.

Pemetic Mountain, Mount Desert Island. This is one of the best hikes on the coast and perhaps the very best on the island. It lets you warm up on a nice, easy stretch, then gets tougher as the trail gets steeper. It passes through what some call a "storybook forest" to great views of Mount Desert's hills and the nearby islands and ocean. The climb begins at Bubble Pond and continues for one mile with an elevation gain of 1,000 feet. You can make this walk into a 3.75 mile loop by following the trail down to Jordan Pond, then the carriage trail back to Bubble Pond.

Penobscot and Sargent mountains, Mount Desert Island. A wonderfully varied walk with excellent views of Cadillac and the island panorama. This begins tough with a somewhat difficult ascent up Jordan Cliffs, but the rest is relatively easy. After the cliffs, follow the trail from the summit of Penobscot about 1.5 miles past a pretty lake to Sargent, the island's second highest mountain. The climb is about 1,200 feet from Jordan Pond to the top of Sargent.

Flying Mountain, Southeast Harbor. Short, brisk climb through pleasant woods to a plateau and outlook, with great views of Somes Sound and Cadillac. (Possible loop, descending via Valley Cove; slippery in spring.) Fernald Cove to overlook, 1/2 miles; elevation gain 200 feet. (Loop, 1 1/4 miles.)

Schoodic Mountain, Winter Harbor. An easy climb that offers a short backward-looking view of Frenchman Bay and the more populated section of Acadia. It's a winding road to the top of this rocky headland (400 feet).

East of Schoodic

West Quoddy Head State Park, south of Lubec. This is the easternmost point of the United States, an elemental and majestic beginning. A two-mile trail outlines the 100-ft. cliffs and Carrying Place Cove. Several miles out, you can see Grand Manan, looking like a giant humpback whale.

HORSEBACK RIDING

South Coast

Bush Brook Farm (284-7721; 463 West St., Biddeford). Lessons, boarding, indoor riding arena, wooded trail rides.

Whistlin' Willows (282-5103; 52 McKenney Rd., Saco).

Horseback Riding Plus (883-6400; Scarborough). Public trails.

Long Horn Equestrian Center (883-6400; Scarborough). Indoor arena, lessons, boarding.

The thrill of learning to ride a pony.

Diana Lynn Doherty

Casco Bay

100 Acre Wood Farm (729-4415; Hacker Rd. Brunswick). Lessons, jumping, dressage and everything.

Highland Dressage Center (797-6207; 77 Babbidge Rd., Falmouth). Lessons, training, riding, driving, boarding, indoor and outdoor rings.

Hurricane Valley Stables (797-2280; 21 Shaw Rd., Falmouth). Indoor arena, boarding, polo.

Midcoast

Cherrydale Horse Farm (443-6782; Old Brunswick Rd., West Bath). Trails, boarding.

Gallant Morgan Horse Farm (443-4170; Days Ferry Rd., Rte. 128, Woolwich). Lessons, boarding, training, indoor facilities, tack shop, girls' riding camp.

Ledgewood Riding Stable (882-6346; Rte. 27, Edgecomb). Lessons, boarding, transporting, trails, summer camp.

Hill-N-Dale Farm (273-2511; Western Rd., Warren). Lessons, trail rides, sleigh rides, hay rides, day camp and carousel tack shop.

Fall Foliage in Maine

Leaf peeping is relatively new to Maine. For years, devoted foliage aficionados have chosen New England neighbors to the south and west of Maine. That wasn't for any lack of color, say state tourism officials, but merely because the state had failed to promote the fall season. The truth is the coast does have a lovely foliage season, and it is often less crowded than coinciding seasons in New Hampshire and Vermont.

The change begins almost immediately after Labor Day, when the temperature begins to drop. The big change comes about a month later, when warm days and cool nights cause trees to begin storing energy to get them through the winter. Trees extract sugars, starches and other nutrients from their leaves, causing leaves to turn from green to red, yellow and orange. First trees inland change, then those on the coast.

Down East from Acadia to Washington County is the first region on the coast to turn — generally around the end of September or early October. The western coast stretching from Kittery to Bucksport usually turns about a week later. Peak foliage usually lasts for about three to four weeks. This can all change from year to year, depending on the prevailing temperatures, the rainfall and other weather factors. For an inside tip on color conditions, call the *Foliage Hotline* (582-9300; out-of-state 800-533-9595) after September 15. The state publishes a leaf peepers' guide with several coastal leaf routes between 100 and 250 miles long; ask for it at any of the state information centers listed in *Information*, Chapter Eight.

If you want to find your own way, here are some tips on colorful routes. *St. George's Peninsula* near Port Clyde usually has great color. So does the *Blue Hill Peninsula. Acadia* is a favorite spot, particularly if you drive or hike up Cadillac or the other Mount Desert hills. The *Camden Hills* are another excellent site for autumn foliage. The *Saco River* near Biddeford and the *Royal River* in Yarmouth are two great canoe trips for viewing the foliage. One of our favorite sights are the blueberry barrens that cover the hillsides way Down East. As the weather cools, they turn a brilliant scarlet. We also think the shortcut (See "Shortcuts" in *Transportation*, Chapter Two) on Rte. 182 between Ellsworth and Cherryfield is one of the prettiest autumn drives in New England.

MOTORCYCLING

In 1991 biker clubs went on a lobster run in Brunswick, a surf & turf run from Biddeford, held a swap meet in Portland and a Halloween Party in Hallowell. See a local bike shop for scheduled gatherings.

The state urges all riders to wear helmets. The law requires only passengers under 15 years of age, cyclists operating on a learner's permit and riders who have had their license for less than one year to wear one. The law also requires all motorcyclists to ride with their lights on during the day. The number for the *Motorcycle Safety Foundation* is 800-447-4700. They will give you motorcycle course information.

NATURE PRESERVES

The state may seem vast and unpopulated to visitors from the north and south, but the fact is that less than four percent of Maine's lands are publicly held. That makes Maine 47th in the union in the preservation of public access lands. Three groups are actively trying to increase the supply of lands protected from commercial development. The Maine chapter of the *Nature Conservancy* (729-5181; 122 Main St., Topsham 04086) has been able to convert more than 50,000 acres of wilderness to protected preserves since it was founded in 1956 at the urging of naturalist Rachel Carson. The *Maine Audubon Society* (781-2330; 118 U.S. Rte. 1, Falmouth 04105) operates several nature centers on the coast as well as inland. Founded in the early 1970s by Peggy Rockefeller and Tom Cabot, the *Maine Coast Heritage Trust* (729-7366; 167 Park Row, Brunswick 04011) has worked to preserve and protect more than 49,000 coastal acres through conservation easements.

These and several smaller conservation organizations have established a network of nature preserves that grace the coast like pearls on a loosely strung necklace. Beginning in the South Coast with the *Wells National Estuarine Sanctuary* and the *Rachel Carson National Wildlife Refuge,* these few small preserves are rich with avian and plant life, and they are fragile havens for birdwatchers, ecologists and the garden variety of nature lover. Spring, summer and fall are good times to walk the trails and observe nature in action. Many of the preserves turn over their trails to cross-country skiers in the wintertime (see below).

South Coast

East Point Sanctuary, Biddeford Pool. A 30-acre sanctuary on the largest tidal pool in Maine. Two trails ring the water and give views of nesting and migratory birds as well as harbor seals at high tide.

Laudholm Farm, Wells. Part of the Wells Reserve that also links the Carson Refuge, this is a saltwater farm that boasts soils more fertile than the richest Iowa farmland. More than 300 years ago the first European farmers in the New World tilled land like that at Laudholm Farm, and visitors can tour buildings and grounds to get a taste of this endangered agricultural tradition.

Rachel Carson National Wildlife Refuge, Rte. 1, Wells. The naturalist summered on the coast, and during her lifetime she was instrumental in establishing the national environmental movement with the writing of environmental classics including *Silent Spring* and *At the Edge of the Sea.* Her estate was willed to the Sierra Club and the Nature Conservancy. Today, this refuge is a living reminder of her crusade — and a wonderful place to observe nature. The mile-long trail built by volunteers in 1988 is handicap accessible.

Refuge at Brave Boat Harbor, Seapoint Rd., Kittery Point. Small refuge on a tidal inlet with good birdwatching and an interesting trail through a salt marsh.

Scarborough Marsh Nature Center, Scarborough. Maine Audubon operates this nature center on the coast's largest saltwater marsh. Self-guided nature walk, as well as several special events and educational programs. You can rent a canoe here, too, to visit marsh animals in their natural habitat.

Wells National Estuarine Research Reserve, Rte. 1, Wells. An educational and research facility set on 1,600 acres of coastal marshland and woods with seven miles of nature trails. There are guided nature, birding, sky watch and wildflower tours in the summer. Admission is free, but there is a nominal fee for guided tours and parking in July and August.

Casco Bay

Fore River Sanctuary, Portland. A 76-acre preserve on the Fore River Estuary. This small pocket of nature includes a portion of the old Cumberland and Oxford Canal and the city's only waterfall; 2.5 miles of nature trails through hemlocks, red oaks and white pine.

Gilsland Farm, Rte. 1, Falmouth. The headquarters for Maine Audubon sits on 60 acres of salt marsh just minutes from Portland with 2.5 miles of trails. Good walks, great cross-country skiing and one of the region's best selection of natural history books in the society's gift shop. Open year round.

Mast Landing Sanctuary, Freeport. Another of the small refuges set aside by Maine Audubon, this one winds through the hills, fields, woods and salt marshes near busy downtown Freeport. There are self-guided nature walks, and you can tent, camp and picnic here.

Wolf Neck Woods State Park, Freeport. This small park is truly one of nature's gems. Well-marked, self-guiding nature trails through coastal woods on Casco Bay and the Harraseeket River. Lovely picnic area. Nominal fee in summer time.

Midcoast

Fernald's Neck Preserve, off Rte. 52, Camden—Lincolnville. Four miles of trails through woods, bog and along 200-ft. cliffs on a 315-acre preserve near Lake Megunticook. Managed by the Nature Conservancy.

Josephine Newman Wildlife Sanctuary, Rte. 127, Georgetown. A 119-acre preserve on the ocean with more than two miles of natural trails. The sanctuary is bounded on two sides by salt marsh and contains a small pond. Managed by Maine Audubon.

Lane's Island Preserve, Vinalhaven. The Nature Conservancy manages a 43-acre refuge here made up of rolling moors and shoreline pounded by rough surf. Trails lead to several beaches. Access is by a stone causeway from Vinalhaven (a car ferry from Rockland services the island of Vinalhaven).

Rachel Carson Salt Pond Preserve, Rte. 32, Bristol. Part of the network of protected lands willed to the public by the late naturalist Rachel Carson. A great place to observe marine life from the point of view of a tidal pool. Good views of Muscongus Bay. A map published by the Nature Conservancy (729-5181) points out interesting rock formations along the shore.

Robert P. Tristam Coffin Wildflower Sanctuary, Rte. 128, Woolwich. The New England Wildflower Society owns and operates this 180-acre refuge. It is home to more than 200 species of flowers, grasses, trees and other plants. Nature trails follow the edge of Merrymeeting Bay.

Down East/Acadia

Crockett Cove Woods, Stonington. A 100-acre preserve managed by the Nature Conservancy, this is a good example of an eastern coastal rain forest. It is a great place to visit on a foggy summer day. Self-guided nature trail.

Indian Point — Blagden Preserve, Mount Desert Island. One of the few forested portions of Mount Desert Island that survived the disastrous 1947 fire, this 110-acre preserve is managed by the Nature Conservancy. Pick up a map and guide from the caretaker and explore the intertwined trails leading through spruce, fir and cedar forests and along the water. Seals like to sun on nearby islands.

Ship Harbor Nature Trail, Rte. 102A, Mount Desert Island. Thirteen stations describe the geology, flora and fauna of the island along a 1.4-mile trail. This is a good, self-guided trail for the family. The trail is named for the famous 1739 shipwreck of the *Grand Design* from Ireland.

East of Schoodic

Great Wass Island Preserve, Rte. 187, Beals Island. Almost 1,600 acres of land with two wooded trails through spruce and fir forests edging a long, narrow cove. Magnificent views of the ocean and eastern islands. Managed by the Nature Conservancy.

Petit Manan National Wildlife Refuge, Rte. 1, Milbridge. A pleasant trail leads 1.5 miles through a wild blueberry barren and woods to a rugged shoreline. Part of a 1,841-acre refuge that includes Petit Manan Peninsula, Petit Manan and Nash islands and part of Bois Bubert Island. The islands — except for the northern end of Bois Bubert — are open to the public and can be reached by private boat.

PUFFIN WATCHING

Their feathers once graced the heads of fashionable women during the 19th century, so much so these colorful sea birds were almost plucked from the species list. Their eggs were also a favorite meal of gourmands. Also known as sea parrots because of their colorful curled beaks, their population is on the increase with help from their friends at the Audubon Society, which launched a major campaign in 1973 called Project Puffin. The project has been successful to date, although puffins may never reach their pre-1800 population. The society relies on private donations to fund the repopulation. To make one, write to Project Puffin, National Audubon Society, HC 60, Box 102-P, Medomak, ME 04551.

The struggle to repopulate off the coast is understandable. Puffins prefer to nest on the remote islands stretching from mid-Maine to Canada. They don't reproduce until after their fifth year, and each mating pair produces only one egg each year. Today puffins flourish to the north in Newfoundland, Iceland and

Britain. In Maine, colonies of the birds nest on Matinicus Island, Machias Seal Island, Eastern Egg Rock in Muscongus Bay and Seal Island in Penobscot Bay. Early summer is the best time to see them. Several tour boat operators split ticket sales with the National Audubon Society, which watches over these puffin sanctuaries.

Midcoast
Pink Lady, **R. Fish and Son** (633-3244; 65 Atlantic Ave., Boothbay Harbor).
Dorothy Diane, **Albert Bunker** (366-3737; Matinicus Island).
Hardy III, **Hardy II Tours** (677-2026; Shore Rd., North Edgecomb).
Captain's Lady, **Lively Lady Enterprises** (863-4461; Vinalhaven Island).
Mary Donna, **Offshore Passenger & Freight** (366-3700; Maine State Ferry Service, Rockland).

East of Schoodic
Barna Norton (497-5933; Jonesport).
Seafarer, **Butch Huntley** (733-5584; Lubec).

ROCK CLIMBING

In spite of this being the rock-bound coast, rock climbing is not one of the most popular pastimes. Consequently, good rock climbing spots have not

Tom Hindman

Otter Cliffs in Acadia National Park is one of the best places in Maine to go rock climbing.

yet been well mapped. The coast of Maine offers climbers both challenges and solitude. *Acadia National Park* is the obvious place; the Precipice, Great Head and Otter Cliffs offer a handful of quality climbs. *Camden Hills State Park* provides moderate climbs as does *Fort Williams Park* in Cape Elizabeth just south of Portland. These places are easily accessible. For further information or gear, call or stop by one of the nearby sporting goods stores (See "Sporting Goods" in *Shopping*, Chapter Seven).

RUNNING

Don't let us stop you. Seriously, *Runner Magazine* readers voted the *Schoodic 10K Road Race* on the Schoodic Peninsula as one of the five best in the country. The terrain is relatively flat, the scenery beautiful, the air and the light clear. Here is a short list of some of the more popular annual runs and the approximate time of year they are held. Call the number supplied for further information.

10,000 Meter Run, Camden (236-4032) Early June.
13-Miler, Bar Harbor and Acadia National Park (288-3511) Mid-September.
5K Road Race & Fun Run, Bar Harbor (288-3511) Early June.
Maine Lobster Festival 10K Road Race, Rockland. (Contact Rockland-Thomaston Area Chamber of Commerce, 596-0376.)

Old Orchard Beach, which stretches for seven miles, challenges visiting runners. The snow fence is to protect new grass.

John Metzger

SKATING

If it has to do with water — frozen included — it's available on Maine's coast. Skating is popular on the coast during the winter. Outdoor listings are free. Indoor listings cost a couple of dollars. Call for times and fees.

South Coast
The Arena (283-0615; Alfred Rd., Industrial Business Park, Biddeford). October 15–April 1. Indoors.

Casco Bay

Dayton Arena (725-3332; Bowdoin College Campus, Brunswick). November – March. Indoors.

Brunswick Parks & Recreation (725-6656; on the Mall, Brunswick). December– March. Outdoors.

Deering Oaks Park (775-5451, Ext. 300; State St. and Park Ave., Portland). December–February. Outdoors.

Payson Park (874-8300, Ext. 300; Baxter Blvd., Portland). December–February. Outdoors.

Portland Ice Arena (774-8553; 225 Park Ave., Portland). Open through April. Indoors.

Mill Creek Park (799-7996; Cottage Rd., South Portland). December–February. Outdoors.

Yarmouth Community Services Park (846-9680; Main St., Yarmouth). December–February. Outdoors.

North Yarmouth Academy Ice Arena (846-2384; Rte.1, Yarmouth). Indoors. Friday nights, 7–9.

Midcoast

Camden Snow Bowl Ski Area (236-3438; Hosmer Rd., Camden). Open December–March. Outdoors.

Walker Park Ice Rink (236-9648; Sea St., Rockport). Outdoors.

SKIING

DOWNHILL SKIING

There are not many people who come to the coast to go downhill skiing; the state's biggest ski areas are inland near Bethel and Rangeley. But you can be one of the few to escape the crowds and feel the ocean breezes at the *Snow Bowl* (236-3438; Camden). There the vertical drop is about 900 feet, the mountain has nine trails and is serviced by a double chairlift and two T-bars — one 4,100-ft. long. Best of all, lift tickets are inexpensive.

CROSS-COUNTRY SKIING

Cross-country on the coast is another story. There are dozens of summer hiking trails that are converted to ski trails with the first snowfall. Skiing the carriage roads at *Acadia* is a beautiful way to experience the park; further Down East, *Cobscook Bay State Park* offers great oceanside ski trails. We also recommend the *Lincoln House* in Dennysville for a good cross-country ski B&B (See *Lodging,* Chapter Three). The inn has its own trails cut through almost 100 acres of woods, and they serve a wonderful dinner as well. Almost every town along the coast has a park and trails that cross-country skiers take over in the wintertime. We've listed some of the better-known areas, but you can find out more by contacting the local chamber of commerce where you plan to visit.

Most of the areas listed below are unstaffed. Remember that it can be unsafe to ski alone. Stay on the trails, and be prepared for Maine's mercurial weather. Also, don't forget to carry out litter. Call beforehand for snow and trail conditions.

South Coast

Vaughan Woods State Park (289-3821; Old Fields Rd. off Rte. 236, South Berwick). Six miles of snow-covered hiking trails that take you by Salmon Falls River and Cow Cove. Two miles are classified "easy"; the other four miles are more difficult.

Casco Bay

Gilsland Farm (781-2330; 118 U.S. Rte. 1, Falmouth). This is the home of the Maine Audubon Society. Three-and-a-half kilometers of trails through their country backyard. Open 7:30 to dusk.

Mast Landing Sanctuary (781-2330; Upper Mast Landing Road, Freeport). Also owned and operated by Maine Audubon Society. Five kilometers of estuary trails through forests and orchards. Open from dawn to dusk.

Bradbury Mountain State Park (688-4712; 6 mi. west from the Freeport exit of I-95, Pownal). From the top of Bradbury Mountain (460 feet) you can see past L.L. Bean to the ocean. There's an easy 1/2 mile, a more difficult 2 miles, and a most difficult 1/2 mile. Trail maps are available at the entrance.

Midcoast

Camp Tanglewood at Camden Hills State Park (594-2104 or 789-5868; off Rte. 1, Lincolnville). Ten miles of ungroomed trails, graded for entry level to the most skilled skiers. Ask for a map available at the gate. January through March, dawn to dusk.

Samoset Ski Touring Center (594-2511; P.O. Box 78, Rockport). Ten kilometers of groomed trails split evenly between entry level and more difficult.

Down East/Acadia

Holbrook Island Sanctuary State Park (326-4012; Cape Rosier, Brooksville). Seven kilometers along wood roads and hiking trails through upland forests and fields offering views of Penobscot Bay.

Acadia National Park (288-3338; Mount Desert Island). Forty miles of well-marked carriage roads and trails. A trail map can be had from park headquarters on Rte. 233. Wilderness facility.

Roy Zalesky

There are more than 40 miles of well-marked cross-country ski trails in Acadia National Park on Mount Desert Island.

East of Schoodic

Cobscook Bay State Park (726-4412 for snow and trail conditions; off Rte. 1, Dennysville). Six miles of roads through woods with terrific views of the bay.

Moosehorn National Wildlife Refuges (454-3521) adjacent to Cobscook State Park also allows skiing.

SURFING

I t's a South Coast sport. That's where the best waves are, and, in the fine tradition of Moon Doggie and Gidget, that's where the best beaches are. Don't plan on sunbathing when you surf. The truth is that the best surfing is in the fall and winter. Even then surfing here is mostly for beginners. Here are some prime surf apprentice spots.

Fortune Rocks, Biddeford. Surfing on the incoming tide. Then the waves are steep, hollow and break to the right.

Gooch's Beach, Kennebunkport. Best surfing is at low to mid-tide. The waves are steep, thick waves, and they break both right and left.

Moody Beach, Wells. Best waves at high tide. They break close to shore.

Old Orchard Beach, Old Orchard Beach. There is a designated surfing area on the north side of the pier.

Wells Beach, Wells. Surfing best during the incoming tide. The waves break both right and left over sandbars.

York Beach, York Beach. Best waves are at low to mid-tide, and they break right and left.

TENNIS

I n addition to the courts listed, call the town halls for the location of free municipal tennis courts. Several motels and hotels also make their courts available to the public, sometimes for a fee.

South Coast

Biddeford (283-0841; Mayfield Park, May St.). Three courts with night lights. Also Clifford Park, Pool St., has two courts.

Kennebunk (985-6890; Parsons Field, Park St.). Two courts, plus courts at Kennebunk High School. Total of six courts with night lights.

Ogunquit (646-3032; Agamenticus Rd.). Three courts.

Old Orchard Beach (934-2500; high school, T for Turn Rd.). One court; two courts at Ocean Park and two more at Memorial Park.

Wells (646-6171; Congdon's Resort, Rte. 1). Three courts.

York Recreation Area (363-1040; Organug Rd.). Two courts with night lights.

Casco Bay

Bath (443-8360; Congress Ave.). Four courts with night lights.

Brunswick (725-6656; Stanwood St. Courts). Five courts with night lights; bring change. Merrymeeting Health & Fitness Center (729-8433; 120 Harpswell Rd.).

Falmouth (Tennis of Maine, 781-2671; 196 Rte. 1, Falmouth).

Portland (874-8793; Deering Oaks Park). Eleven courts, and six more across the street at Deering High School; four courts on the Eastern Promenade; four courts at Payson Park on Baxter Blvd.; the Racket & Fitness Center (775-6128; 2445 Congress St., Portland).

Midcoast
Boothbay Harbor (633-2855). Two courts.
Damariscotta (563-3477; YMCA). Two courts with night lights.

Down East/Acadia
Bar Harbor (288-5801; Atlantic Oaks, Rte. 3). Four courts. Night lights.
Trenton (Maine Racquet & Fitness Club, 667-3341; Rte. 3). Three indoor courts.

VOLLEYBALL

Volleyball is as much a part of Old Orchard Beach as the boardwalk. The *Eastern State Volleyball* tournament is played here the end of July and the *Granite State Tournament* is held in August.

WACKY FAMILY FUN

There's recreation and then there's recreation. If you get tired of going to the beach, herewith is some more good stuff, kids.

South Coast
Aquaboggan Water Park (282-3112; Rte. 1, Saco). Can't miss it. Kids love it. Water slides, splash pools for kiddie tots, bumper boats, races cars, shuffleboard. A real fun time.

Cascade Water & Amusement Park (284-6231; Rte. 1, Saco).

The rides along the boardwalk at **Old Orchard Beach.**

Fun-O-Rama (363-4421;13 Beach, York Beach).

Funtown U.S.A. (284-5139; Portland Rd., Saco). Need we say more?

Jellystone Park (324-7782; Rte. 109, Sanford/Wells). Family camping at Yogi Bear's place! Wacky fun all night long!

Maine Aquarium (284-4511; Rte. 1, Saco). Fish under glass.

Pirate's Cove Adventure Golf (First Street, Old Orchard Beach). 36 holes. "Explore the wonderful and mysterious hideout of pirates!"

York Wild Kingdom (363-4911; Railroad Ave., York). Contained wild animals and more.

Casco Bay

Hot Shots (773-1441; 87 Marginal Way, Portland). Indoor family fun for a rainy day. Mini-golf, video games, airhockey, bankshot basketball. Enough to hold you and the kids over until the sun comes out.

Westerly Winds (854-9463; 771 Cumberland St., Westbrook). Pitch n' Putt golf course, driving range, miniature golf, and pitching machines for hardball and softball.

Down East/Acadia

Kart Land (667-2920; Trenton).

Odyssey Park (667-5841; Bar Harbor Rd., Trenton).

Pirate's Cove Adventure Golf (Rte. 3 near Hulls Cove, Mount Desert Island). 36 holes of miniature golf.

WHALE WATCH

F inbacks, pilots, minkes, rights and humpbacks cruise the coast along the continental shelf. From early spring through late fall from shore you can see whales at *East Quoddy Head Lighthouse, West Quoddy Head Lighthouse* and *West Quoddy State Park* looking out toward Grand Manan Island. The Gulf of Maine is also home to dolphins, harbor porpoises, seals, osprey, storm petrels, puffins and other sea birds (see Birdwatching, above) and fishermen. Most of these charters run through the summer and into mid-September or October.

Whales are frequent summer visitors off the coast of Maine.

Tom Hindman

South Coast

Indian Whale Watch (967-5912; Arundel Wharf Restaurant, Ocean Ave., Kennebunkport).

Casco Bay
Indian II (642-3270; Long Wharf, Commercial St., Portland).
Odyssey Whale Watch (775-0727 or 642-3270; Long Wharf, Commercial St., Portland).

Down East/Acadia
The Acadian Whale Watcher (288-9794; Bar Harbor).
Frenchman Bay Co. (288-3322; 1 West St., Bar Harbor).
Maine Whalewatch (276-5803 or 800-339-5803; Northeast Harbor).

East of Schoodic
Capt. Butch Huntley (733-5584; Lubec). If he can't make it, he'll tell you who can.

WINDJAMMERS

Today the only cargo these sea trains carry are tourists. Life on a windjammer was never the cruise it is today. Work for the crew was never optional; private cabins were unheard of for all but the captain; and there never were gourmet meals served at respectable hours.

The *Lewis R. French*, built in 1871, is the oldest. *Angelique*, a steel-hulled ketch launched in 1980, is the youngest member of the fleet. That new ships still are being built and the industry is prospering is testament to the enjoyment windjammers provide. The newest windjammers are built true to old ways, only with a few added comforts. In fact, most of the old fleet has been rebuilt or refurbished to serve the cruise business in the style to which its tourists are accustomed. Some of the old ones are still pushed by yawlboats to open water.

Every year near Rockland, home to much of the fleet, there is an annual *Great Schooner Race* in early July. People with timely reservations take part. There are *Windjammer Days* in Boothbay Harbor around the end of June, and *WoodenBoat* magazine's annual sail-in during mid-September.

If you aren't lucky enough to visit during one of these events, there are always the cruises. They last from three days in the off-season to six days during the summer. Most windjammer cruises cost between $300—$600. On some windjammers you can take a two-hour ride for $16 per person. For more information about the old sailing vessels, you can contact the *Maine Windjammer Association* (800-624-6380; P.O. Box 317, Rockport 04856).

Midcoast

American Eagle (594-8007 or 594-7617 or 800-648-4544; Capt. John Foss, P.O. Box 482, Rockland 04841).
Angelique (236-8873 or 800-282-9989; Capts. Mike & Lynne McHenry, Box 736, Camden 04843).

Appledore (236-8353 or 800-233-PIER; Sharp's Wharf, Camden 04843). Four two-hour sails daily in July and August; three two-hour sails in June, September and October.

Grace Bailey (236-2938 or 800-736-7981; Maine Windjammer Cruises, Capts. Ray and Ann Williamson, P.O. Box 617, Camden 04843).

Heritage (800-648-4544, 800-542-5030; Capt. Doug and Linda Lee, P.O. Box 482, Rockland 04841).

Isaac H. Evans (594-8007 or 800-648-4544; Capt. Ed Glaser, P.O. Box 482, Rockland 04841).

J & E Riggin (594-2923 or 800-896-0604; Capt. Dave Allen, Box 571, Rockland 04841).

Lewis R. French (594-8007 or 800-648-4544; Capt. Dan Pease, Box 482, Rockland 04841).

Mary Day (236-2750 or 800-922-2218; Coastal Cruises, Capt. Steve Cobb, P.O. Box 798, Camden 04843).

Mercantile (236-2938 or 800-736-7981; Maine Windjammer Cruises, Capts. Ray and Ann Williamson, P.O. Box 617, Camden 04843).

Mistress (236-2938 or 800-736-7981; Maine Windjammer Cruises, Capts. Ray and Ann Williamson, P.O. Box 617, Camden 04843).

Nathaniel Bowditch (326-4098 or 800-288-4098; Capt. Gib Philbrick, General Delivery, Harborside 04642).

Olad (236-2323; Capt. John Nugent, P.O. Box 432, Camden 04843).

Roseway (236-4449 or 800-255-4449; Yankee Schooner Cruises, Capts. George Sloane and Stephen Gold, Box 696, Camden 04843).

Stephen Taber (236-3520 or 800-999-7352; Capts. Ken and Ellen Barnes, Windjammer Wharf, 70 Elm St., P.O. Box 1050, Rockland 04841). This is the only windjammer to be listed on the National Historic Register.

Surprise (236-4687; Atlantic Ave., Camden 04843).

Timberwind (236-0801 or 800-624-6013; Capt. Bill Alexander, P.O. Box 247, Rockport 04856).

Victory Chimes (594-0755; Capt. Kip Files, P.O. Box 1401, Rockland 04841).

Wendameen (236-3472; Capt. Neal Parker, Box 506, Camden 04843). Overnight cruises on a 67-foot schooner.

Down East/Acadia

Natalie Todd (288-4585 summer, 546-2927 winter; Downeast Windjammer Cruises, Capt. Steven F. Pagels, P.O. Box 8, Cherryfield 04622). A three-masted schooner that offers two-hour cruises and sails from Bar Harbor Inn Pier, Bar Harbor.

Frenchman Bay Company (288-3322; 1 West St., Bar Harbor 04609). 21 trips a day from whale watching to windjamming.

Summertime Cruises Inc. (359-2067; Capt. Bill Brown, Box 20, North Brooklin 04661).

WINDSURFING

This is not an easy sport to learn. It's even harder in the ocean. Lakes are the place for lessons. *Back Cove* in Portland is a popular spot. It's lakelike enough to learn on, and the wind can blow like the ocean in a storm. *Pine Point* in Scarborough is another good spot. So are *Eagle Lake, Echo Lake* and *Long Pond* on Mount Desert Island. The beaches in the south are popular once you've mastered the sport. Wherever you windsurf in Maine, a wetsuit is required, because the water can be very cold. If you want tips from experienced coastal windsurfers, look up the folks at *Port Sports* in Portland (775-6080; 127 Marginal Way) or *Latitude 44* in Bar Harbor (288-5805; 39 Cottage St.). Both offer lessons, gear and rentals.

SEASONAL SPORTING EVENTS

Beyond the annual events mentioned in the above categories, the coast has dozens of events that lure sportsmen and women from around the world. Following are a few favorite events you should know about.

South Coast

Sand Building Contest, mid-July. On the beach in Ogunquit, the time of this contest is governed by the tides (phone 636-2939 for information).
Great Inner Tube Race, mid-August. On the river in Ogunquit. (646-2939 for information).
Kite Flying Contest, late August. On the beach in Ogunquit (phone 646-2939).

Diana Lynn Doherty

A father and daughter enjoy the cool waters in Echo Lake, on Mount Desert Island.

Casco Bay

Peaks Island-to-Portland Swim, late July. Strong-armed swimmers often finish the two-mile swim from Peaks Island beach to East End Beach in Portland in under one hour (contact YMCA, 874-1111).

The Multiple Sclerosis Regatta, late August. Takes place in Casco Bay (contact the Portland Chamber of Commerce, 772- 2811).

Midcoast

Friendship Sloop Days and Friendship Sloop Races, late July. Beautiful wooden boats compete for attention and prizes (contact the Friendship Sloop Society, 633-2353).

The Great Schooner Race, early July. Sponsored by the Maine Windjammer Association, this all-day race begins at North Haven and ends in Rockland (contact the Rockland Chamber of Commerce, 596-0376).

Maine Retired Skipper's Race, late August. You have to be over 65 to enter (contact the Retired Skipper's Race Committee, Castine, 326-8579).

The Monhegan Island Yacht Race, mid-August.

Owls Head Transportation Rally, mid-August. Planes, trains and automobiles. More than 300 of them (contact the Owls Head Transportation Museum, 594-4418).

Schooner Days, early July (Rockland area Chamber of Commerce, 596-0376).

Windjammer Days, late June. Windjammers of all shapes and sizes (contact the Boothbay Harbor Chamber of Commerce, 633- 2353).

East of Schoodic

The World's Fastest Lobsterboat Races, early July. Takes place near Moosabec Reach (contact the Jonesport 4th of July Committee, P.O. Box 106, Jonesport 04649; 497-2804).

CHAPTER SEVEN

Something Old, Something New

SHOPPING

Maine these days is known for its outlets as well as its inlets. The outlet trail stretches north and eastward from Kittery all the way to Ellsworth near Bar Harbor. The descendants of L. L. Bean, the man who invented the Maine Hunting Boot, still keep shop in Freeport on Casco Bay and in two "factory stores," one in Ellsworth and another in Freeport.

Photo courtesy of L. L. Bean, Inc.

The old L. L. Bean store, a name that is almost synonymous with the coast of Maine.

Mainers have been commercially adept since the early 1600s. The Pilgrims of Plymouth Colony sent their most industrious members north to establish a fur trade out of Bagaduce (now known as Castine) on the Blue Hill peninsula. They paid off the debts for their voyage in just a few years. The earliest trade with Europe and their fellow colonists was in furs and lumber, then ships and granite. Later, coastal residents began selling manufactured goods to the rest of the world: fabric woven in textile mills to the south; shoes from leather tanned and handsewn at factories inland; paper made at pulp mills on many of the state's rivers; and herring and sardines canned at factories Down East.

Not all the selling was one-sided. Mainers were world-class shoppers, and during the 18th and 19th centuries world travelers — ship captains and merchants filled their homes with riches from Europe, the Far East and ports to the south.

Shoes, paper, lumber and seafood still comprise much of the industrial base for the state. Yet since the days the "rusticators" discovered Bar Harbor and summer resorts began to sprout up along the coast and inland, much of the state's economy has focused on catering to seasonal residents and tourists. From paintings and artwork to decorate summer homes, and nautical gear to outfit visiting yachts, to T-shirts, balsam sachets, blueberry pottery and lobster magnets — everything to remind the visitor that they had been here.

There are a profusion of art galleries on the coast. Many of them are very good. Antiques, pottery and other handcrafts are big here. Until the past decade, many of the stores along the coast would close after the tourists went home on Labor Day. Now, in towns like Camden and Bar Harbor, they are open all year long.

In this chapter we mention some — but by no means all — of the shopping stops on the coast. Rte. 1, from where it first enters Maine at Kittery to far Down East, is a virtual shopper's paradise with outlets, galleries, junk stores, flea markets and the occasional yard sale all along the way.

ANTIQUES

S hopping for antiques on the coast is almost as popular as outlet hopping, but slower paced. Most antique shopping is done in two places: the region in the South Coast between York and Kennebunkport, and between Belfast and Searsport in the Midcoast. There is plenty of good stuff in between and beyond, only antique shopping in those places isn't as concentrated an experience.

To really know who has what and what it's selling for, pick up a copy of the *Maine Antique Digest*, the bible for coastal and inland antique shoppers. It's published in Waldoboro and can be found at most newsstands in the state.

South Coast

Antiques on Nine (967-0626; 75 Western Ave., Rte. 9, Kennebunk). A mishmash of American and continental furniture, architectural elements, books, art and textiles — even old garden accessories.

The Barn at Cape Neddick (363-7315; Rte. 1, Cape Neddick). Recognized for its selection of American country furniture, accessories and folk art.

The Farm (985-2656; Mildram Rd. off Rte. 1, Wells). Fine English antiques from the 18th and 19th centuries and oriental porcelain. *Yankee* magazine calls this one of the best in New England.

R. Jorgensen Antiques (646-9444; Rte. 1, Wells). Eleven rooms of period furniture and antiques from North America, the British Isles, France and Scandinavia.

MacDougall-Gionet Antiques Associates (646-3531; Rte. 1, Wells). For more than a quarter of a century dealers — now there are 60 — have gathered in an old barn to show and sell formal and country period antiques.

Kenneth & Ida Manko (646-2595; on Seabreeze, one half mile off Eldridge Rd., Moody). An intriguing selection of Americana and folk art, including old weathervanes.

Partridge House Antiques (646-7922; Rte. 1, Wells). A multi-dealer shop with good values in furniture and antique accessories.

York Antiques Gallery (363-5002; Rte. 1, York). Renovated three-story barn with an extensive selection of American country furniture.

Casco Bay

F.O. Bailey (774-1479; 141 Middle St., Portland). Great showroom and a terrific mix of stuff from rustic pottery to highly polished highboys.

Mystic Indian (865-1811; Rte. 1, Freeport). Artifacts, relics and handmade crafts by Native Americans.

Red Wheel Antiques (865-6492; Rte. 1, So. Freeport). We think some of this mix of old dishes, tools, furniture and paraphernalia is overpriced. Still we keep going back to find that occasional bargain. On summer weekends, it becomes an open air flea market.

Phelps & Phelps (775-5004; 43 Silver St., Portland). A beautiful selection of art glass, art pottery and art nouveau on a cobbled Old Port side street.

Midcoast

Apex Antiques and Design Service (338-1194; 98 High St., Belfast). Eclectic mix of American and formal furniture, painted furniture and custom-designed quilts.

Avis Howell's Antiques (338-3302; corner of Pearl and Court, Belfast). Avis has collected and sold Shaker furniture for more than a quarter of a century.

Ben & Leslie Blumenberg (832-6734; 1015 Main St., Waldoboro). An eclectic collection of old fishing tackle, antique tools and Staffordshire china. The Blumenbergs also collect old glass and are open most or the year.

F. Barrie Freeman (442-8452; Quaker Point Farm, West Bath). Old American maps. They also specialize in printed Americana and ephemera.

Eagull Antiques (367-5050; Main St., Stonington). Antique furniture and art. They are only open for the season (July—September).

The Ditty Box (882-6618; Rte. 1 at the No. Edgecomb/Newcastle town line). Antiques and collectibles including old samplers, china, Currier & Ives prints and American country furniture.

Dot's Good Deals (Rte. 1, Woolwich). Odds, ends and maybe even the kitchen sink. More than one person has called this "the attic of America." If Dot has a phone, she's not telling.

Patricia Anne Reed Fine Antiques (563-5633; Bristol Rd., Rte. 129, Damariscotta). American antiques and collectibles, including children's toys.

Schueler's Antiques (236-2770; 10 High St., Camden). Antique American furniture, accessories, porcelain and decoys.

Tools & Antiques (832-6344; 1015 Main St., Waldoboro). Old tools, old fishing lures and old photos and prints.

Wee Barn Antiques (354-6163, 354-6347; 4 1/2 Georges St., Thomaston). Gwen Robinson and Lee-Ann Upham have gathered a fun collection of antique "smalls," glass, furniture, jewelry and silver.

A flea market in Searsport. Flea markets, yard and garage sales yield some of the coast's best selections of antiques and other treasures.

Tom Hindman

Acadia/Down East

The Big Chicken Barn (667-7308; Rte. 1, Ellsworth). With hundreds of tiny windows rising several stories, this really is an old chicken barn. The feathers are gone, and it now is packed with a giant collection of old books, antiques and fun junk.

Hulls Cove Tool Barn (288-5126) and **Geronimo Cafe Bookshop and Sculpture Garden** (288-5503; Breakneck Rd. off Rte. 3, Hulls Cove). Old tools and antiques of all descriptions at the Tool Barn; old books, paintings and prints at Geronimo's, which is also a vegetarian cafe and has two acres of sculpture garden showing the work of three to four artists.

Auctions on the Coast

If you're looking for antiques or just a Victorian knick-knack to take back to your Aunt Pearl, auctions provide the chance to cut out the middleman and get a feel for the worth of something by competing against professional buyers. Estate auctions are even more fun, because they give you a truer sense of time and place than many historic homes or museums. Most of the auction houses listed below will be glad to put you on their mailing lists. *The Maine Sunday Telegram* and the *Maine Times* often run notices of upcoming auctions in their classified sections. In addition, the *Maine Antique Digest* has auction announcements, solid news and an entertaining column of auction gossip complete with photographs.

South Coast

Bacon's Auction Co. (985-1401; Rte. 1, Arundel).
J. J. Keating (985-2097; Rte. 1, Kennebunk).
Richard Oliver (985-3600; Rte. 1, Kennebunk).
Hap Moore Antiques Auctioneer (363-6373; York).

<u>Casco Bay</u>
F.O. Bailey Antiquarians (774-1479; 141 Middle St., Portland).
Northern Lights Auction Hall (829-3063; Yarmouth).

<u>Midcoast</u>
Foster's Auction Gallery (563-8150; Newcastle).
Andrews and Andrews (338-1386; Atlantic Ave., Northport).

<u>Downeast/Acadia</u>
Mayo & Mayo Auctioneers (667-2586; Rte. 3, Trenton).

BOOKS

F riends who visit us love our bookstores. While many of the bookstores are small mom-and-pop affairs, they cater to a literate clientele. Several are known for their specialties — like women's studies or new age essays or fine old volumes only a bibliophile could love. Others you can count on for having a good translation of Homer as well as the top 10 from *The New York Times* Book Review section. Maybe it's the long winter, and the fact that people here really do curl up by the fireplace with a good book. A couple of years ago Maine's preeminent weekly, *Maine Times*, surveyed its readers and found they read, on average, fifty books a year.

South Coast
Kennebunk Book Port (967-3815; Dock Square, Kennebunkport). Books sold in an old rum warehouse.
Harding Book Shop (646-8785; Rte. 1, Wells). A book collector's paradise with old and rare books, maps and prints. Bring your favorite first edition and they will do an appraisal.

Casco Bay
Allen Scott Books (774-2190; 89 Exchange St., Portland). Old, used and rare books bought and sold. Good browsing for a rainy day.
Carlson & Turner Antiquarian Books (773-4200; 241 Congress St., Portland). We love to survey these dimly lit shelves. Ask to be put on their mailing list to receive their annual collectors' calendar.
DeLorme Mapping Company (865-4171; Rte. 1, Freeport). The company is responsible for charting the state's wilderness — urban and otherwise — from every possible point of view. You see DeLorme maps everywhere in Maine, but you don't truly understand the scope of their accomplishment until you see all the maps in their store. These days they continue to branch out in their charting the world, and now they use satellites.
Harbour Books (846-6306; 40A Lafayette St., Yarmouth). Books for children and mariners in this small shop near the harbor.
Harding Book Shop (761-2150; 538 Congress St., Portland). This is the younger sister of a well-known collectors' store in Wells (see above).
The Maine Writers Center (729-6333; 12 Pleasant St., Brunswick). More than 1,400 works by Maine writers, publishers and small presses are represented,

as well as Maine-related books. This is the home of the Maine Writers Alliance, a non-profit organization that sponsors seminars and workshops.

Raffles Cafe and Bookstore (761-3930; 555 Congress St., Portland). Munch on a vegetarian BLT and browse through a well-chosen selection of recent and classic books.

The Store at Maine Audubon Society (781-2330; 118 U.S. Rte 1, Falmouth). A good collection of books for those interested in natural history.

Midcoast

ABCDef, Lillian Berliawsky, Bookseller (236-3903; 23 Bayview St., Camden). Fine, old, hard to find and rare books.

Canterbury Tales Books (338-1171; 52 Main St., Belfast). Books for all ages, in addition to topographical maps and nautical charts.

A Children's Bookstore (236-4141; 24 Bayview St., Willey's Wharf, Camden). Books for the little people.

The Fertile Mind Bookshop (338-2498; 13 Main St., Belfast). New and "recycled" books and a book and cassette rental collection.

Maine Coast Book Shop (563-3207; Main St., Damariscotta). Penguin novels and coffee table books, as well as a full selection of paperback and hardcover books.

New Leaf Books (596-0040; 348 Main St., Rockland). New age titles for women and those interested in alternative health care and spiritual matters.

Owl & Turtle Bookshop (236-4769 or 800-876-4769; 8 Bayview St., Camden). Not only do they encourage browsing, but if you get really absorbed in something, they have a few rooms available. Possibly the only B&B&B in Maine, or anywhere else. Children's and nautical books.

Stuart Phelps (338-5234; Miller St., Belfast). Buys and sells old collectible books.

Thomaston Books & Prints (354-0001; Main St., Thomaston). Books for kids, adults and everyone in between, plus limited edition prints and art posters.

Down East/Acadia

Mr. Paperback (288-3232; 24 Cottage St., Bar Harbor). Also carries Mr. Magazine.

Memories of Maine (288-9766; 1 West St., Bar Harbor). Regional books, maps, papers and cards.

Blue Hill Books (374-5632; 2 Pleasant St., Blue Hill). A healthy selection of books about Maine and New England. Books for children. Fiction for adults.

The Compass Rose (800-698-9366 or 326-9366; Main St., Castine). Books and antique prints.

Oz Books (244-9077; Main St., Southwest Harbor). Books for kids. Books about Maine for grownups.

East of Schoodic

Eastern Maine Books (255-4908; 65-67 Main St., Machias). One of the few book stops East of Schoodic, and the easternmost selection of rare and collectible books in the U.S.

L. L. Bean, the original outlet store, is the second most visited spot on the coast of Maine.

Photo courtesy of L. L. Bean, Inc.

Maine Outlets

Maine's outlet trail runs from Kittery to Freeport, and it begins almost immediately after you cross the state line. There are few things an experienced shopper will need to know to conquer the outlets, but here are a few tips anyway. Try to avoid shopping on rainy days. Take note that even outlets have sales, and many times those coincide with sale seasons in regular retail stores (July 4, late summer and early fall are particularly popular sale times here because of the summer tourist traffic). Remember that not all outlet bargains are real bargains — usually there's a reason, good or otherwise, these items did not sell elsewhere.

In Kittery, most of the outlets are for products you can purchase at many other outlet havens throughout the country. Anne Klein, Brooks Brothers, Corning/Revere, Timberland, Puma, Capezio, Villeroy & Boch, Crate & Barrel, Dansk, Black & Decker and more.

It's much more of the same in Freeport in the Casco Bay region, except there you have L. L. Bean. You'll also find an outlet for high end Maine shoe manufacturer Cole-Haan (The Company Store), Calvin Klein, Reebok, The Gap (upstairs there are some great bargains), Banana Republic, J. Crew, Patagonia and G. H. Bass (based just south of here in Falmouth). My thrifty, quality-minded father-in-law especially likes to shop the Ralph Lauren store during their late summer sale. There he finds great bargains on his favorite polo shirts.

There are more than outlets in Freeport. If it weren't for Freeport's outlets it would be just another pretty Maine coastal village. As it is, behind the scenes there are facsimile machines, complicated phone systems and everyone in town is a marketing expert and aware of the square foot cost of floor space.

Ellsworth, the youngest outlet community on the coast, has the smallest selection of stores, but if you're an outdoors person, you'll want to check out the L. L. Bean Factory Store. Unlike their off-price store in Freeport, you occasionally can find significant markdowns on store samples of their sporting equipment — mountain bikes, steppers, tents, stoves and the like. If you find something you like, grab it. It's usually the only one in stock.

Meanwhile, there are hundreds more true factory stores and outlets along the coast. Here are some of our favorites:

Cuddledown Factory Store (865-1713; 6 Mill St., Freeport). Lush down comforters, comforter covers, sheets and other linens sewn at a factory in nearby Portland. Buy them here and save 30 to 80 percent. Or ask to receive their catalog.

Maine State Prison Showroom Outlet (354-2535; Rte. 1, Thomaston). Everyone needs an outlet. Handcrafted furniture and gift items usually with a nautical theme. Here you can find patio furniture, lamps, ship's wheel mirrors, hutches, handcarved novelties, desks and cedar chests. All are at reasonable prices.

The Moss Tent Outlet (at Maine Sport, 236-7120; Rte. 1, Rockport). Moss Tents, designed and manufactured in nearby Camden, are considered by many experts to be the finest. Firsts, seconds and discontinued models are sold at up to 30 percent off retail.

Tom's of Maine (985-3874; 106 Lafayette Center, Kennebunk). In 1990 more than 4000 visitors stopped by Tom's Natural Outlet to stock up on toothpaste in slightly battered tubes, shaving cream, shampoo and other natural personal care items and bathroom staples. Tom Chapell, the founder, recently graduated from Harvard Divinity School and is looking for new ways to fill the spiritual void in corporate America, as well as prevent tooth decay naturally.

The Visitor's Loft Store (at the Rockport Apprenticeshop, 236-6071; on Rockport Harbor, Rockport). Buy a beautiful wooden boat made by the apprentices here and support a Maine coast way of life. Friendship sloops, Lawley tenders, Rangeley guide boats, peapods, melon seeds and Nomans Land boats. In the shop they also sell wooden boat mementos and hardware. Join the apprenticeshop for only $35, and receive the newsletter *On the Ways*, a discount at the shop and other good wooden boat things.

CLOTHING

South Coast

Dock Square Clothiers (967-5362; Dock Square, Kennebunkport; and 646-8548; Perkins Cove). Classic, natural-fiber clothing for men and women sold at two locations.

Casco Bay

Amaryllis (772-4439; 41 Exchange St., Portland). Unusual women's clothing, shoes and hats.

The Company Store (865-6321; 66 Main Street, Freeport). An upscale "outlet" for Cole-Haan, the high-end shoe manufacturer that has its offices in nearby Yarmouth. Downstairs they stock beautiful shoes. Upstairs it's clothing from around the world.

Joseph's (773-1274; 410 Fore St., Portland). The men's and women's clothing stores are as *haut* as Maine gets.

Levinsky's (774-0972; 278 Congress St., Portland; and 865-6868; Rte. 1 just past the Big Indian, Freeport). This is a bargain hunter's institution among tight-fisted Mainers, so much so the store had been immortalized in the pages of *Down East* magazine. This is a good place to outfit the kids for school.

Portmanteau (774-7276; 36 Wharf St., between Fore and Commercial streets, Portland). Tapestry and leather clothing, bags, luggage and accessories made on the premises.

Midcoast

Tea Hill Threads (367-2292; Tea Hill Rd. off Rte. 15, Stonington). Be nice to the rabbits and goats hanging around Carol Collin's workshop and store. They provide the fibers for her handwoven, quilted and knitted apparel, rugs and wall hangings.

Down East/Acadia

Darthia Farm (963-7771; Rte. 186, West Bay Rd., 1.7 miles off Rte. 1, Gouldsboro). Ikat dyed and handwoven clothing and accessories by Cindy Thayer, as well as handspun yarns and handknit items by other local craftspersons. In season you can purchase organic produce raised by Ms. Thayer and her husband on the saltwater farm.

Island Supply Company (367-5558; Stonington). Great sweaters.

East of Schoodic

The Sow's Ear (255-4066; 7 Water St., Machias). An engaging collection of clothing, books, toys and gifts.

COLLECTIBLES

Midcoast

Duck Trap Decoys (789-5363; Cannan Rd., off Rte. 1, Lincolnville Beach). Hand-carved decoys by Walt Simmons and 32 other carvers. Furry animals, too. Prices range from under $10 to several thousand.

Ducktrap Trading Co. (236-9568; 28 Bayview St., Camden). Decoys, ships' models, carvings, prints and original art.

Howard G. Jones Nantucket Lightship Baskets (236-4042 or 800-437-8899; Rockport). Nantucket basket purses with fossil-walrus scrimshaw and brass fittings. All signed and dated.

Ye Olde Coin Shop Fine Jewelry (338-2663; High St., Belfast). A collector's mix including old comic books and collectors' supplies. If there has to be an Ye Olde anything, then, okay, this place.

Yesterday and Today Doll Shoppe (548-2793; Rte. 1, 227 W. Main, Searsport). Old, new and collector dolls, doll supplies, books and miniatures. Also porcelain doll-making classes.

Stephen Hensel (354-8526; Friendship). American songbirds, seabirds, gamebirds, and raptors mostly carved from basswood and painted with acrylics. Birds displayed outdoors are waterproofed. Call for an appointment.

Down East/Acadia

Belcher's Country Store (348-9938; Reach Rd., Deer Isle). They are big on Christmas here, all year round. Antique and collectible tinware, hooked rugs, handblown glass, ceramics. Recently the owners opened a baby Belcher's on Water St. in Blue Hill.

Downeast Decoys (469-2158; Rte. 1, Orland). Antique and old decoys, as well as new ones carved by Bill Conroy. He will appraise yours, if you ask.

Merrill's Decoys and Wooden Fish Lures (469-3108; Rte. 166, Orland). Merrill Clement was born and has spent his life on the coast. At one time he served as the local fish commissioner; now he carves beautiful fish lures and duck decoys. Clement has studied carving with several New England master carvers, and many of his pieces are modeled on fine old antiques he has collected on travels throughout New England.

Nancy Neale Typecraft (244-5192; Steamboat Wharf Rd. off Rte 102, Bernard). Irving Silverman and Nancy Neale began collecting antique wood type in 1969. Today they have the largest selection in the country in a shop near Bass Harbor on Mount Desert Island. In addition, Ms. Neal creates what she calls "framed assemblages" — type collages — for anniversaries, birthdays and other events. Open by chance or appointment.

The Scrimshaw Workshop (288-4380; Rte. 3, north of Bar Harbor). Conservationist, scrimshaw engraver, and friend of elephants, Chris Cambridge uses mostly old walrus and woolly mammoth ivory.

Diana Lynn Doherty

Looking for a find at the St. Savior's church sale in Blue Hill.

Yard Sales

There's nothing more Maine than a good yard sale. A yard sale begins when a homeowner piles the contents of his attic and garage on the lawn, hangs signs around town and then sits and waits for the people to come.

The people do come, and they'll buy anything. Mainers hate to see anything go to waste. In fact it's noble to take something your neighbor outgrew or grew tired of and transform it into a family heirloom. We bought a dining room set for pennies that would have cost a thousand in a tony antique store. Why buy new, when used is as good as this?

From mid-August through mid-September is good yard sale season. Spring after the ritual spring cleaning can mean good yard sales in an economic boom time. Pick a road lined with large, prosperous-looking single-family homes. Then watch for the signs. Rte. 115 through Yarmouth and Rte. 88 through Falmouth are good yard sale routes. Read the Sunday classifieds; they often list good upcoming sales.

CRAFT SUPPLIES

South Coast

York River Trading Store (363-7734; 90 U.S. Rte. 1, York). Craft supplies including stencil patterns, basket supplies, tole painting supplies, as well as local crafts.

Casco Bay

Martha Hall Natural Fibre Yarns (846-9334; 46 Main St., Yarmouth). Yarns from Maine and all over, plus unusual buttons and knitting patterns. Sign up for their knitting newsletter/catalog, the *Natural Fibre News.*

Midcoast

The Cat's Meow (548-2546; Rte. 1, Searsport). Patchwork quilts. Calicoes and solids. Also quilting supplies.

GALLERIES

South Coast

Barn Gallery (363-6131; Bourne Line and Shore Rd., Ogunquit). This gallery has been going strong since the 1950s and is known for launching new and young artists. Recent exhibits have included works by Lincoln Perry, the husband of author Ann Beattie (they recently bought a summer home in nearby York).

Mast Cove Gallery (967-3453; Main St., Kennebunkport). This gallery offers what art critic Gail Glickman calls a "solid introduction to Maine Art."

Casco Bay

Abacus (772-4880; 44 Exchange St., Portland). Jewelry, sculpture, furniture and other handcrafted items by more than 400 American craftspeople and jewelers.

Evans Gallery (879-0042; School St., Portland). Betsy Evans, a former assistant to photographer Robert Mapplethorpe, opened her photography gallery during the late 1980s. She represents an impressive stable of photographers including Todd Webb. By appointment only.

Frost Gully Gallery (773-2555; 411 Congress St., Portland). Drawings, prints and sculpture by contemporary Maine artists, including works by Dahlov Ipcar.

Icon Contemporary Art (725-8157; 19 Mason St., Brunswick). Works by contemporary Maine artists.

Nancy Margolis Gallery (775-3822; 367 Fore St., Portland). Nationally known artists. Features contemporary American crafts, especially ceramics and fine jewelry.

Meander Gallery (871-1078; 40 Pleasant St., Portland).

O'Farrell Gallery (729-8228; 46 Maine St., Brunswick). Works by local artists.

Dean Velentgas Gallery (772-2042; 60 Hampshire St., off Congress, Portland). Locally one of the most respected galleries along the coast. Works by Salle and Longo, as well as prints and paintings by Dean Nimmer.

Midcoast

Blue Heron Gallery (348-6051; Church St., Deer Isle). A barn full of contemporary crafts by faculty members of the nearby Haystack Mountain School. Open June through September.

Deer Isle Artists Association (second floor, Seamark Bldg., Rte. 15, Deer Isle). Revolving, two-week exhibitions of members' sculpture, painting, photographs and drawings. Open June through August.

Frick Gallery (338-3671; 139 High St., Belfast). Exhibits of work by local artists, most of it contemporary and applied art.

Leighton Gallery (374-5001; Parker Point Rd., Blue Hill). Local critics and those from away rave about this gallery, owned by outdoor sculptor Judith Leighton, which shows her work as well as other sculptors and painters.

Maine Coast Artists (236-2875; Russell Ave., Rockport). Their annual juried art show is a good introduction to new and rising local talent. Open June through September.

Gallery Sixty Eight (338-1558; 68 Main St., Belfast). Prints and paintings by Maine coast artists.

Turtle Gallery (348-9977; Main St., Deer Isle). Work by Maine realist painters, abstract sculpture, hollow-ware and jewelry.

Down East/Acadia

Spring Woods Gallery (422-3997; Rte. 299, .2 miles off Rte. 1, Sullivan). Original oils and watercolors by illustrator Paul M. Breeden.

East of Schoodic

Eastport Gallery and Arts Center (853-4166; Dana and Water streets, Eastport). Sculpture, painting and other media by almost two dozen regional artists. The center also sponsors workshops in music, theater, dance, puppetry and poetry. Open June through October.

GIFTS

South Coast

Animal Instinct (646-7728; Main St., Ogunquit). Bear collectors alert! Great stuffed animals, puppets, dolls and toys for the young and young at heart.

Brick Store Museum Shop (985-3639; 105 Main St.; Kennebunkport). Antique reproduction toys including a jacks set, rag doll kit and old-time picture book. The shop also has grown-up gifts.

Brass Carousel & Kite Galleries (646-8225; Rte. 1, Perkins Cove). Kites, brass, travel stuff and gifts.

Compliments (967-2269; Dock Square, Kennebunkport). An unusual gallery of outre pottery, mirrors, jewelry, lamps and objects d'art. The "Time Bomb" clock with sticks of "dynamite" is worth a look alone.

Nestling Duck Gift Shop (883-6705; 350 Pine Point Rd., Scarborough). A collection of New England gifts, including candles, stoneware, jewelry and Maine-made crafts.

Port Canvas (967-2717; Ocean Ave., Kennebunkport). Canvas suit bags, carpetbags, satchels, duffles, totes, raincoats in a variety of sizes and colors. Custom orders taken too.

Midcoast

Bluejacket Shipcrafters (567-3525; School St., Stockton Springs). Museum quality wood ship model kits manufactured right here. Watch how they're made every day from 9 to 4.

The Clipper Trade (442-8671; 110 Front St., Bath). Souvenirs, Maine crafts and goods from the world over in a small shop created to resemble emporiums from the days of the clippers.

Dromore Bay Herb Farm (443-1574; Rte. 209, Phippsburg). Pick out gifts for family and friends in a barn on a working saltwater farm.

Enchantments (633-4992; 16 McKown St., Boothbay Harbor). Crystals, herbs, incense and books. Gifts and stuff for the metaphysical crowd.

Granite Hall Store (529-5864; Round Pond). An old-fashioned country store in an historic building. Penny candy, antiques and woolens. Closes after Christmas.

Laughing Whale (443-5732, out-of-state 800-722-0945; 174 Front St., Bath). Models of Friendship sloops, dories, whaleboats, catboats and distinguished American sailboats such as the *America* and the *Joseph Conrad*. You can get a 23" Muscongus Bay lobster smack gaff rig and a jib — radio controlled if you like. Good selection of nautical books.

The Leather Bench (236-4688; 34 Main St., Camden). During the seventies, this leather goods store began with handmade anti-establishment leather fashions. Today the store caters to the moneyed establishment with more tony leathers by Coach and others.

Maine Gathering (236-9004; 4 Commercial St. on the Public Landing, Camden). Contemporary and traditional crafts by Maine residents with an extensive selection of Maine Native American baskets.

Narragansett Leathers (563-5080; Main St., Damariscotta). Leather goods — bags, belts, briefcases — handmade right here.

The Right Stuff (236-9595; 38 Main St., Camden). A gift and home store crammed with attractive reproductions, period lighting and country-style accessories.

The Sheepskin Shop (273-3061; Rte. 90, Warren). If it can be made from sheepskin, these folks have it: seatcovers, gloves, footwear, hats, purses, blankets, rugs and chamois cloth. A good shopping stop on the shortcut past Rockport to Camden.

Suzy's Searsport Boutique (548-6522; Rte. 1, Searsport). The motto at Suzy's is "Today's investment . . . tomorrow's heirloom." It will take an investment in time to work your way through Suzy's shop jam-packed with Victoriana, folk art, paper dolls, soaps, candles and handmade papers. But it will be fun. Closed on Tuesdays.

Down East/Acadia

Dollhouse Treasures (469-7832; Rte. 1, East Orland; and 288-4241; 61 Cottage St., Bar Harbor). Two stores that carry miniatures, dollhouses, toy replicas. Everything's here for the doll lover, including building materials to make your own dollhouse. Know the building code in your own state.

Glass Workbench (548-2788; Rte. 1, two miles north of Searsport). Original stained glass designs for windows and gifts.

H.O.M.E. Craft Shop (469-7961; Rte. 1, Bucksport). A craft lover's dream, this sprawling store is a cooperative for more than 400 Maine craftspersons — H.O.M.E. stands for "Homeworkers Organized for More Employment." For sale are quilts, toys, jewelry, weaving, pottery and other handcrafted items.

Membership is not required to shop at H.O.M.E. (Homeworkers Organized for More Employment), a rambling complex of booths and stores, with everything from crafts to home-canned foods.

Tom Hindman

U. S. Bells (963-7184; Rte. 186, Prospect Harbor). Sculptor Richard Fisher began crafting bells more than 20 years ago. Now his bronze and brass bells are sold around the world. They're in all shapes, all sizes and for all purposes — including windchimes for letting you know it's windy and doorbells for letting you know someone's at the door. He also sells beautiful handmade quilts in a "factory outlet" that sits next to the bell foundry.

East of Schoodic

J. E. B. Baskets (733-2434; Rte. 189, Lubec). What a find. Janice Bronson and her mother Susan weave baskets from Belgian reeds all winter in anticipation of summer. Some are Shaker style. Some are similar to those made by the region's Native Americans. The rest are J. E. B. originals. They also publish the *Basket News Letter*, a hand-typed 8" x 11" sheet that describes their latest designs and reminds you to order in time for Christmas. They will be happy to put you on their mailing list. You can't miss their place. From the road you can see some of their baskets hanging on the clothesline out front.

JEWELRY

South Coast

Swamp John's (646-9414; Oar Weed Rd., Perkins Cove). They've been making and selling jewelry, including rings, earrings and pins of Maine tourmaline, for more than two decades,

Casco Bay

Tracy Johnson and Devta Doolan — Fine Jewelry (775-2468; 142 High St., Portland). A couple of the best jewelers in Maine. Specializing in wedding rings and fine art jewelry using high karat gold, silver and precious gemstones. By appointment only.

Geraldine Wolf Antique Jewelry (774-8994; 26 Milk St., Portland). Pretty baubles from the past.

Midcoast

A Silver Lining (633-4103; 21 Townsend Ave., Boothbay Harbor). Blueberry pendants and other originally designed memories of the Maine coast in metals past cast in sterling, gold, copper, brass, titanium or gold electroplated.

KITCHEN & HOME FURNISHINGS

Master cabinetmaker Thomas Moser.

Courtesy of Thomas Moser

Maine Cabinetmakers

What is it about Maine and cabinetmakers? Ever since Thomas Moser quit his teaching job at Bates College to make his signature Shaker-style tables and chairs, dozens of other fine cabinetmakers have sprung up nearby. Some have worked in Moser's workshops.

For the most part the spare, elegant desks, tables, chairs and bureaus they design and build by hand look like they truly belong in the Maine landscape. Beautiful dovetails, smooth hardwood finishes. As Phil Patton wrote in *Esquire* magazine, "In the best Yankee tradition, this furniture has no sides that it is embarrassed to show."

Here are a few of the cabinetmakers in residence on the coast.

South Coast

Great Works Woodworking (James Taylor, 439-1176; 39 Frost Hill Rd., York). Shaker and colonial reproductions and custom pieces.

Casco Bay

Thos. Moser (774-3791; 415 Cumberland Ave., Portland). The most famous of Maine's cabinetmakers, Moser was instrumental in making Shaker furniture fashionable again. Now, he lords over a small furniture empire with several dozen carpenters, a store in Washington, D.C., and one in Portland. Recently they've introduced a line of arts and crafts-style pieces called the New Century collection.

Midcoast

David and Susan Margonelli (633-3326; 2585 W. River Rd., Edgecomb). Fine, handmade furniture.

Roy Gillespie's Carriage House (529-5555; New Harbor Rd., Round Pond). Cabinetmaker, antiques dealer and used book seller owns enough used books to fill a barn.

Studio Mnemosyne (389-2027; HC 31 Box 323, Popham Beach). Jerry Moser designs and builds modern hardwood furniture with plenty of right angles.

Thomas C. Hinchcliffe — Cabinetmaker (326-9411; Rte. 176, Blue Hill). Hinchcliffe uses old woods and 18th-century joinery to make handmade copies of antique chairs, tables, cupboards and armoires.

William Evans, Cabinetmaker (832-4175; 804 Main St., Waldoboro). Reproductions, restorations and contemporary furniture.

Windsor Chairs (789-5188; Rte. 1, Lincolnville). They make chairs. Windsor chairs. Watch them work. They also make other furniture, providing it complements their Windsors.

Down East/Acadia

Louis Charlett (244-5643; Kings Ln., Manset). Custom- designed furniture.

Robert Newton (846-3412; 11 South St., Yarmouth). Furniture builder and designer.

Seamark Designs (348-9955; Seamark Bldg., Rte. 15, Deer Isle). Original designs in native woods by cabinetmaker/artist Bruce Bulger.

South Coast

Viale Parioli Designs Inc. (284-0370; River Dam Millyard, Biddeford). European ironwork, handpainted furniture and custom fabrics and home accessories.

Casco Bay

Heritage Lanterns (846-3911; 70A Main St., Yarmouth). Handcrafted reproductions of 18th-, 19th- and early 20th-century lanterns, sconces, chandeliers and lamps.

Pemaquid Floorcloth (529-5633; Rte. 32, Round Pond). Decorative floor cloths, used exclusively by refined citizens from colonial days to the Age of Linoleum. Heavy canvas hemmed, coated with a background paint, hand-decorated with some design in typically repetitive checkerboard fashion and stiffened with eight coats of varnish. Good for high traffic. Open by chance or appointment.

Maine Cottage Furniture (846-1430; Lower Falls Landing, Rte. 88, Yarmouth). Summer furniture in colors that will appeal to modern day rusticators. Also, hooked rugs, quilts, lighting, vintage-cloth pillows and sisal flooring.

The Whip & Spoon (774-4020; 800-937-9447; 161 Commercial St., Portland). From Cuisinarts to lobster potholders, what to stock for the well-kept kitchen.

Midcoast

Dancing Blanket Studio (372-8625; Tenants Harbor). One-of-a-kind handmade blankets woven by Cynthia McGuirl. Also limited edition clothing and jewelry. Call for an appointment.

The Maine Sale (563-9599; River Rd., Newcastle). Folk art for the home, from cupboards to coverlets. Open July and August only.

New York Clay Co. (338-4728; 74A Main St., Belfast). Tiles with fish. Tiles with animals. Tiles with boats. We liked the garden vegetable series. The owner makes the ceramic tiles in the back.

Down East/Acadia

Rooster Brother (667-8675; 18 W. Main St., next to Union River Bridge, Ellsworth). Cooking equipment and tableware, plus gourmet foods and wine.

Scottish Lion Blacksmith (529-5523; Rte. 32, Round Pond). Blacksmith Andrew Leck's hand-forged iron home accessories include pot racks and fireplace tools.

Sleepy Hollow Rag Rugs (789-5987; Rte. 173, Lincolnville Beach). Hand-loomed rag rugs woven on antique looms and sold right in the studio.

Weatherend Estate Furniture (596-6483; 374 Main St., Rockland). Reproductions of lawn furniture first crafted using yacht joinery techniques and considered by many to surpass the originals in style, construction techniques and durability.

Wildfire Run Quilt Boutique (422-3935; off Rte. 1, Sullivan). Quilt heaven. Peg and Chris McAloon have brought together an extensive collection of antique and newly made quilts, wall hangings and pillows. They also run a B&B on the premises.

NAUTICAL EQUIPMENT

Casco Bay

Chase Leavitt & Company (772-3751; 10 Dana St., Portland). Half a block away from Portland's "working" waterfront, this old-fashioned marine store caters to pleasure boaters with a good selection of charts, marine hardware, navigation equipment and foul-weather gear.

Midcoast

Bohndell Sails (236-3549; Commercial St., Rockport). They've been making sails since 1870, which is nothing sailors around here don't know.

Hamilton Marine (548-6302; East Main St., Searsport). Everything you need for your sailboat or motor boat. Should your radar — or any other nautical doodad — break down in some exotic far off port, call these guys. They ship replacement parts and hardware daily via UPS.

Down East/Acadia

RainWise, Inc. (288-5169; 25 Federal St., Bar Harbor). Electronic weather instruments known world-wide; barometers, weather stations with television displays.

POTTERY

Casco Bay

Pottery by Peg & Dick Miller (846-4981; 7 Smith St. off Rte. 88, Yarmouth). The Millers fashion their wheel-thrown, slab, shingle and coil pottery from local materials including native clay, beach sand, wood ashes, seaweed, clam and mussel shells. Then they fire it in their own kiln. Their glazes are lead-free and all of their works are ovenproof and dishwasher safe.

Sawyer Street Studios (767-4394; 131 Sawyer St., South Portland). One of the first artist-owned studios in Maine. Great pottery. Classes taught.

Maine Potters Market (774-1633; 376 Fore St., Portland). Local potter's cooperative featuring stoneware, porcelain and earthenware. An interesting mix of traditional to funky one-of-a-kind pieces.

Midcoast

Andersen Studio (633-4397; Rte. 96 and Andersen Rd., East Boothbay). Clay rendered and glazed to resemble seals, gulls and ducks. Also stoneware vases and bowls.

Arrowsic Pottery (443-6048; Rte. 127; Arrowsic). Nan Kilbourn-Tara learned her craft at Bennington College during the mid-60s. Now she creates hand-thrown, functional stoneware and majolica earthenware. She also works on commission. Open year round.

Edgecomb Potters (882-6802; Rte. 27, Edgecomb). Chris and Richard Hilton founded their potter's studio in 1976. Today their staff produce striking and functional pottery for the home.

Hand in Hand Galleries (865-1705; 8 School St., Freeport; 633-4199; McKown St., Boothbay Harbor; 882-6802; Rte. 27, Edgecomb). Three craft galleries featuring work by the Edgecomb Potters, jewelry by Maine artist Patricia Daunis, bells by Richard Fisher, handwoven rugs, Maine tourmaline jewelry and jewelry boxes.

Down East/Acadia

Gull Rock Pottery (422-3990; 325 Eastside Rd., Hancock). Torj and Kurt Wray create wheel-thrown pottery decorated with birds, fish and scenes from nature.

Rowantrees Pottery (374-5535; Union St., Blue Hill). They've been in business a long time — 50 years. Their glazes, made from locally found minerals, are famous.

Rackliffe Pottery (374-2297; Rte. 172, Ellsworth Road, Blue Hill). Younger than Rowantrees, but just as famous.

East of Schoodic

Columbia Falls Pottery (483-4075; Main St., Columbia Falls). Potters April Adams and Alan Burnham have set up shop in a Victorian country store halfway between Cherryfield and Machias and next to the Ruggles House Museum. You can get a tour of their studio or just browse through their collection of majolica and terra cotta pottery. They also sell baskets, candles and paintings by Maine artists and crafts people.

Dog Island Pottery (853-4775; 224 Water St., Eastport). Functional and decorative stoneware handcrafted by the shop's owner, Barbara Smith.

SPORTING GOODS

South Coast

Black Bear Trading Post (883-5003; 581 Rte. 1, Scarborough). Hunting, fishing, camping equipment and stuff for the offshore angler. Fresh- and saltwater bait and canoes.

Kittery Trading Post (439-2700; Rte. 1, Kittery). Just as Freeport's outlets grew up around Bean's, the shopping mecca here seemed to spring from the roots established by this rambling outdoor store full of canoes, sleeping bags, parkas and pocketknives.

Casco Bay

Eastern Mountain Sports (772-3776; 50 Maine Mall Rd., So. Portland). Clothing, footwear and gear for campers and hikers.

L. L. Bean (865-4761; Main St., Freeport). The big daddy of all outdoor stores in Maine. The store stays open 24 hours every day of the year. The best time to shop — if you can stay awake — is in the wee hours. Then you have more time to chew the fat with the staff, who often have great stories to tell about fellow customers and their own outdoor exploits. (See sidebar.)

Peregrine Outfitters (800-331-5162; 865-1455; 274 U.S. Rte. 1, one half mile no. of the Big Indian, So. Freeport). A fly fisherman's heaven. What they don't know, neither do the fish. They even have a registry so friends and family will know just what fly to get for a birthday or anniversary. They also arrange fishing trips. Plus they post daily fishing conditions throughout the state.

Port City Fly & Tackle (761-4278; 20 Danforth St. near the Old Port, Portland). Shoot the breeze with an experienced fisherman or just browse quietly in this shop set in an old warehouse.

L. L. Bean

The lore that surrounds L. L. Bean is almost as numerous as the items sold in the Maine company's mail order catalog, but here are some salient Bean facts.

√ L.L. Bean was born Leon Linwood Bean in 1872, a name he changed soon after the turn of the century to Leon Leonwood.

√ He was orphaned in 1884.

√ He invented the Maine Hunting Shoe in 1911.

√ He sent potential customers his first mailing in 1912, a small circular with an illustration and description of the Maine Hunting Shoe.

√ In 1951, he threw out the keys to his famous store, making it one of the first stores in America to stay open 24 hours a day, 365 days a year.

√ Since then the store has closed only four times: two Sundays in 1962 before L. L. got town permission to counter the state's new blue laws; the day in 1963 when President John F. Kennedy was assassinated; and the day L. L. Bean died in 1967.

Photo courtesy of L. L. Bean, Inc.

The interior of the L. L. Bean store in Freeport.

Surplus Store (775-0201; 28 Monument Sq. on Congress St., Portland). Before there were Marshalls, Loehmans and shopping warehouses, surplus stores were the place to buy discounted jeans and old army fatigues. This store has all that, plus a good selection of respectably inexpensive camping and fishing gear.

Tommy's (772-5357; 273 Congress St., Portland). Equipment and clothing for kayaking, boating, ice skating, diving, fishing and snowshoeing. For some reason, we think of this local institution more as a hardware store than a run-of-the-mill recreational outfitter. Maybe that's because you always walk out with plenty of advice.

Midcoast

Maine Sport (236-7120; Rte. 1, Rockport). They sell and rent mountain bikes, sea kayaks, canoes, camping gear, backpacks and fishing equipment. They also serve as a true factory outlet for Moss tents.

Down East/Acadia

L. L. Bean Factory Store (667-7753; Rte. 1, Ellsworth). Brighter and more airy than their Freeport bargain basement, this store often has one-of-a-kind bargains on tents, bicycles, canoes and sleeping bags, as well as outdoor clothing.

Life Sports (667-7819; Rte. 1, Ellsworth and 288-9641; Main St., Bar Harbor). Gear and clothing for camping, hiking, canoeing, kayaking, fishing, running, swimming, tennis and sailboarding.

Cadillac Mountain Sports (288-4532; 26 Cottage St., Bar Harbor). If you can do it outdoors on the island, you can find the gear and clothing to do it here. They have one of the best selections of sports footwear in the area, including more than 100 types of hiking boots. They have the stuff you need for rock and ice climbing and cross-country and telemark skiing. Open seven days a week throughout the year, and until 11 p.m. during the summer.

East of Schoodic

Currier's Sport Shop (255-4344; 26 East Main St., Machias). Canoes, kayaks, camping gear and clothes.

Only in Maine

During the Civil War one Maine paper manufacturer ran out of cotton rags from which to make his paper. As legend goes, he began importing the cotton wrapping from Egyptian mummies to use in his factory. Today, Maine entrepreneurs are equally as resourceful, if not as ghoulish, in finding ways to make a living. Every family has at least one yard sale a year. Here are a few of the coast's most unusual producers of one-of-a-kind products.

Bar Harbor Weathervanes (667-3868; Rte. 3, Trenton). For centuries weathervanes in the shape of boats and animals have been used by sailors and farmers to tell which way the wind blew. This store serves that tradition with handwrought copper, brass or cast aluminum weathervanes by Phil Alley. You can buy a whole cupola.

Downeast Dog Kennels (236-8622; 21 Elm St., Camden). Using Maine lobster trap technology, these people create custom doghouses that are North Atlantic tough and certainly worth a look. This is also home to *Maine Boats and Harbors*, the magazine boat owners just love to sink their teeth into.

Joseph Gray Flagpoles (359-4448, Reach Rd., Sargentville). Handhewn flagpoles measuring 20' to 40'. Mr. Gray prefers to make his poles from Maine cedar because the wood is naturally water repellent. He'll deliver free of charge within 30 miles.

Dakin's Quality Crafted Miniatures (548-6500; Prospect St., Searsport). Wooden Breyer horses, horse show stalls and accessories.

Product testing outside a typical Maine coast country store.

Tom Hindman

CHAPTER EIGHT

Practical Matters
INFORMATION

Maine high tides, low tides, shown here in Mintum.

Tom Hindman

T his chapter is meant to be a modest encyclopedia of useful information about the coast of Maine. Visitors can refer to it when planning trips to the coast and when on vacation here. It covers the following topics:

AMBULANCE/FIRE/POLICE

Emergency numbers differ throughout the coast. Here is an abbreviated listing for the major destinations. For other locations, check the local phone listings or dial "O" for operator.

Town	Ambulance	Fire	Police
Bar Harbor	911	911	911
Bath	911	911	911
Belfast	338-1340	338-2420	338-1340
Blue Hill	374-2435	667-7575	374-9900
Boothbay Harbor	911	911	911
Brunswick	911 or 725-5521	911 or 725-5521	911 or 725-5511
Camden	236-2000	911	236-2000
Castine	326-4322	667-7575	326-4421
Damariscotta	563-3131	563-3444	563-3200
Eastport	853-4221	853-2544	853-4828
Ellsworth	667-2525	667-2133	667-3200
Freeport	865-4211	865-4212	865-4211
Jonesport	483-2993	800-432-7303	497-2385
Kennebunkport	967-3323	967-3323	967-3323
Kittery	439-2262	439-1638	439-0100
Lubec	733-4321	733-4321	733-4321
Machias	255-3535	255-4033	255-3535
Ogunquit	646-5111	646-9361	646-5111
Old Orchard Beach	911	911	911
Portland	911	911	911
Rockland	911	911 800-432-7381	911
Stonington	367-2655	667-7575	348-2300
Thomaston	354-2424	354-2511	354-2424
Waldoboro	911 or 832-5211	911 or 832-4500	911 or 832-5211
Winter Harbor	963-2222	963-7144	667-3200
Wiscasset	911	911	911

AREA CODE/TOWN GOVERNMENT & ZIP CODES

AREA CODE

Maine's area code is 207.

TOWN GOVERNMENT

There are more than 250 cities, towns, villages and "plantations" (see definition below) along the coast of Maine from Kittery to Eastport. There are 16 counties in Maine and eight that line the coast. From west to east, they are: York, Cumberland, Sagadahoc, Lincoln, Knox, Waldo, Hancock and Washington.

Cities have their own charters and city councils. In Maine you don't have to be big to be a city; if you're big, there's nothing to prevent you from being a town. There are 2,000 city people in Eastport and 10 times that number of townspeople in Brunswick.

During the 19th century the annual town meeting was the social event of the year for most of Maine. Over the course of the day, men managed the town business; women set the noon table. Although more towns are electing officials and hiring professionals to govern and manage their communities, and women are regular fixtures in town hall, the annual town meeting still predominates. At a town meeting, usually held in March, everyone who shows up has as much pull as the next person.

In addition to towns and cities, Maine has 33 plantations — a holdover from the time when the region was part of the Massachusetts Bay Colony. Originally intended to be temporary forms of government, many of Maine's plantations, such as Monhegan and Matinicus islands, have annual meetings, do not have home rule powers and are incorporated by county commissioners.

The state government, according to New England tradition, exercises relatively little power over the towns and cities — home rule, in other words. The government of the towns through the medium of the town meeting has been called the only existing type of "pure" democracy.

Don't forget that Maine had a thriving democracy long before European settlers arrived. Today, two Native American reservations, at Old Town near Bangor and Perry outside of Eastport, are self-governed nations and exist outside of U. S. federal jurisdiction.

For more information regarding the governing bodies of Maine's coastal plantations, towns and cities, contact the following town hall offices.

ZIP CODES

Town	Telephone	Zip Code
Bar Harbor	288-4098	04609
Bath	443-8330	04530
Belfast	338-3370	04915

Town	Telephone	Zip Code
Blue Hill	374-2281	04614
Boothbay Harbor	663-3671	04538
Brunswick	725-6659	04011
Camden	236-3353	04843
Castine	326-4502	04421
Damariscotta	563-5168	04543
Eastport	853-2300	04631
Ellsworth	667-2563	04605
Freeport	865-4743	04032
Jonesport	497-5926	04649
Kennebunkport	967-4243	04046
Kittery	439-0452	03904
Lubec	733-2341	04652
Machias	255-6621	04654
Newcastle	563-3441	04553
Ogunquit	646-5139	03907
Old Orchard Beach	934-5714	04064
Portland	874-8300	04101, 04102, 04103, 04104
Rockland	594-8431	04841
Stonington	367-2351	04681
Thomaston	354-6107	04861
Waldoboro	832-5369	04572
Winter Harbor	963-2235	04693
Wiscasset	882-6331	04578

BANKS

The major banks in Maine and several of the smaller local banks are linked to national and international instant teller machine networks. Following is a list of many of the banks with offices along the coast.

Bank	Phone	Instant Teller Networks
Camden National Bank	236-8821	Plus, Yankee24
Casco Northern	800-635-2265	NYCE, Plus, Yankee24
Citibank	800-345-2484	Cirrus, Yankee24
Coastal Savings Bank	774-5000	Instacard, Plus
Bangor Savings Bank	338-4270	Yankee24, Passkey, Plus, Encore24
Bar Harbor Banking and Trust	800-924-7787	Cirrus, Plus, Yankee24

Bank	Phone	Instant Teller Networks
First National Bank		
of Damariscotta	800-564-3195	Plus, Scott 24-Hour, Yankee24
Fleet Bank	800-922-2882	Cirrus, NYCE, Yankee24
Key Bank	874-7222	NYCE, Cashere, Cirrus, Passkey, Plus
Peoples Heritage Bank	761-8500	InstaCard, NYCE, Passkey, Plus, Yankee24

There is an American Travel Service representative at 2 Portland Sq., Portland, 774-1424.

BIBLIOGRAPHY

<u>*Books You Can Buy*</u>

AUTOBIOGRAPHY, BIOGRAPHY & REMINISCENCE

Ames, Polly Scribner. *Marsden Hartley in Maine.* Orono, ME: University of Maine Press, 1972. 36 pp., illust., $7.95. Polly Scribner Ames writes about fellow painter Marsden Hartley's final three years living with lobsterman Forrest Young and his wife Katie in Corea, Maine (near Winter Harbor).

Caldwell, Bill. *Islands Of Maine.* Portland: Guy Gannett Publishing Co., 1981. 241 pp., index, illust, photos, $12.95.

Caldwell, Bill. *Maine Coast.* Portland: Guy Gannett Publishing Co., 1988. 398 pp., $12.95. Two collections of a journalist's rambling monologues about the people he has met and places he has visited.

Small, Constance. *The Lighthouse Keeper's Wife.* Orono, ME: University of Maine Press, 1986. 226 pp., photos, $13.95. Constance Small and her husband Elson tended a Maine island lighthouse for 28 years. This is her wry and moving account of that life.

FICTION

Caldwell, Erskine. *Midsummer Passion and Other Tales of Maine Cussedness.* Camden, ME: Yankee Books. 192 pp., $11.95. Fifteen short stories Erskine Caldwell wrote while living in Maine.

Lecker, Robert and Kathleen R. Brown, eds. *An Anthology of Maine Literature.* Orono, ME: University of Maine Press, 1982. 260 pp., index, $13.95. A collection of works by native and out-of-state writers, including E. B. White, Nathaniel Hawthorne, Henry David Thoreau, Harriet Beecher Stowe, Sarah Orne Jewett and Kenneth Roberts.

McCloskey, Robert. *Blueberries for Sal.* New York: The Viking Press, 1948. 55 pp., illust.

McCloskey, Robert. *One Morning in Maine.* New York: The Viking Press, 1952. 64 pp., illust. Two of the best books about Maine to read, for adults as well as children.

Monroe, Judith. *Widdershins.* Durham, NC: Crone's Own Press, 1989. 240 pp., $9.95. Quirky, comic feminist novel about a group of women on a Maine island who discover their own power and independence.

Phippen, Sanford, Charles G. Waugh and Martin Greenberg, eds. *The Best Maine Stories.* Camden, ME: Yankee Books. 316 pp., $10.95. Short stories set in Maine written by some of America's most famous authors from Henry James to Caroline Chute.

Shain, Charles and Samuella Shain. *The Maine Reader.* New York: Houghton Mifflin Company, 1991. Illust., $29.95. Four hundred years of Maine through the eyes of explorers, writers, painters and photographers.

HISTORY

Doty, C. Stewart, ed. *The First Franco-Americans: New England Life Histories from the Federal Writers' Project, 1938-1939.* Orono, ME: University of Maine Press, 1985. 163 pp., photos, $12.95. Collected interviews of first-generation immigrants from Acadia and Quebec.

Eckstorm, Fannie Hardy. *Indian Place Names of the Penobscot Valley and the Maine Coast.* Orono, ME: University of Maine Press, 1978. Map, index, $7.95. An interesting journey through Maine by way of the exploration of Penobscot Indian language and legend.

Rich, Louise Dickinson. *The Coast of Maine.* New York: Thomas Y. Crowell Co., (published simultaneously in Canada by Fitzhenry & Whiteside Ltd. Toronto), 1975. 371 pp., index, illust, photos. A wonderfully rambling history of the coast from the Ice Age to the mid-1970s that is punctuated with the author's idiosyncratic interpretations of historical facts.

PHOTOGRAPHIC AND PAINTING STUDIES

Joseph, Stanley and Lynn Karlin. *Maine Farm: A Year of Country Life.* New York: Random House, 1991. Photos, $32.50. Beautifully photographed, warmly told account of life on a saltwater farm.

Skolnick, Arnold ed. *Paintings of Maine.* New York: Clarkson/Potter Publishers, 1991. 123 pp., illust., $27.50. Luscious reproductions of paintings of Maine by artists including Georgia O'Keeffe, Winslow Homer, Andrew Wyeth and Edward Hopper.

Tragard, Louise, Patricia E. Hart and W.L. Copithorne. *A Century of Color: Ogunquit, Maine's Art Colony 1886-1986.* Ogunquit, ME: Barn Gallery Associates, 1986. $24.95 Interviews and commentary from 100 years in the southern Maine art community.

RECREATION

Getchell, Dave and Kate Cronin. *The Maine Island Trail Book.* Rockland, ME: Maine Island Trail Association, 1991. The Maine Island Trail Association publishes this guidebook packed with charts and information for its members. It's worth joining just to get tips touring the coast from the water. For information, or a copy of this great book, write to: Maine Island Trail Association, 60 Ocean St., Rockland, ME 04841.

Isaac, Jeff and Peter Goth. *The Outward Bound Wilderness First-Aid Handbook.* Lyons & Burford, 1991. 252 pp., index, illust., $13.95. A must-have for anyone discovering the coast by kayak, canoe, sailboat, foot or bike.

Pierson, Elizabeth Cary and Jan Erik Pierson. *The Birder's Guide to the Coast of Maine.* Camden, ME: Down East Books. $13.50. Birds that nest and visit, summer and winter on the coast and its islands.

Taft, Hank and Jan Taft. *A Cruising Guide to the Maine Coast.* Camden, ME: International Marine Publishing Company, 1988. 363 pp, illust., $32.50. The definitive guide for ocean-going travelers.

Venn, Tamsin. *Sea Kayaking Along The New England Coast.* Boston: Appalachian Mountain Club, 1991. 205 pp., maps, photos, $14.95.

TRAVEL

Hacinli, Cynthia. *Down Eats: The Essential Maine Restaurant Guide.* Gardiner, ME: Tilbury House Publishers, 1991. 191 pp., $8.95. A former New Yorker's reviews/essays about Maine restaurants make for a good guide, as well as excellent reading.

Monegain, Bernie. *Natural Sites: A Guide to Maine's Natural Phenomena.* Freeport, ME: DeLorme Mapping Company, 1988. 44 pp., index, maps, photos, $3.95.

Monegain, Bernie. *Coastal Islands: A Guide to Exploring Maine's Offshore Isles.* Freeport, ME: DeLorme Mapping Company, 1988. 43 pp., index, maps, photos, $3.95.

Tree, Christina and Mimi Steadman, *Maine: An Explorer's Guide,* fifth edition. Woodstock, VT: The Countryman Press, 1991. 417 pp., index, illust, maps, photos, $16.95. A traveler's encyclopedia of Maine from the islands to the mountains.

Books You Can Borrow

Brault, Gerard. *The French-Canadian Heritage in New England.* Hanover and London: University Press of New England, and Kingston and Montreal: McGill-Queen's University Press, 1986. 264 pp., index, illust.

Carson, Rachel. *The Edge of the Sea.* New York: Houghton Mifflin Company, 1955. The famous naturalist and ecologist's essays on the coast. If you like this, you'll enjoy her other books, *The Sea Around Us* and *Silent Spring.*

Coffin, Robert Tristam. *Saltwater Farm.* New York: Macmillan, 1939. 114 pp., illust. Poetry by the premier poet and prose writer of Maine's middle coast.

Conkling, Philip. *Islands in Time.* Camden, ME: Down East Books, 1981. 222 pp., illust. Former Outward Bound naturalist, now head of the Island Institute, provides a lyrical history of Maine's coastal islands from an ecologist's point of view.

Federal Writers' Project of the Works Progress Administration, State of Maine. *Maine: A Guide 'Downeast.'* Boston: Houghton Mifflin Co., 1937. 458 pp., index, illust, photos. Try to get hold of this thick volume or the revised version, which was published in 1970 by Dorris Isaacson and the Maine Historical Society. It is a thorough account of all Maine: its history, natural wonders and recreation.

Jewett, Sarah Orne. *The Country of the Pointed Firs.* Boston and New York: Houghton Mifflin Company, 1929. 306 pp.

Williamson, William D. *History of the State of Maine (2 vols.) 1602-1820,* 1832. This is an overview of Maine's history and geography before it became a state.

Willis, William, ed. *Journals of Rev. Thomas Smith and Rev. Samuel Deane,* 1849. The author of this book was a Portland minister whose record of daily life during the Revolutionary War is interesting in its thoroughness.

Enjoying the summer season in Ogunquit.

State Development Center

CLIMATE, WEATHER & WHAT TO WEAR

Whoever once said "character takes four seasons to make" must have been familiar with the seasons of coastal Maine, which add drama to the already variable landscape from Kittery to Eastport. Spring bulbs will often bloom as late as mid-June. Summer generally remains temperate throughout July and August. Autumn frequently lasts well past the foliage's fall, and although it has been known to snow up to 70 inches in one winter (it snowed that much in Portland during the winter of 1970-71), harsh northern winter winds are usually softened by warmer ocean temperatures.

The state's climate is governed by the "prevailing westerlies," the belt of eastward-moving air that encircles the globe at the middle latitudes. The westerlies and warm currents of the Atlantic ensure that prolonged hot and cold spells are rare, although coastal weather — with the added moisture from the ocean — can be extremely changeable. Fogs frequently descend upon the coast, and are a reason why Maine mariners are famed the world over for their navigation skills. There are an average of 59 foggy days every year at Quoddy Head Light near Lubec.

Summer temperatures on Maine's coast range from 60 to 90 degrees, with the steadily warmest temperatures around 80, in July. Even when the temperature climbs during the day, coastal nights are almost always cool and comfortable. Autumn generally brings sunny days, cool nights and a brilliant display of fall foliage colors ranging from vivid golds (birches, poplars and ginkgos), oranges (mountain maples, hickories and ashes) to dazzling scarlets (red maples, red oak and sassafras).

Frosts and freezing temperatures can occur from October to May, although Portland experiences only 132 freezing days every year and is usually only 4 degrees cooler than Boston. The coast receives about 46 inches of precipitation annually. Of that precipitation, it snows only 15 or 20 days, and there are only 10 to 20 thunderstorms every year.

Meteorological extremes do occur. There was "the year without summer" in 1816 when it snowed in July. Hurricanes strike the coast about once every decade, but often Maine's coast misses their most destructive blows. The last hurricane to land on the coast was Bob, which hit on the southern coast in August 1991 and averaged winds from 90 to 100 mph. The coast also experiences what have become known as "100-Year Storms," when severe wind and weather peak with high tide, creating tides 10 to 20 feet higher than normal. The most recent 100-year storm was on January 12, 1978. More common are "Nor'easters," coastal storms that come up the coast and pummel it with high tides, heavy rain — or snow — and gale force winds.

People who enjoy reading about the weather will want to look for The Weather Report column in the weekly newspaper *Maine Times*. The rambling weather-and-natural life accounts are gathered from residents who regularly observe the weather from their windows onto the harbor or field. People from all places along the coast and inland give colorful reports of "flaming swamp maples" or a jack-in-the-pulpit discovered while out looking for mushrooms or pulling up the boat.

For frequently updated coastal and marine weather information, call the *National Weather Service, 207-775-7781.*

What to Wear in Maine

"Rainy days are tough on pedestrians, but I grew up in Maine, so I have no qualms about wearing really dorky clothes when it rains."

— Al Daimon, Maine's "walking" newsman, quoted in *Casco Bay Weekly*

"As I write this, I am wearing heavy long underwear, wind pants, three layers of insulation under a water-resistant jacket, wool socks, a wool hat and fingerless gloves. I look ridiculous, especially since it is now early June. But I'm on a small boat, and it is wicked cold out here."

— Jeff Isaac, Maine sailor

One could say fashion is a stranger to Maine. Dressing for a visit to the coast of Maine has everything to do with form and function. Versatility and comfort are respected. Strict formality is highly unusual, and probably transplanted from somewhere else. Any color is okay as long as it is brown, green or gray.

Knowing how to dress for coastal weather requires understanding the relationship between wind, water and land. The overall climate of Maine is Northern Temperate with cold winters and warm summers. The effects of the ocean can significantly moderate the weather on the islands and for a few miles inland, depending on the direction of the wind. The water off the coast is part of an upwelling of the Labrador Current that has its origin under the polar ice cap. Although the water has traveled hundreds of miles to get here, it still feels like icebergs. The air — or wind — passing over coastal waters is cooled and humidified before it arrives ashore.

On a typical sunny summer day, warm air rises over the mainland and the cool and dense air over the ocean is drawn in to replace it. This produces the summer southwesterly sea breeze. Temperatures along the immediate coast and islands will reflect that of the ocean, which only reaches 60 degrees by late summer. Approaching the coast on a hot day you can feel the air temperature drop 10 or 15 degrees, often accompanied by a thick fog.

If you're headed for the shore, carry a jacket and a pair of long pants, no matter what the TV weather personality says. This is especially true if you're boarding a boat. Rain is almost always associated with larger and more predictable weather systems. Unless a frontal passage or storm system is expected, you can leave your foul-weather gear in the trunk.

Clothes should be loose and comfortable for scrambling over rocks and through spruce and raspberry bushes. Garments should be versatile enough to handle rapid changes in temperature. Shorts are fine for strolling or trail hiking during the day when it's warm. If you're going any distance, bring wind pants for protection against the sea breeze and bugs. Summer nights are almost always cool. A medium-weight sweater will get plenty of use. If you cannot bring all of them, choose wool or bunting over cotton. Those fabrics will keep moisture away from your skin, and therefore keep you warmer.

Hiking shoes are also a good idea. Maine is really just a very thin layer of topsoil over a very thick layer of coarse-grained granite. Since you don't want to damage the soil layer, most of your walking will be on the rocks. The soft soles of sandals and sneakers are quickly worn smooth by avid hikers. One of the most useful items is a pair of knee-high rubber boots. The tide range in Maine runs from eight to 20 feet, exposing thousands of tide pools and clam flats for exploring. Bare feet would be shredded by shells and barnacles, and sneakers can get lost in the mud. A good pair of "worm boots" can make your whole trip.

Never mind what the calendar says, fall can begin on the coast during the third week of August. By this time, summer has lost its grip. Increasingly frequent cold fronts bring the prevailing winds to the west and northwest. With the wind off the land, temperatures reflect the cooling mass of the North American continent.

This is a great time to visit Monhegan or Vinalhaven, because summerlike conditions often extend well into the fall on the islands. While the mainland cools, the islands' temperature is moderated by the still-warm ocean water.

For fall and winter travel in coastal Maine, bring everything from shorts to winter gear, and expect to change often. Good foul-weather gear is essential unless you plan to spend a lot of time indoors. When an approaching winter storm swings the wind to the south or east, the breeze brings relative warmth. Wind off the water can melt the snow out from under your skis as fast as it fell. The day can seem downright balmy, until the next front sends the temperature plummeting. Precipitation can alternate quickly between rain and snow as the conflicting land and ocean air masses meet.

Spring on the coast can be a real tease. The ocean is very reluctant to warm up. This creates a drastic difference between inland and coastal temperatures and an even more drastic difference between your expectations and reality. You pull out your bathing suit, head for the beach and find that the water is still 43 degrees. The key is to expect it. Remember your fall and winter wardrobe? Bring it. If the wind is off the water, you'll need it. Away from the shore, or with a shore breeze, you can lie around with little on as at a summer picnic. It all depends on the wind.

Fogs in Maine

E. B. White gave us one of the best descriptions of a Maine fog in his 1948 *Atlantic Monthly* essay titled "Death of Pig."

"We had been having an unseasonable spell of weather — hot, close days, with the fog shutting in every night, scaling for a few hours in midday, then creeping back again at dark, drifting in first over the trees on the point, then suddenly blowing across the fields, blotting out the world and taking possession of houses, men, and animals."

GUIDED TOURS

Guided and sightseeing tours on the coast of Maine can be divided into three categories. You can travel by bus or trolley in many of the more popular destinations such as Ogunquit, Kennebunkport, Portland and Bar Harbor. You can travel by water on regular guided boat cruises, including whale, seal and puffin tours. You can also travel by air in a small plane because there are many small private airstrips and flying services along the coast. In this section we will discuss guided land and air tours. For lists of ocean-going guided tours, including windjammer cruises, whale, puffin watch tours and harbor tours, see *Recreation,* Chapter Six.

South Coast

During the summer months, the **Ogunquit Chamber of Commerce** operates a free, unnarrated trolley that covers the town's high spots from Perkins Cove to the west and Footbridge Beach to the east. The four trolleys — all named after garden flowers — operate daily from Memorial Day weekend through Columbus Day.

The **Intown Trolley Company** in Kennebunkport (967-3686) has provided old-fashioned narrated tours of the seaport for more than 10 years, including historical notes, a drive-by of the Bush family summer home at Walker Point and stops at the Franciscan monastery, major inns, hotels and shopping. There is a nominal fee for the service, and the fare is good for the entire day. The Intown Trolley leaves from the bottom of Ocean Ave. near Dock Sq. During July and August it is good to line up 15 minutes before scheduled departure.

Casco Bay

On-land tours are harder to come by in the Casco Bay region. The best opportunities are for charted bus, taxi and van tours operated by various companies. Two of those, **Custom Coach of Portland and Great Atlantic Travel** (797-8688) and **VIP Tour and Charter Bus Company** (772-4457) have limousines they rent from $40 an hour to $250 a day. A driver will meet a party at the airport, an inn or hotel and provide a personalized tour of the coast from Kennebunkport north. When you book your tour, let them know of your personal preferences — whether you'd like to antique or visit a working lobster port — and they will comply. Their specialty is the Portland area, where they will point out architecture and historical sites. Both companies will arrange a "midnight madness" trip to L. L. Bean in Freeport, which is open 24 hours, 365 days a year. VIP Tour and Charter Bus Company also will lease a van to larger groups. **Town Taxi** (772-0111 or 773-1711) in Portland offers a similar, custom tour service. You can book one of their Chrysler taxis or 10-seater vans for $15 an hour.

Midcoast

Guided tours in the Midcoast are just as difficult to come by. **Bill and Mary Sweet** (548-2190), who also operate a three-room bed and breakfast in Searsport, will hire out their Lincoln Town Car for a full-day narrated tour of the area's historical, architectural and natural highlights. One tour runs from Rockland to Acadia and back. The second is a guided tour of the Blue Hill peninsula and Ellsworth. Bill Sweet, a retired schoolteacher and history buff, was born and raised on Mount Desert Island. He also operates the **Sweet William Tour Guide Service** (288-5443) in Bar Harbor. Cost for each tour is $100 per day for up to four people. It's important to book at least 24 hours in advance during July and August.

If you want to view the region by air, **Downeast Flying Service** (800-752-6378 in state or 207-882-9401 out-of-state) offers regular half-hour scenic flights over the coast near Wiscasset for $45. Their Cessna 172 seats three passengers.

Regular routes include Boothbay, Pemaquid Point and the small fishing villages nearby including Damariscove, one of the first fishing villages established in the New World; they also regularly offer an aerial view of Popham and Reid state parks on the Kennebec River where it empties into Sheepscot Bay. The flying service is open year round, although it's important to book at least a day in advance for summer weekend flights.

The *Penobscot Air Service* (596-6211) provides custom air tours. The company offers flights in one-hour increments for $100-$200 and operates out of the Knox County Airport in Owls Head near Rockland. Suggested flights are east to Acadia (20 minutes from airport) and west toward Portland. Owner Charlie Jones grew up in the region and often will narrate the scenic flights. The flying service has four other pilots who fly five Cessnas that seat from three to five passengers. Penobscot Air also provides air service to Portland and the islands in Penobscot Bay.

Down East/Acadia

One of the best ways to see Bar Harbor and Acadia without having to deal with the summer traffic is on *Oli's Trolley* (288-9899), a two-and-one-half hour ride. The old-fashioned brown bus seats 40 and travels the park loop with stops at Cadillac Mountain, the Wild Gardens of Acadia and Thunder Hole. The guided tour also includes Sieur de Mont Spring, Otter Cliffs and a running historical narrative of Mount Desert Island from prehistoric times through present day. Two daily tours run from late May through mid-October. The summer months are busy, and reservations can be made the day before at the Acadia Restaurant on Main St. The bus leaves from near the fountain and the "Welcome to the Bar Harbor" sign at the entrance to Acadia National Park.

To view Acadia by air, you have two options, including the *Penobscot Flying Service* (see "Guided Tours," *Midcoast*, above) and *Acadia Air* (667-5534), which operates out of Bar Harbor Airport in Trenton. Acadia Air offers several scenic flights ranging from $12 per person to $275 for five. The shorter, less-expensive flights tour Acadia, Deer Isle and Stonington in a Cessna 172. They also have whale watch and lighthouse flights ranging as far Down East as Machias. Acadia Air operates scenic flights on demand from June 1 through mid-October.

HANDICAPPED SERVICES

Almost all state and national parks in Maine provide access and facilities for the physically impaired. Most motels and hotels also have rooms easily accessible to the handicapped. We have tried to provide information on individual restaurants in Chapter Five, and on inns and bed-and-breakfast establishments in Chapter Three that are accessible. To confirm, please call ahead.

To find out more about tourist facilities for the handicapped, contact the *Maine Publicity Bureau*, P.O. Box 2300, Hallowell, ME 04347; 207-582-9300 in state and 800-533-9595 out-of-state.

HOSPITALS

South Coast

BIDDEFORD

Southern Maine Medical Center 1 Mountain Rd., Biddeford 04005; 283-7000; Emergency Room open 24 hours.

YORK

York Hospital 15 Hospital Dr., York 03909; 363-4321; Emergency Room open 24 hours.

Casco Bay

BATH

Bath Memorial Hospital 1356 Washington St., Bath 04530; 443- 5524; Emergency Room open 24 hours.

BRUNSWICK

Parkview Memorial Hospital Upper Maine St., Brunswick 04011; 729-1641; Emergency Room open 24 hours.

PORTLAND

Brighton Medical Center Brighton Ave., Portland 04102; 879-8000; Emergency Room open 24 hours.

Maine Medical Center 22 Bramhall St., Portland 04102; 871-0111; Emergency Room open 24 hours.

Mercy Hospital 144 State St., Portland 04101; 879-3000; Emergency Room open 24 hours.

Jackson Brook Institute 175 Running Hill Rd., South Portland 04106; 761-2200.

Midcoast

BOOTHBAY

St. Andrews Hospital 3 St. Andrews Ln., Boothbay 04538; 633-2121; Emergency Room open 24 hours.

BELFAST

Waldo County General Hospital Northport Ave., Belfast 04915; 338-2500.

DAMARISCOTTA

Miles Health Care Center Bristol Rd., Damariscotta 04543; 563-1234; Emergency Room open 24 hours.

ROCKLAND

Penobscot Bay Medical Center Glen Cove, Rockland 04841; 596-8000; Emergency Room open 24 hours.

Down East/Acadia

BAR HARBOR

Mount Desert Island Hospital Wayman Ln., Bar Harbor 04609; 288-5081

BLUE HILL

Blue Hill Memorial Hospital Water St., Blue Hill 04614; 374-2836.

ELLSWORTH

Maine Coast Memorial Hospital 50 Union St., Ellsworth 04605; 667-5311.

East of Schoodic

Down East Community Hospital Upper Court St., Machias 04654; 255-3356; Emergency Room open 24 hours.

LATE NIGHT FOOD AND FUEL

The coffeepot is always on all night at the service desk at L. L. Bean, the famous store that remains open 24 hours every day, including Christmas and Thanksgiving. If you need more than coffee — say fuel for your car or your body — here is a short list of notable late-night or all-night stores, restaurants and gas stations.

South Coast

Howell's Auto Truck Stop (food and fuel), Rte. 1 bypass, Kittery. Open 24 hours.

Rapid Ray's (food), Main St., Saco. Weekdays, 11 a.m.–1:30 a.m.; weekends, 11 a.m.–3:30 a.m. High quality burgers.

Casco Bay

Cumberland Farms (food market and fuel), 801 Washington Ave., Portland. Open 24 hours.

Denny's Restaurants (food), 1101 Congress Ave., Portland (Congress St. exit off Rte. 295). Open 24 hours.

Midcoast

Mullen's Country Store, Rte. 1, Belfast. Daily 5:30 a.m.–midnight.

The Belfast Cafe (food), 90 Main St., Belfast. Daily 11 a.m.–1 a.m.

Red's Eats (food), Rte. 1, Wiscasset. Open Mon.–Thur., 11 a.m.–11 p.m.; Fri.–Sat., 11a.m.–2 a.m.; Sun., noon–9 p.m.

Cappy's Chowder House (food), 1 Main St., Camden. Daily 7:30 a.m.–midnight.

MEDIA

"Tr. [Trooper] Joseph Tibbets investigated a burglary at a private camp in Twp. 24. The only item stolen was a hand-operated well pump, however, a chain saw was used to gain entrance through the door."
— *The Downeast Coastal Press*, Sept. 16, 1991

The news business on the coast of Maine is dominated by two major newspaper companies, which publish the *Bangor Daily News* to the north and the *Portland Press Herald* and *Maine Sunday Telegram* to the south. To really learn about the area is to read about it through the eyes of the people who live and work here. For that reason, we recommend reading one of the several flourishing weeklies published on the coast.

Downeast, based in Camden, is the granddaddy of Maine magazines, but during the past decade dozens of younger magazines have sprung up, from *Ocean Navigator*, rumored to be Walter Cronkite's favorite magazine, to *WoodenBoat*, *National Fisherman and Coastal Fisheries News*. Many of these reflect the mariners' lifestyle. Then there are specialty magazines and newspapers like *Maine Antique Digest*, a thick tabloid packed with articles on art, antiques, and Americana, where to get it, and if you missed it, what it went for. Following is a roundup of the media you will find on the coast.

South Coast

NEWSPAPERS

Biddeford Journal Tribune P.O. Box 627, Biddeford 04005; daily. Known as a photographer's paper, and a pleasant place to do serious journalism.
York County Coast Star P.O. Box 979, Kennebunk 04043; weekly. Founded in 1877; considered a good training paper for the *Boston Globe*.
The York Weekly 17 Woodbridge Rd., P.O. Box 7, York 03909.

RADIO
WPKM-FM 106.3; Scarborough; Classical.

TELEVISION
WPBN-TV Channel 12; Biddeford; PBS.

Casco Bay

NEWSPAPERS

Brunswick Times Record Industry Rd., Brunswick 04011.
Coastal Journal 361 High St., Suite 3, P.O. Box 575, Bath 04530.
Portland Press Herald/Maine Sunday Telegram 390 Congress St., P.O. Box 1460, Portland 04101; daily. The only game in town.
Casco Bay Weekly 551A Congress St., Portland 04102; free weekly. New and growing, their writers have appeared in *The New York Times*, the *Utne Reader* and *Garbage* magazine. Good arts and entertainment coverage.
Maine Times The Great Bowdoin Mill, One Main St., Topsham 04086; weekly. Appeals to environmentally oriented readers. The movie reviews are brutal; worth getting for the weather report alone.

MAGAZINES
Boating Digest P.O. Box 996, Yarmouth 04096.
Golf Course News 38 Lafayette St., Yarmouth 04096. Trade tabloid for the greens crowd.
Greater Portland Magazine 142 Free St., Portland 04101. Features regional stories; the Portland magazine.
Ocean Navigator 18 Danforth St., Portland 04101.
Salt Magazine 119 Pine St., Portland 04102. Journalistic interviews and studies of the "real people of Maine"; great photos.

RADIO
WBLM-FM 102.9; Portland; Album-oriented rock, classic rock.
WGAN-AM 560; Portland; Talk, news, sports.
WHOM-FM 94.9; Portland; Easy listening.
WJTO-AM 730; Bath, ABC; Oldies.
WMEA-FM 90.1; Portland; Public radio.

WMPG-FM 90.9; Portland; Full service, eclectic.
WPOR-AM 1490; Portland; Country.
WPOR-FM 101.9; Portland; Country.
WTHT-FM 102.9; Portland; Contemporary hits.
WSJB-FM 91.5; Windham; Alternative, new music, progressive.
WWGT-FM 97.9; Portland; Contemporary hits.
WYNZ-AM 970; Portland; News and talk.

TELEVISION
WCSH-TV Channel 6; Portland, PBS.
WGME-TV Channel 13; Portland, CBS.
WPXT-TV Channel 51; Portland, Fox.

Midcoast

NEWSPAPERS
Bucksport Free Press P.O. Box 340, Bucksport 04416; weekly.
The Boothbay Register 95 Townsend Ave., Boothbay Harbor 04538; weekly.
The Camden Herald Box 248, Camden 04843; weekly.
The Courier-Gazette 1 Park Dr., P.O. Box 249, Rockland 04841; published Tuesday, Thursday and Saturday.
Lincoln County News Box 36, Damariscotta 04543; weekly.
The Republican Journal Box 327, 4 Main St., Belfast 04915-0327; weekly.
Waldo Independent 47 Church St., Belfast 04915; weekly.

MAGAZINES
Down East Magazine Box 679, Camden 04843. Bills itself as the magazine of Maine; two-thirds of their 72,000 readership live out of state.
Maine Antique Digest 71 Main St., P.O. Box 645, Waldoboro 04752.
National Fisherman 120 Tilson Ave., Box 908, Rockland 04841. A color glossy founded in 1903, they cover commercial fishing and boat building, as well as other marine-related stories.
Rod & Reel P.O. Box 370, Camden 04843.
WoodenBoat P.O. Box 78, Brooklin 04616. Beautiful to look at. Covers the design, building, care, preservation and use of wooden boats, both commercial and pleasure, old and new, sail and power.

RADIO
WCME-FM 96.7; Newcastle; Easy listening.
WMEW FM 91.3; Waterville; Classical.
WRKD-AM 1450; Rockland; Talk, news, sports, big band/nostalgia.

Down East/Acadia

NEWSPAPERS
The Bar Harbor Times 66 Main St., Bar Harbor 04609; weekly.
Castine Patriot P.O. Box 205, Castine 04421; weekly.

The Ellsworth American 63 Main St., P.O. Box 509, Ellsworth 04605; weekly.
  One of America's truly great small-town papers.
Island Ad-Vantages P.O. Box 36, Stonington 04681; weekly.
The Weekly Packet Townsend Ave., Blue Hill 04614; weekly.

RADIO
WDEA-AM 1370; Ellsworth; Full service, eclectic.
WKSQ-FM 94.5; Ellsworth; Adult contemporary, light/soft rock.
WWMJ-FM 95.7; Ellsworth; Contemporary hit radio.

East of Schoodic
NEWSPAPERS
County Wide Newspaper 26 Main St., P.O. Box 497, Machias 04654.
Machias Valley News Observer P.O. Box 357, Machias 04654; weekly.
The Quoddy Tides 123 Water St., Eastport 04631; weekly.

RADIO
WMCS-AM 1400; Machias; Country, easy listening.
WMEA-FM 90.1; Calais; Public radio.

REAL ESTATE

I f, after visiting the coast, you decide you want to own a piece of it, you can
write to the *Maine Board of Realtors,* 122 Northern Ave., Gardiner 04345
(582-8727) for a list of real estate agents in the areas you like. That office also
can provide names of agents who handle seasonal rentals in coastal areas.

  Also, good references for those looking to rent or own along the coast are
the *Maine Times* and *Down East* magazine. During late spring, the *Maine Times*
publishes a special summer vacation guide with classifieds for rental proper-
ties. The supplement is usually available all summer at newsstands throughout
the state. *Down East* runs a monthly real estate classified section as well. See
"Media," above, for further information about these publications.

ROAD SERVICE

Portland
AAA Maine 425 Marginal Way; Mailing Address: P.O. Box 3544, 04104; Mon.–
  Fri. 8:30–5, Sat. 9–1. 774-6377.

South Portland
AAA Maine Marshall's Plaza, 443 Western Ave., 04106; Mon.–Fri. 9–6, Sat. 9–
  1. 775-6211.

TOURIST INFORMATION

What is the right way to Acadia?

Tom Hindman

There are several publicly funded information centers and state agencies that provide visitor information. In addition, most chambers of commerce will gladly send packets of information to people planning a stay in their area. Here is an abbreviated list of agencies and chambers for coastal Maine.

FISHING AND HUNTING REGULATIONS
Dept. of Inland Fisheries and Wildlife, 284 State St., Augusta 04333; 289-2871.

VISITOR INFORMATION
Maine Publicity Bureau P.O. Box 2300, Hallowell 04347; 582-9300 in state, 800-533-9595 out-of-state.

New England Vacation Center Shop #2, Concourse Level, 630 Fifth Ave., New York, New York 10020; 212-307-5780.

South Coast

Kennebunk—Kennebunkport Chamber of Commerce P.O. Box 740, Kennebunk 04043; 967-0857.

Kittery Information Center I-95 and Rte. 1, P.O. Box 396, Kittery 03904; 439-1319.

Kittery/Eliot Chamber of Commerce P.O. Box 526, Kittery 03904; 439-7545.

Ogunquit Chamber of Commerce P.O. Box 2289, Ogunquit 03907; 646-2939.

Old Orchard Beach Chamber of Commerce P.O. Box 600, Old Orchard Beach 04064; 934-2500.

Casco Bay

Bath Area Chamber of Commerce 45 Front St., 04005; 443-9751.

Brunswick-Topsham-Harpswell-Bowdoinham Chamber of Commerce 59 Pleasant St., Brunswick 04011; 725-8797.

Chamber of Commerce of the Greater Portland Region Middle St., Portland 04101; 772-2811.

Freeport Merchants Association P.O. Box 452, Freeport 04032; 865-1212.

Yarmouth Information Center U.S. Rte. 1/Exit 17, I-95, P.O. Box 1057, Yarmouth 04096; 846-0833.

Midcoast

Belfast Area Chamber of Commerce P.O. Box 58, Belfast 04915; 338-2896.

Boothbay Harbor Region Chamber of Commerce P.O. Box 356, Boothbay 04009; 633-2353.

Damariscotta Region Chamber of Commerce P.O. Box 13, Damariscotta 04543; 563-8340.

Rockland/Thomaston Area Chamber of Commerce P.O. Box 508, Rockland 04841; 596-0376.

Rockport-Camden-Lincolnville Chamber of Commerce P.O. Box 919, Camden 04843; 236-4404.

Waldoboro Chamber of Commerce Box 698, Waldoboro 04572; 832- 4883.

Down East/Acadia

Acadia National Park Headquarters P.O. Box 177, Bar Harbor 04609; 288-3338.

Bar Harbor Chamber of Commerce P.O. Box 158, Bar Harbor 04609; 288-5103.

Blue Hill Chamber of Commerce P.O. Box 520, Blue Hill 04614.

Deer Isle-Stonington Chamber of Commerce P.O. Box 268, Stonington 04681; 348-6124.

Ellsworth Area Chamber of Commerce P.O. Box 267, Ellsworth 04605; 667-2617.

East of Schoodic

Calais Information Center 7 Union St., Calais 04619; 454- 2211.

Eastport Chamber of Commerce P.O. Box 254, Eastport 04631; 853-4644 (seasonal).

Lubec Chamber of Commerce School St., c/o Town Office, Lubec 04652; 733-2223.

Machias Bay Area Chamber of Commerce P.O. Box 606, Machias 04654; 255-4402.

Index

Index

LODGING BY PRICE

Price Codes

Inexpensive	Up to $50
Moderate	$50 to $110
Expensive	$110 to $180
Very Expensive	$180 and up

Offshore Lodging
MODERATE TO VERY EXPENSIVE
Harbor Boat & Breakfast

South Coast
INEXPENSIVE – MODERATE
Econo Lodge
Atlantic Birches Inn

MODERATE
Breakers
Dockside Guest Quarters
Green Heron Inn
Gundalow Inn
Old Village Inn
Scotland Bridge Inn
Trellis House

MODERATE - EXPENSIVE
Beachfront
Cape Arundel Inn
Cliff House
White Barn Inn
Wooden Goose Inn

EXPENSIVE
Captain Lord Mansion
Hartwell House

EXPENSIVE – VERY EXPENSIVE
Edwards' Harborside Inn
Inn by the Sea

VERY EXPENSIVE
Black Point Inn

Casco Bay
INEXPENSIVE - MODERATE
Inn at Carleton
Isaac Randall House

MODERATE
Bagley House

Chebeague Inn
Harpswell Inn
West End Inn

MODERATE - EXPENSIVE
Atlantic Seal Bed & Breakfast
Captain Daniel Stone Inn
Pomegranate Inn
Portland Regency

MODERATE - VERY EXPENSIVE
Harraseeket Inn

Midcoast
INEXPENSIVE
Hiram Alden Inn

INEXPENSIVE - MODERATE
Hichborn Inn
Roaring Lion
William & Mary Inn

MODERATE
Bradley Inn

Carriage House Inn
Fox Island Inn
Gosnold Inn
Maine Stay
Navigator Motor Inn
Newcastle Inn
Owl and Turtle Inn
Penobscot Meadows
Squire Tarbox Inn
Trailing Yew

MODERATE - EXPENSIVE
Five Gables Inn
Inn at Bath
Newagen Seaside Inn

EXPENSIVE
Samoset Resort
Spruce Point Inn
Whitehall Inn

**EXPENSIVE - VERY
EXPENSIVE**
Norumbega

Down East/Acadia
INEXPENSIVE
Jeannie's Place B & B

INEXPENSIVE - MODERATE
Captain's Quarters Inn &
    Motel
Oceanside Meadows B & B
    Inn

MODERATE
Castine Inn
Lindenwood Inn
Sunset House

MODERATE - EXPENSIVE
Blue Hill Inn
Inn At Canoe Point

EXPENSIVE
Asticou Inn
Le Domaine
Pentagoet Inn
Pilgrim's Inn

VERY EXPENSIVE
Keeper's House

East of Schoodic
INEXPENSIVE
Moonraker Bed & Breakfast

**INEXPENSIVE -
MODERATE**
Peacock House Bed &
Breakfast Inn
Todd House
Weston House

MODERATE
Riverside Bed & Breakfast

MODERATE - EXPENSIVE
Lincoln House Country Inn

RESTAURANTS BY PRICE

Price Codes
Inexpensive   up to $10
Moderate $10 – $20
Expensive $20 – $30
Very Expensive $30 or more

South Coast
INEXPENSIVE
Carson's Family Restaurant
Flo's Hotdogs
Maine Diner
Rick's All Seasons Restaurant

**INEXPENSIVE TO
    MODERATE**
Cap'n Simeon's Galley
Jackie's Too
Spurwink Country Kitchen

MODERATE
1810 Eatery
Alisson's

Billy's Chowder House
Chauncey Creek Lobster
    Pound
Jonathan's
Joseph's By the Sea
Rose Arbor Tea Room
Village Inn

MODERATE - EXPENSIVE
Hurricane
Ogunquit Lobster Pound
Roberto's
York Harbor Inn

EXPENSIVE
Cape Neddick Inn
Cornforth House
One Fish, Two Fish

VERY EXPENSIVE
Arrows

Casco Bay
INEXPENSIVE
Estes Lobster House
Rosita's

**INEXPENSIVE -
    MODERATE**
Dolphin Marina Basin
Five Islands Seafood
Harraseeket Lunch & Lobster

MODERATE
Alberta's
Cannery, The
Jones's Landing
Richard's
Street & Company
Uncle Billy's Southside BBQ's
    & Takeout

MODERATE - EXPENSIVE
Chebeague Inn
Muddy Rudder

RESTAURANTS BY CUISINE

SEAFOOD
Dolphin Marine Basin
Estes Lobster House
Five Islands Seafood
Harraseeket Lunch & Lobster
Street & Company

Midcoast
AMERICAN
Cappy's Chowder House
Captain's Table
Darres
Kristina's
Le Garage
Lobsterman's Wharf
Moody's Diner
Newcastle Inn
Nickerson's Tavern
Penobscot Meadows Inn
Peter Ott's Steak House
Squire Tarbox Inn
Waterfront

ECLECTIC
90 Main Restaurant
Brown Bag
Truffles Cafe

FRENCH
Cassoulet

SEAFOOD
Harbor View Tavern
Haven

Down East/Acadia
AMERICAN
Castine Inn
Chase's
Dennetts Wharf
Dick's
Duffy's
Firepond
Jordan Pond House
Porcupine Grill

ECLECTIC
Left Bank Bakery & Cafe

FRENCH
Le Domaine

SEAFOOD
Charlie's Lobster Hut
Eaton's Lobster Pool
Fisherman's Inn Restaurant
Fisherman's Landing
Tidal Falls Lobster Pound

East of Schoodic
AMERICAN
Helen's Restaurant
Micmac Farm
Sandwich Shop

ITALIAN
Rolando's

SEAFOOD
Officer's Mess

Maps

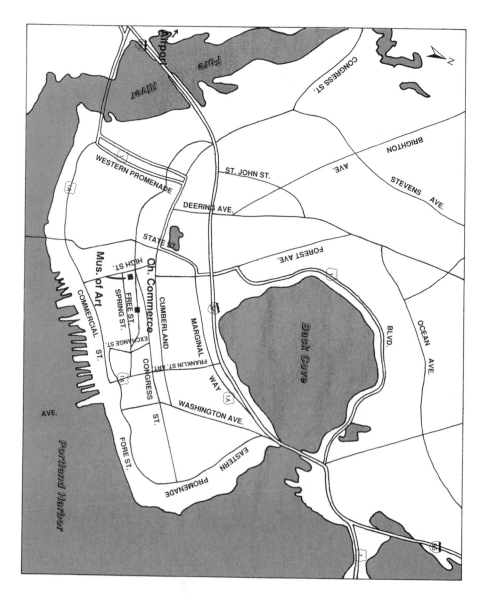

CITY OF PORTLAND

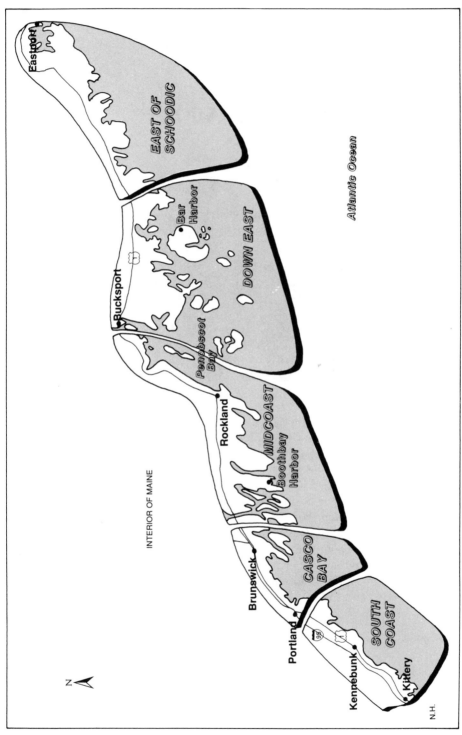

COAST OF MAINE — FIVE REGIONS

About the Authors

Rick Ackermann is a former journalist and Kathryn Buxton is a former film critic. They met while working for the *Palm Beach Post* in West Palm Beach, Florida. Their first cooperative writing efforts were as restaurant critics for *New England Monthly*.

Separately, they have written for several publications including *Town & Country*, *The Washington Post*, *The Palm Beach Daily News*, Reuters, *Yankee* and *Variety* magazines, *The Columbia Journalism Review*, *The Washington Journalism Review*, the *Maine Times* and the *Maine Sunday Telegram*. The authors live in Portland, Maine, where Ackermann is completing his first novel and Buxton writes advertising and promotions for companies and business clients including L. L. Bean, Bass, and the Norwegian Salmon Marketing Council.